PENGUIN BOOKS

THE VOTIVE PEN

Nilanjana Sengupta is a notable author of Singapore who has built a reputation in writing books which travel to unchartered territories. In *A Gentleman's Word* she chronicled the legacy of a forgotten war hero, Subhas Chandra Bose across Southeast Asia. In *The Female Voice of Myanmar*, she wrote of the latent masculine bias of Burmese culture and women voices which have managed to cut through the clutter. *Singapore, My Country-Biography of M Bala Subramanion* was a nuanced look at the Tamils of Singapore who though the majority Indian community, struggle with vulnerabilities of their own. Sengupta, who has been a research scholar at NUS and ISEAS-Yusof Ishaak Institute, is critically acclaimed, widely read and her books have been translated and included in the university course.

T0150030

PRAISE FOR THE VOTIVE PEN

'I am large, I contain multitudes.' To those who have read his poems and spoken with him, let alone worked with and come to know him, Edwin Thumboo so truly exemplifies what Whitman said. Reading his best-known poems, you recognize some of the most iconic explicit and extroverted assertions in the canon of a successful and still young country, and yet also encounter finely poised questions about the national condition. To have the opportunity to sit and talk with him is an even more complex, rich and even magical encounter.

The Votive Pen is an encounter with Thumboo as poet and personality. It is studied and erudite, yet unconcerned with orthodoxy and rigid order. This book explains and enrichens and also risks to entertain us with the man and his work. What results is not only an examination of this fine poet and powerful personality in his own work and words, but in the context of the universe—no, multiverse—of ideas, histories, experiences and imaginations that Thumboo contains and has carried forward for so many decades as a unique writer and immense and human soul.

Simon Tay
Writer and Singapore Literature Prize Winner 2010
Nominated Member of Parliament (1997-2001) and Ambassador

Edwin Thumboo lives the single most interesting literary Singaporean life of his generation. *The Votive Pen* makes sure that this fact stays with a people whose literature has been amnestic. The stories here cross many decades to weave the child and man of the past into the rememberer before a new scribe. Nilanjana Sengupta has achieved something superbly lyrical and historical: this book is for the ages.

Gwee Li Sui
Poet and Literary Critic

This wonderfully rich and detailed biography illuminates Edwin Thumboo's work with consummate skill. Sengupta delves deeply into the poet's inner journey, connecting the man and his life to the work and the process of creation. The importance of Thumboo's poetry and its relevance to the making of the Singapore identity is revealed with laser-eyed sympathy.

Dr Meira Chand
Author

A valuable read for anyone wishing to get into the mind of a pioneer poet in Singapore and one of the country's first Cultural Medallion recipients. *The Votive Pen* adds to the much-needed discourse on Singapore's literary history, in which Edwin Thumboo plays a critical role, and helps us understand how the enterprise of nation building and poetic aesthetics intertwine.

Paul Tan
Poet, former Director, Singapore Writers Festival,
Deputy Chief Executive, National Arts Council

Edwin Thumboo's biography and poetry, so beautifully captured in this volume, reflects the dramatic transformation of our world from late colonialism to nationhood. His is very much a Singapore story - the coming of age through an uncovering of layered identities.

Prof. Tan Tai Yong
President, Yale-NUS College

This biography captures the heart and mind of Singapore's widely accepted 'poet laureate'. It is the first book I know which peers into the soul of one of the leading figures of the arts in our country. This is a worthy tome to accompany the life's works of Edwin Thumboo.

Hsieh Fu Hua
Chairman, National University of
Singapore and National Gallery Singapore

The Votive Pen

Writings on Edwin Thumboo

NILANJANA SENGUPTA

PENGUIN BOOKS

An imprint of Penguin Random House

PENGUIN BOOKS

USA | Canada | UK | Ireland | Australia
New Zealand | India | South Africa | China | Southeast Asia

Penguin Books is part of the Penguin Random House group of companies
whose addresses can be found at global.penguinrandomhouse.com

Published by Penguin Random House SEA Pte Ltd
9, Changi South Street 3, Level 08-01,
Singapore 486361

Penguin
Random House
SEA

First published in Penguin Books by Penguin Random House SEA 2020
Copyright © Nilanjana Sengupta 2020

ISBN 9789814882132

Typeset in Adobe Garamond Pro by Manipal Technologies Limited, Manipal

www.penguin.sg

To you, my kryptonite

CONTENTS

FOREWORD

Nilanjana Sengupta has done us a great service. First, she persuaded Edwin Thumboo to agree to be interviewed about Edwin the man and Edwin the poet. Second, she galvanized Edwin so much so that he began to enjoy helping her to link his life to his poetry and led him to write the illuminating introduction that opens this book. And, not least, she has drawn from her encounters with Edwin's life some distinctive threads that enable us to understand many layers of Edwin's mind and several features of his soul-searching.

I have a personal reason for being grateful. When she asked me to write this foreword, it reminded me that I had not followed Edwin's writings closely since the 1960s. I did read some of what he wrote in the 1970–80s, notably in the collection, *Gods Can Die*, but only intermittently and from far away. Since coming to Singapore in 1996, I realized I had missed so much of the literary developments of the city-state that I could no longer place Edwin in that story. What Nilanjana did was to link bits of Edwin's life and poetry to a coherent frame. In her own way, she made it possible for me to rediscover the Edwin that I remember and also managed to project on a stark canvas the Edwin that I did not know.

By coincidence, her invitation came when I had just finished writing about the second stage of my education, most of which had to do with the University of Malaya of the 1950s in Singapore that

Edwin and I had attended. That period was when I discovered that I was an outsider who could qualify to become a future 'Malayan' while Edwin was being schooled to believe that the ideal of Malaya was already achievable. In different ways, as we learnt to make words and images do new things for us, we were wading in the same literary pool. We imagined that we could bring to life a new national identity with poetry that would enable us to swim in ever larger waters.

I soon realized that I was not a poet and my contact with writers in the maritime Malay world, in Indonesia and the Philippines, had convinced me that national literature could only be written in a language native to the country. I recalled that my fellow students at the university held a debate in 1950 where the motion 'that English rather than Malay should be the national language of a self-governing Malaya' was carried by 33 votes to 31. I was not convinced and decided to turn away from literature to the study of history.

Edwin, however, was to find that nothing but poetry could satisfy his personal quest for identity as 'the first *Malayan*', especially when Singapore separated from Malaysia in 1965 to become the only place where the idea of Malaya might yet be possible. He turned away from working in the civil service to seek his own path to this unexpected nationhood. I was in Kuala Lumpur when I heard of his 'return' to the world of literature and I marvelled at the Edwin that was keeping faith.

Nilanjana describes how he had expanded his mentalité by exploring the history of the many cultures of Asia that had been pushed off course by colonial rule towards an alien modernity, and also the way he was further inspired by African capabilities with Anglophone literature. Edwin himself saw how these encounters combined with his love of Yeats had helped to lift his imagination to a different level. Nilanjana further uncovers what mental and visual landscapes had helped Edwin to appreciate the changes in the new Singapore. The constraints of national survival and the city-state's reinvention as a distinctive plural society were producing a new citizenry in which Edwin's own mixed ancestry could become desirable and normal.

Any remaining thoughts about wandering ghosts could now settle freely in a crucible of calculated choices. Above all, he emerged as the leader of new generations of poets for whom their first language was English. It became possible to think of the poetry written with local cadences as national.

Edwin's poetry after 1965 captures the slew of changes around him. I see both celebration and relief. Thereafter, he could turn more consciously to his own place in the cosmos. I am not sure which came first, his turn to lyric verse to explore the dimensions of love or the rediscovery of his inherited belief in the church of Jesus Christ. It seems to me that the two may only be different parts of the search for the simpler and purer lines of modern life.

This is perhaps what I am most grateful to Nilanjana for. Had I not been given the chance to see Edwin the man afresh and encouraged to read more closely Edwin's recent poems, notably those in *Still Travelling* (2008) and *A Gathering of Themes* (2018), I would not have understood the mature Edwin who is still seeking a new comprehension of the human condition. I hope others who read her book and Edwin's introduction will agree with me that Nilanjana has given us a wider window on a remarkable poet.

Wang Gungwu
Singapore, January 2020.

INTRODUCTION

We compose poems; we don't write them. Very clearly the aim of Nilanjana Sengupta's book is to explain the difference.

We sometimes have a stray thought. It flashes, a manifestation of something at the back of our mind. If our minds like puzzling over things by turning them over, then the flash persists. We spread it out, feed it with memory, emotion, imagination, intellect and try to uncurl its edges. We hold it close, like a mother her precious baby, and think about it and piece it together till we know it well, till the image is complete. And this thing that has taken shape in our mind then broadens our own inner reality.

What Nilanjana attempts to do in this volume is to capture some of this process that I have gone through in the six and a half decades of my poetic career. She started this study in early 2018. Frankly, I was not too willing to initiate such a commitment but, like my old Volks which would croak and cough reluctantly before taking off on a smooth ride, very soon I started enjoying our interviews. Before we knew it, we were cruising along. Nilanjana's is an intelligent, sharp mind which readily reads into nuances, grips an idea and studies it fully, leaving no part unturned.

We met regularly. I commented on poems and answered a mounting series of questions as she read them, starting with the earliest composed at Victoria School (1948–53) and at the

University of Malaya (1953–57) whose Arts and Science faculties were at the old Raffles College campus. *The Votive Pen* is the sixth investigative book on my work. The previous five had been done by academics.[1] Nilanjana herself has written four books.[2] I was confident that given her background, cumulative experience, and deepening interest in Singapore, especially in its literature in English, her study would be lively. This continued to strengthen as she proceeded. The titles of her chapters cover the main trends of my work. Moreover, when taken as a whole, they provide ample space to study what I have done and am likely to do.

The first chapter, *Crossing Boundaries*, takes us to the interior heartlands—my childhood during Japanese Occupation and then proceeds to fan outward (or maybe I should say move inward) to understand how my Indian and Chinese roots shaped my eventual philosophy and how my life and context mature. The chapter begins with a bit of an epiphanic moment during a brooding Easter day in 1945 when at the age of eleven, I first became aware of the multiple worlds that could coexist in an instant, the emotional underpinnings to a physical world. This very naturally turns to a discussion of my family—as anyone with a racially symbiotic family

---

[1] Ee Tiang Hong, *Responsibility and Commitment: The Poetry of Edwin Thumboo*, ed. Leong Liew Geok (Singapore University Press, 1997); Peter Nazareth, 'Edwin Thumboo: Creating a Nation Through Poetry', Interlogue, in *Studies in Singapore Literatures*, Volume 7 (Ethos Books, 2007–2008); Jonathan J. Webster, *Essays on Edwin Thumboo: JJ Webster, T Kandiah, Wong Phui Nam & Lily Tope* (Ethos Books, 2009); Jonathan Webster, *Understanding Verbal Art: A Functional Linguistic Approach* (Springer, 2015); Gwee Li Sui and Michelle Heng, 'Edwin Thumboo: Time Travelling—A Select Annotated Bibliography', in *Singapore Literary Heritage*, Series 1 (National Library Board, 2012).

[2] *Netaji Subhas Chandra Bose: The Singapore Saga* (Nalanda-Sriwijaya Centre, ISEAS, 2011); 'A Gentleman's Word: The Legacy of Subhas Chandra Bose' in *Southeast Asia* (ISEAS-Yusof Ishak Institute, 2012); *The Female Voice of Myanmar: Khin Myo Chit to Aung San Suu Kyi* (Cambridge University Press, 2015); *Singapore, My Country: Biography of M Bala Subramanion* (World Scientific Press, 2016).

would know—and the natural dexterity with which one learns to cross cultural boundaries from an early age. I saw difference but was not divided. This then turns to my early exposure to literature in the cluster of second-hand bookshops of Bras Basah, restricted largely till then to English books. In a long view of the volume, these twin themes dominate Nilanjana's understanding of me: my family and the literature I read. It is only in the later chapters that Singapore emerges to play an important role and so does my nascent spiritual life and larger global understanding.

Nilanjana concludes the first chapter with the thought that I understood early the connections and patterns that hold together cultures and people. But the one experience that deeply affected me and many in my generation was colonization. It divided us into the Westernized 'outer' and the Asian 'inner', a mixture which we saw and had to accept. We were, therefore, Chinese-Indian-Eurasian-and-Malay Singaporeans. A hyphenated people who, in perhaps 200 years from now, would be more Singaporean than of our original ethnicity. We were evolving, some faster than others. There was a need to see connections. It was with a sense of relief that I later turned to unifying cultural symbols like the Hanuman for instance, who makes an easy transit from the faithful follower of Ram in Indian mythology to the legendary Wu Kong of the Chinese pantheon.

The first chapter, undoubtedly the longest and the most complex in setting out the ground structures, ends with Nilanjana pointing at the importance of both the 'individual' as well as the 'collective' experience in shaping Singapore's multiracial ethos. But it is in the second chapter that my external life, tethered to Singapore to this very day, starts. Aptly titled 'The Isle is Full of Noises', it is an interesting exploration of our challenging and exciting university days, the rising sense of Malayanization and the Fajar Sedition Trial of August 1954. For those interested in Singapore's literary traditions, this chapter has some fascinating insights into the works of my friends and seniors, Wang Gungwu, Beda Lim, Goh Sin Tub,

Ee Tiang Hong, or Phui Nam, and such fledgling magazines such as *Youth* or the *New Cauldron*.

At a personal level, it looks at one of my first poems, *The Cough of Albuquerque*, written around 1955–56. Though definitely not one of my favourites, Nilanjana finds in it my inner journey of the time, from an inherent sense of duality to self-discovery and rootedness and the eventual awakening of a restless mind that seeks the birth of a new nation. The mind is splintered yet again and the time is ripe to shake off colonization.

Here Nilanjana also delves into my reading of William Butler Yeats from whom I learnt the power of poetic language, but more importantly perhaps, the link between language and country. Yeats was an Irish nationalist whose poetic psyche was shaped by an evolving sense of Ireland. She also points to the other streams that fed into my own sense of nationalism—Bose's INA or my literature teacher, K.C. Owen, a Welshman who sang Welsh songs full of nostalgia. Nilanjana ends with an analysis of some of the poems from my first collection, *Rib of Earth* (1956). She comments: '*Rib of Earth* also makes him aware of his inner dualities—the way even when he looks in front, his past pulls him back or when he breathes a casual whisper into his lover's sleeve he stops to wonder of the legacy he will leave behind,' as what she sees as the inner duality obviously lingers.

The third chapter, *Tribes*, is a detour, albeit an important one. In it Nilanjana embarks on an African journey, tracing my discovery of Africa in the mid-60s for a master's degree thesis. It is a part of my life that has not been dwelt on much and yet perhaps is important for it introduced me to a new literature of the colonized, a literature that very firmly believed awareness begins with history. Even more intriguing is the relevance of African literature to a freshly independent Singapore—the residue of distrust between communities that the pre-Independence racial riots had left in their wake being a major lesson.

The chapter in parts reads like a travelogue but eventually ends up taking a deep look at the 'drumbeats' of a tribal way of living that had continued to echo in a mint-fresh Singapore—the gangsterism and buying of votes, the pig and poultry farms, secret societies and clans which formed powerful networks of nepotism. Like a triptych, the chapter looks individually at the three African greats (among many others), Christopher Okigbo, Gabriel Okara and of course the Nobel Laureate, Wole Soyinka.

Okigbo is a poet in whom the oral traditions of West Africa came together beautifully with the musical compositions of Europe. He helped to reinforce my belief in the Singaporean four cultures: Malay, Chinese, Indian, and Eurasian. I lived in two, the Chinese far more fully than the Tamil, the latter a part of the larger Indian community. Okara is a poet whose one sustained experiment is in moving the sensibility of one culture into another language, while maintaining a 'mobile sensitiveness'. While Soyinka is an author of symbolism who used this sensitivity to symbolism to bridge the different elements of his life.

Nilanjana ends the third chapter with an analysis of my second book of poems, *Gods Can Die* (1977). By the time of its publication, I had married, become a father, and my career in the university had progressed. Yet rather than the sense of fulfilment, what Nilanjana sees percolating through the lines of the poems, is the complexity of response. She quotes Virginia Woolf in this context, suggesting, like a good biographer, I hold up mirrors at odd angles to view myself, in the fullness of my environment, to check my response to different situations of not only an adult world but also of a more prosperous Singapore. She concludes: it is a set of personal ethics that give my public and personal selves a certain calming unity.

The fourth chapter is titled *City on the Mind* and returns to Singapore. But this time it is Singapore with a difference. If earlier in the second chapter, the city was dwelt on more for purposes of setting the stage and providing the atmosphere, now it is a more theoretical take on our cityscape. Starting with a comment on the possibility of infinitude that is embedded in the very idea of a city of intersecting streets, the chapter goes on to zoom into my Singapore poems using three different lenses: the intersection of Time and History, the intersection of Culture and Mythology and the intersection of the Visible and Invisible. The chapter ends with a commentary on yet another of my collection, *Ulysses by the Merlion* (1979).

History has been a recurrent theme for me. I have dwelt on it in many areas, at many levels and on many platforms. Here Nilanjana narrows down the focus to the author's role in representing history as the past, present and future which are but reflections of each other and speaks of my predilection for choosing symbols, images and metaphors from the past which simultaneously happen to incorporate the national literary discourse of Singapore. Similarly, when discussing culture and mythology, Nilanjana mentions what has been my poetic mission of many years, the need to give voice to a tradition—which is already part of a cultural fabric—and to provide significant correlatives to an emerging culture in terms of 'events' or 'types' or 'places'. Fundamentally, the answer for Singapore as it evolves and reincarnates itself time and again, is for the poet to re-discover, re-negotiate, re-educate, re-work on the imagination of readers to create a new body of metaphors, a new paradigm and a new identity.

To Nilanjana, *Ulysses by the Merlion* represents my central, regenerative unifying vision. It is the midpoint of my poetic career: 'Before this he is on a quest for unity, after this it is a journey to find extensions to this central thought.' For her the Merlion remains the overwhelming symbol of unity, it towers over the milling multitude, standing both as the perceiver and the perceived. In the Merlion coalesce the complex network of overlapping grids—the visible present prosperity and the invisible past of Singapore when lions roared in the jungles and mermaids disappeared into the sea.

The pace visibly relaxes in the concluding chapter, *Still Travelling*, as Nilanjana obviously senses that the major unifying discoveries are over. They have to be worked on, modified and pursued as circumstances require. Nevertheless, it is an interesting chapter because it dwells at length on what has been my preoccupation for the last many years—the identity of a 'hyphenated Singaporean', a new aspiration that the 'SG' part of the Singaporean's identity would gradually gain in importance and the country's ethnic inheritance would eventually be resolved. She refers to my sense of poetic responsibility and the lifelong urge to speak of the softer elements, the language, the poetry, the words, elements that often get pushed aside in a nation's journey towards economic progress.

Nilanjana starts with some of my more lyrical poems, my personal pieces dedicated to my wife, Swee Chin, and then continues to write about the three key volumes of poems: *A Third Map* (1993), *Friend* (2003) and *Still Travelling* (2008) that have followed *Ulysses by the Merlion*. According to her, as the titles suggest, they are on different themes but what brings them together is the gestalt identity they hold forth: 'It was this identity that was his central discovery in *Ulysses by the Merlion* . . . It is this third identity born of syncretic cultures that constitute the "third map" of his existence. Thus, if *Ulysses by the Merlion* was his *bildungsroman*, then the later volumes are variations of the essential unity he had discovered within himself.'

An important section in this chapter is the one dealing with my poems of Christian themes. I have never been an atheist, have always known and believed in a creator but, with the panoply of religious influences in my family, it was more of an eclectic belief. It was with my conversations with my friend, fellow academic, linguist and lay minister Jonathan Webster, that my faith took firmer roots. Subsequently, on 22 August 1992 yet another friend of mine had me baptised—S. Dhanabalan, former Singapore politician and Elder at the Bukit Panjang Gospel Chapel. Nilanjana's comment is interesting that a theme that surfaces recurrently in my Christian poems is one of love, that however great the sin, God's mercy is implied to be greater and that love is the only path to reach Him. And also, that my purpose in my Christian poems remains the same as in my explorations of identity: I attempt to enter the world of spirituality as much for personal reasons as for aesthetic ones.

An urgent search for the aesthetic and lyrical and the need to see my public self as an extension of my personal beliefs and experiences, remain a preoccupation in the last chapter. One of Nilanjana's concluding comments is on the long distance traversed from when I saw Singapore's multiracial unity projected in the Merlion to the unity that I seek today which is more cosmological, making all barriers not only flimsy but also meaningless.

The traveller has been one of my favourite leitmotifs right from the beginning when I wrote *The Cough of Albuquerque*. I have always felt that it is the traveller as he crosses boundaries, dismantles them and peers over walls who is best equipped to see the founding unities that hold together, not only religions, but cultures and histories and even human stereotypes. Keeping this in mind even as I enter my eighty-sixth year, I travel on.

In late 2018, I decided to publish *A Gathering of Themes*. Its poems include those meant for two volumes, one religious and the other for Chin, my wife. Both had not reached the point where they could be published separately. Various circumstances convinced me that it was time for a volume of my poems, unpublished and published, in anthologies. From late October to near the end of November 2018, I worked steadily, placing the poems under different broad headings which sum up the themes that have engaged me over nearly seventy years. In November 2019, the National Gallery Singapore published *Ayatana*. It's in two parts. The first consists of poems touching on paintings and other aspects of the Gallery, the second, poems on painters that had written earlier.

What next? Well, I hope *The Votive Pen* will be widely accepted. It provides some required clues to a fuller, more comprehensive understanding of my poems and the overarching vision behind them. For long have the arc lights remained trained on the public purpose of my poems rather than my private quest. It is that quest which is behind my poetry, as it makes me what I am. I hope with this volume the compass will somewhat change direction. Nilanjana's work started with the poems which gave her the necessary overall perspective of how the poetry reflects my own growth over the last seven decades. She goes where the poems take her so that her book provides the necessary anchorages with which the reader is able to have a larger sense of what I was doing and have done and she does this more comprehensively than earlier studies. For that I am most grateful.

Edwin Thumboo
Phoenix Park
Singapore, December 2019.

AUTHOR'S NOTE

The first time I met Professor Thumboo, he looked at me rather intently over his glasses and said, 'I wrote myself into the centre of Singapore.'

In the breathless pause that followed he seemed to gauge my response and I knew for some reason this was important to him. Maybe this was the scale against which many had weighed him before. In my mind I wriggled a bit under that fixed gaze, thinking, 'And did you get yourself trapped there?'

And so, our journey started—with him a bit anxious and I a bit chary of what lay ahead, on a mission to find the cracks of discord between Thumboo the imaginative creator and Thumboo the engaged citizen.

Very soon after sketching out my first thoughts on the book, I knew none of my previous publishers would touch it with a barge pole. Poetry = niche, elitist, arcane. The arguments had withstood the test of time. Yet, this released me like nothing else could. Afterwards it just soared—the ideas, the discussions, the writing—everything. Maybe because I was no longer writing to impress, but simply to understand. Maybe because I lost my self-consciousness and eased myself into the flow, setting aside what Cocteau calls, 'the agony of the act'.

I remain grateful to Professor for allowing me to paddle down the river the way I chose—to question, to contradict, to badger. To tease open his mind like the complex, interlocking chambers of a Japanese *enro*. It was like leafing through the catalogue of an old-fashioned, non-digitized library. Afterwards we would compare notes, stand back and smile at what we had discovered.

Thus, despite Professor's protests, I continued to maintain that there was a difference between the man and the poet. As a poet he naturally keens towards disorder, following the idea rather than the precision of words. Yet as a man he clings to the comfort of structure, cannot reconcile himself to an unrestrained existence of the LGBTQ community. As a poet he speaks of the difference only in form and not in substance, but as a man is a full-blown Christian. After a lifetime of struggling with contraries, this is a final unity he cannot achieve without sacrificing one for the other. He cannot be a poet of his choice without silencing the man within, nor can he, as a man be stamped 'approved' without sacrificing the poet.

As for me, I sign off happy in my understanding that he is both—a poet and a man.

Nilanjana Sengupta
Kew Crescent,
Singapore, December 2019.

I

CROSSING BOUNDARIES

The Way has never had boundaries; language has never been constant. Borders exist because of affirmations.

—Chuang Chou, *Chuang-tzu*

My place is placeless, my trace is traceless, no body, no soul, I am from the soul of souls. I have chased out duality, lived the two worlds as one.

—Anonymous Sufi poem

In the moonless gleam of midnight, I asked her, 'Maiden, what is your quest, holding the lamp near your heart? My house is all dark and lonesome, lend me your light.' She stopped for a minute and thought and gazed at my face in the dark. 'I have brought my light,' she said, 'to join the carnival of lamps.'

—Rabindranath Tagore, *Gitanjali*

Reflections on a guava tree[1]

Edwin Thumboo (ET) begins the interview with a snippet of a childhood memory. He seems completely immured in the moment as it comes back to him in clear, incisive pictures. The spreading guava tree, the strength of its flaking branches under his fingers, the failing southern light. It was a tree with a mind of its own—gnarled branches that twisted at odd angles—not one of the easiest trees to climb or straddle. Yet, it was his favourite and that day he had sat surrounded by the silence of leaves that barely rustled in their new-born tenderness, immersed in thoughts that were as new. And then, when his mother's call floated up, 'Eddie! Where are you?' in a voice that demanded immediate deference, he had glanced up one last time at the fading sun, the gathering gloom in the trelliswork of branches and then jumped down.

1st April '45, 42 Monk's Hill Terrace, Newton

After Easter Sunday Service
The walk home from Short Street
Is pensive. 'On the third day He rose'
Keeps ringing in my head. I can't grasp it,
Am anxious, in distress. But He is God,
Phoebe says, for Whom all things are possible.
You will know when you are older.

Then Sunny tricks us: Hello, 'April fool'!
We joke and laugh as we romp home.

Late in the afternoon, I sit on my branch of
Our guava tree, still after-service, still unsure,

---

[1] Details from ET's poems *1st April '45, 42 Monk's Hill Terrace, Newton; Government Quarters Monks' Hill Terrace, Newton, Singapore* and interviews 29 May and 06 June 2017.

Sombre. I brooded over three Japanese years,
A stretch of suffering, from the day we fast-fled
Mandai driven by their shelling. The family got
Dispersed into a seemingly long sadness, split
Between Lorong 41, Minto Road and SGH.

In Syonan-to we younger ones grew fast. Only
Ten, eleven, twelve, did earnest work, played less,
Our pre-war comforts stolen away. Tilled sweet
Potato, tapioca, bananas, plantains, yam, all easy
Growing. We had kachang botol and green peas,
Full of vitamin B, good top-ups against beriberi.
Neighbours shared, swapped seeds and saplings.

I herded Uncle Sinna's goats. More fun than
Digging or weeding. Sold two-bite curry puffs,
Rain or shine, at Makenzie Road to Traction Co.
Mechanics, then Jubilee Cinema, and finally
Buyoung Road's cluster of motor repair shops.
Bigger boys shoved me from my spot. One tough,
Rough-speaking foreman interceded when he saw,

Telling me to be careful of that bullying, nasty lot.
Grateful, I took extra care when heading home via
Clemenceau, wondering why they were unfair. So I
Watch people, old, young; friend, stranger. Others
Had similar adventures, moments of knowing in joy,
In pain, in uncertainty; in little corners of our lives.

Days thus settled down into routine responsibilities.
Papa taught school in Nippon-go. Uncle Hock Seng,
Uncle Ratna, and Uncle Ryan, fellow teachers, met
Often after the bombs of last November,* before
My birthday. I was hoping for a steel pang-see top.

They chatted in the hall, whispered when saying
Mountbatten, the big chief, King Georgie's cousin.

There were many air raids. Shining silver planes in
Groups were B 20-something, Papa explained, smiling.
Bombed only the Japanese who claimed white-black
Ack-Ack puffs corroded the planes. They will crash,
En route home.
Suddenly 'Eddie! Where are you?' Mama
In that voice! Go get the vegetable! Enough lengkuas
To tumis her special curry chicken for Uncles tomorrow.

A last look up before jumping down. Light of the South
Is fading. I think I know why Papa and Uncles smile.

*November 1944 is the time of the air raids by the Allied Forces
on Japanese-occupied Singapore

The day was 01 April 1945. That same night the fabled Awa Maru
capsized in the South China Sea, torpedoed till a lone steward was
left to tell the story of its astonishing treasures. The sunken ship was
perhaps a symbol of the turn in the Pacific War—the Japanese sun
was setting, the Allies were on an ascent. And Eddie, no longer the
little boy he was when Singapore fell, could sense that their life was
going to change—yet again. The years under the Japanese had not
exactly been of peace and plenty. Yet after the initial flurry, their life
had settled into a familiar rhythm. His uncles, Cha-kong-ku and Ah-
hia-ku with their crammed wooden office between Crawford Street
and the Rochore River opposite Minto Road and the Lee's family
twakows (light boats on Singapore River) berthed behind for easy
loading to the Riau Islands had supplied them with the occasional
sack of rice and dried fish.[2] Father, with the few words of Japanese

---

2   Jonathan J. Webster, *Return to origins: the poet and the Tao—Edwin Thumboo's
     'Uncle Never Knew'* (Singapore: Ethos Books, 2009), p. 29. Cha-kong-ku is his

he had learnt from makcik (aunt), held a steady if poorly-paid job as a teacher. It was true that the family had been split, that Father had to sell off his car, that Mother could never buy the Peranakan jewellery—gold set with brillante stones that shone like tiny mirror chips—for which she had been saving up. It was also true that he hated eating the kachang botol (beans) that was supposed to be an antidote to beriberi caused by their poor wartime diet. But despite the discomforts, the patterns of their life had in the last three years acquired the familiarity of a dog-eared book and to Eddie's twelve-year-old mind, this familiarity was important.

That year, All Fool's Day coincided with Easter and ET (Edwin Thumboo) and his siblings had walked home after Sunday Service at the Short Street Church. It was the old Tamil Methodist Church, since rebuilt, where ET had to sing the hymns in Tamil, a language of which he knew precious little. At home his Mother spoke Teochew and English and his Father only English, and when the adults did not want the children to understand, they spoke Malay to shoo them away. Yet once he and his siblings had mastered the sounds of the Tamil hymns, ET enjoyed singing them, relishing the deep-throated, guttural sounds of the language. The Methodist Church was then presided over by Reverend T.R. Doraisamy who later became the Methodist Bishop of Singapore and also taught ET in the Japanese school. ET received religious instructions from yet another of his father's friend, Uncle Phua Hock Seng, though it was only after the war that he would visit his church. According to ET, Uncle Hock Seng was a zealous missionary. With the usual luscious abandonment with which he embraces words, ET describes him as, 'Uncle was not a reverend and yet he was more reverend than most reverends!' Before the war, Uncle Hock Seng had used his bungalow to start what was probably the first bungalow-church of Singapore which since then has moved to the top of a hill along Pasir Panjang Road. After the war, ET would continue to attend his sermons for about a year and

---

maternal uncle in Teochew. Minto Road has since been expunged. Lee is the family name of the Teochew branch on ET's mother's side. While Kang is the name on the Peranakan side.

a half (1950–51) and would eventually only stop after Father and Uncle fell out over a discussion on the theology of communion.

But that late morning, ET was unusually quiet as they walked back the short distance from Church, down Makenzie Road, past the old Traction Co. which ran trolley buses across the city and finally to Monk's Hill Terrace, where Father occupied #42 government quarter, a modest two-storey with a veranda with a view of the Government House. He would later realize that it was here, in these clusters of identical government quarters that he had seen in a microcosm the future multi-racial Singapore. But that day he had words from the sermon ringing in his head, *On the third day He rose...* He had asked his half-sister Phoebe how resurrection was possible. But she, with the unquestioning acquiescence of those who accept what they hear, had merely replied, *But then He was God! Anything was possible. ET only needed to grow older to understand.* And so, ET had climbed onto his favourite branch of the guava tree and sat in a pensive mood till his mother called him down and sent him off to buy galangal for her stir-fried chicken.

So why is this moment so important, enough to be placed at the beginning of a book? Is it because of the turning tides of history? Would the Thumboo family know a reversal of fortunes that would change their lives forever? Or would theological questioning propel ET towards a new path of spirituality? The answer to both is an unequivocal no, and yet the moment is definitely life-defining in its own way.

It was the first time in his young life that ET realized there were multiple worlds that one could inhabit and traverse in an instant. There was the sensory world of the fruit tree and the burning, dying day in which he was so intensely present. There was the bit more nebulous emotional world, the new adult world of feelings he was waking up to. He had not missed the sharpness of pleasure in Mother's voice as she sent him off to the market. They could see the growing impotence of the Japanese and hopeful little rumours were doing the rounds about the return of the more benevolent British.

But he had not forgotten Father's warning either, when he said in a low, firm voice, with a strange light smouldering in his eyes, *Eddie, never cry*:

> Much else disturbed the peace, brutalised your pride.
> Yet you coped; self-redeemed. Only a fire in your eye
> Revealed nerves sharply pinched during the daily ride
> To school on uncle's dubious Raleigh. Eddie, never cry
> You said, so softly that I feared some terrible thing,
> Without shape or name, had left in you its bitter sting.[3]

ET worried about the vulnerabilities of his apparently resolute, invincible father, his mother who in her wartime anxiety thought only of keeping her family well fed. But he was equally aware of his parents' need to protect him and his sisters from an unkind world—it would not do for him to be susceptible. And even beyond this world of feelings that threatened to engulf him in its sweetness and sorrow, ET felt the presence of a spiritual world where God embraced one with the promise of love and new life. But only, as in most such eventualities, renewal came inseparably intertwined with thoughts of mortality. And maybe thoughts of God came with its attendant guilt at transgressing the moral code—little acts of innocent pleasure committed, white lies told to shirk responsibility that now weighed heavy on his young shoulders.

Other poets have written of such moments, fragments of existence when they suddenly felt themselves stand outside time and saw two different worlds: the binary arrangements of body and spirit, finite and infinite or temporal and transcendental. William Wordsworth writes in the first book of his *Prelude* for instance, when as a boy he rowed across the Ullswater Lake on a moonlit night and watched in awe as a craggy pinnacle emerged from the silent waters. He writes of the proud cliff that reminded him of the eternal nature

---

[3] *Father-4.*

of the universal spirit and of human thought compared to which his skiff and his own act of stealing it from the shadows of the shore, appeared miniscule and irreverent,

> . . . the huge Cliff
> Rose up between me and the stars, and still,
> With measur'd motion, like a living thing,
> Strode after me. With trembling hands I turn'd,
> And through the silent water stole my way
> Back to the Cavern of the Willow tree.
> . . . and after I had seen
> That spectacle, for many days, my brain
> Work'd with a dim and undetermin'd sense
> Of unknown modes of being . . .

Rabindranath Tagore writes of a childhood morning when he read his first primer strewn with isolated words, smothered under the burden of learning spellings.[4] They wearied him in their moth-eaten meaninglessness until he stumbled on to a sentence of combined words, *It rains, the leaves tremble.* The beauty of the line seemed to rescue him from the desert haze of inactive imagination and suddenly his mind touched the eternal realm of truth. In that picture of pattering rain on forest leaves he saw the harmony of existence. Again, Ted Hughes writes of his hunting expeditions when he was a boy to the moorlands of West Yorkshire.[5] As he, as his elder brother's retriever, scrambled into all kinds of places collecting magpies and owls and rabbits and curlews, he grew aware of an un-killable biological optimism, a primeval energy that sprung from the root-filled forest floor that defied everyday living.

---

[4]   Rabindranath Tagore, *My Life in My Words* (India: Penguin Books, 2006), pp. 25–6.

[5]   Ted Hughes, *Poetry in the Making* (UK: Faber & Faber, 2008), p. 16.

Needless to say, more than the crafting of words, poetry is dependent on such power of perception and the sharper the acumen to perceive, the easier it is to cross boundaries and enter other worlds. As ET himself puts it, 'The doors of perception shape our cognition and are in turn shaped by it . . .' and it is perception that defines both the content and the boundaries of the worlds one inhabits, whether simultaneously or otherwise.[6] So what his reflections on the guava tree represent, is his passage into the enchanted world of perceptions—perceptions that would in the future torment and fulfil him in equal measures.

This incident of a brooding Easter Sunday is important because it clearly delineates ET's childhood from his youth: self-confessedly, it is a turning point. He was no longer the boy who in 1942 had clapped in joy when, standing under a frangipani tree in front of the Chemistry Building at the Singapore General Hospital, he had seen the Japanese tanks rolling in and got rapped on his knuckles for doing so. Then the violence of war had been manifested to him in a single rifle that an Australian soldier had left leaning against a coconut tree in Mandai. But in the intervening years he had witnessed much and his childish world had acquired more and more of adult elements. His granduncle had been tortured to death by the *kempeitai*, he himself had sold curry puffs on the streets of Singapore, worked as a sales boy in the Yarl Store along North Bridge Road, herded Uncle Sinna's goats—odd jobs with a distinct element of responsibility. The Japanese education system, less patriarchal than the British and treating as it did children as young adults, had also played a hand in his early maturity.[7] The war had wizened his bones and now when he overheard news of American planes from Kanpur bombing Singapore on Uncle Hock Seng's secret radio or saw the black and white ack-ack puffs released by the Japanese which failed to

---

6 *Perceiving Other Worlds*, edited by ET and Thiru Kandiah (Singapore: Marshall Cavendish, 2005), pp. ix–x

7 *Interlogue*, vol. 4, ed. Ronald D. Klein (Singapore: Ethos Books, 2005), p. 58.

corrode the Allied planes, he did not know the undiluted happiness of childhood anymore.

This moment also proffers an inkling of ET's eventual poetic vision. It is a world that remains warmly populated by family and friends, where half-sister Phoebe or Uncle Hock Seng or Uncle Sinha or Ah-hia-ku can never be expendable. His poetry is a tapestry woven before a cosy fire, though the winter wind whistles through the shutters. It is also a world where the 'self' is important—a personal self as an antithesis to egoism. As in E.M. Forster, of whom ET remains an admirer, in his personalization of the universe there is involved a personalization of the self.[8] It is a self that remains at ease with itself always, scarcely if ever in denial of the 'terrible mistakes' he has committed. As in Forster, as the self evolves and understands better its own mystery and order, it finds itself to be the inhabitant of a precious and mysteriously ordered universe. ET's universe of poetic thought is firmly placed on a time-space continuum where sadness plays its own role but where there is little bitterness. It is a universe that is never free of memories, nor shy of the future, casting and mixing timeless connections of cause and effect in its own earnest light.

And so ET writes poems like *Bitter Ballad* which starts off on a slightly censorious note at the young boy who puffs away on his cigarette but ends up as an exercise in empathy for not only the boy who smokes away his frustrations but for the old father who worries for his son's future:

Little boy smoking cigarette

come blow up your horn

little boy jabbering
old man's language.

---

[8]   C. Bedient, *Architects of the Self* (Berkeley: University of California Press, 1972), pp. 205–6.

He puffs lustily,
ignorant,
burning his body away.

. . . Bits of anger, evil smelling curses,
the father clouts his head.

Old man cries over
fragment bowl:
His son can only have
the symptoms of a man.

A familiar fusion: syncretic beliefs

The first twenty years of his life, till September 1953 when he left for University, ET and his family resided at various homes. He spent the first few idyllic years of his life in Mandai. In 1942, when he was nine, Singapore surrendered to the Japanese. It was in Mandai that he was born in 1933 to Tamil-Christian father, Jabez Thumboo and Teochew-Taoist mother, Kang Sai Eng. The war meant a dispersal of the family from Mandai when his father, mother and sister Lena and he evacuated to the Chemistry Building at the Singapore General Hospital. This was a time when his father, a school teacher, struggled to maintain their middle-class lifestyle. Soon the family moved to government quarters at #42 Monks Hill Terrace, Newton. It was in 1951 that his father retired and the family moved to a home near Kampong Java Road and then, in 1952, his father built a home in Lorong Melayu to where they moved again.

ET's voice distinctly softens when he speaks of Mandai, a whispering gentleness that clothes the place with the magic of Xanadu or the mystical Shangri-La.[9] The fourteenth and a half milestone on the road, deep in the Singapore countryside, surrounded by

---

[9]   NAS interview transcript, 14 February 2005, reel 19.02.

undulating, low-lying hills where a bamboo grove creaked, a secret stream lost its way in the darkness of a well, where the night air was rent by the harsh cry of a nightjar. Where there was the exploding rubber tree, the dainty custard apple and,

> For the inquisitive,
> Slightly disobedient, there were little
> Infinities in sound in light in the ant's
> Unexpurgated sting . . .[10]

His father, Jabez, loved the countryside and the Mandai Hill, with its trigonometrical point, just a little lower than the Bukit Timah Hill, had not been quarried down to a hole in the ground then.[11] It rose on one side in a solid granite wall, reassuring and solemn, behind their home. It was here where panthers had once roamed and grass snakes entwined branches like green glass bangles, that ET's father had built a house.[12] It was a large, oblong house of *attap* and timber, with its wells fed by local streams and a workshop where his bit of a 'frustrated engineer' father put together his steam engines. ET reminisces of his Chinese maternal grandfather who carried him around on his shoulders and the intriguing fragrance of opium that wafted up. Eddie would eventually sell his grandfather's sweet-smelling secret to his grandmother for some candy, perhaps in his first act of misdemeanour!

At Mandai

I
Before the War this countryside was lush;
Enveloping. Winds accosted pert prepositions

---

[10]   *At Mandai.*
[11]   *Interlogue* (2005), p. 57.
[12]   This and other family details from interviews 29 May to 06 June 2017.

To tint our rising sun. Birdsong browsed
Among custard apples. Slightly disobedient
Inquisitives like me, uncovered first lucidities
In sound in light in the whiff of roses, an ant's
Unexpurgated sting, a spider's hexagonal web,
And neat, pungent musang droppings. Every
Bit incited. Even grand-aunty's graphic tales,
All dripping blood, absurd. Where was Nanjing
Anyway? To me, at nine, they were fantasies;
Unreal, indulgent games which adults played.

Exploding rubber seeds; durian trees in flower:

So daily rhythms settled. But that itch to know,
To unpack to argue to discount, sort experience
Into layers, invent quick cadences in the mind,
And that smile to win difficult approval, grew
Gradually confident. They were apt beginnings,
Enactments, ruminations, before shifting dioramas
Of daily life and contacts that choreographed eyes
To track morning light spreading and sliding down
Mandai Hill, into facing valleys to shove off dark
Intimidations, then glorify favourite treetops still
Floating on mist. They, too, construe. First birds
Fly decisively; a breeze carries memories as I feel . . .

II
The potency of origins, the mandate of tradition.

Mandai to town, now global city. We had selves,
Ours only, to stand, prepare and pair departures
And returns. No anointing sky no blessed earth no
Healing waters, then or now. Little in nature ours.
No bounty. Except the spirit's wholeness, Father

To Son and Daughter, sanctified by roads forebears
Canonised when hunger chewed, muscle tested rock.

O City
We made you inch by inch. Blood and sweat redid
Rewrote reforced; stayed focused on means, on ends;
Forged unity, margins, our slim hinterland. Let our
Vision hold. Nothing venture, nothing gain Papa said.
He knew painful history, the hard way ahead. As we
Grew, streets turned avenues; gleaming condos took
Down ancestral homes, an ache, yet necessary.

We move, adjust, discover yet again
There are two imaginings, perhaps
More, between pages, between lines,
Between you and me and us,
And our posterity.

ET remembers occasionally walking with his father down Mandai
Road, which was being surfaced then. Ramaya would emerge out
of his tiny lean-to quarters which was part of the labour lines by the
roadside to speak to them. He was a Tamil labourer from Madras,
part of a team brought in by the British Public Works Department
(PWD) that built roads and dug canals. ET's father eventually
befriended Ramaya and employed him as part-time gardener. As
the adults spoke, ET would look beyond and notice a small statue
of Murugan in the twinkling darkness of Ramaya's little home, the
glowing marigold at his feet, the javelin that was said to spear through
all darkness.

But the image of the young warrior God would soon be
superimposed by a myriad other colourful images when he went with
his mother, Kang Sai Eng, to the Taoist Temple on Balestier Road.
It was most possibly the Goh Chor (Teochew for Rochor) Tua Pek
Kong Temple with its forecourt where the wealthy philanthropist

Tan Boon Liat had built an opera stage, and its ramparts of leaping dragons and rising phoenix. ET remembers the smoke rising from the tall pillar-like joss sticks with dragons moulded on their sides and, on festival days, from the rolls of *yi bao,* in a temple where among the many residing deities was Mazu, the Sea Goddess, protector of the seafaring community of Singapore.

Life coloured by images of various gods continued, and then when he was around seventeen, just before he took his school cert exam, ET fell sick with a terrible fever, one of those influenzas that visit him every twelve years or so and threaten to be fatal. He knew it was no ordinary flu when great aunts visited, telling him soothingly that he was a good boy; that he need not worry. Images of God preyed on his fevered, delirious mind and yet, when he thought about it later, he realized it was not a Christian God—neither the wrathful, punishing God of the Old Testament nor the loving Christ of the New, about whom he had heard in Church. Instead, it was more of an amorphous idea of a superior power that might heal him of his sufferings.[13]

Self-confessedly, though his father was a Christian, ET's formal exposure to Christianity occurred mostly after the war (though he was formally baptised only in March 1992 and according to him full Christian belief came even later), when his family moved to Lorong Melayu and Uncle Hock Seng insisted they visit his bungalow-church every Sunday. What he remembers of the time is that the different religions were neatly compartmentalized in his mind with little overlap. Yet, he could not help but notice the connections: his Buddhist friend, Boey Yew Hock, who unfailingly played the church organ in the Church of Our Lady of Nativity at the junction of Upper Serangoon Road and Punggol Road every Sunday; or when they joined the mayhem of Hari Raya celebration in Geylang Serai and his family feasted with their Muslim friends; or when his Taoist mother visited a Malay mystic.

---

[13]   Ibid.

The connections went even further back. ET's grandfather, Adolphus Jacob Thumboosamy, had migrated from Madras in the 1880s after he converted to Christianity to marry a girl from a convent.[14] He came to Singapore but eventually settled in Muar, working for Abu Bakar, the Anglophile Sultan of Johore, well known for his friendship with Queen Victoria. So, though a Christian, his grandfather grew deep roots in the Malay-Muslim culture of the Muar region with its spreading riverside plantations of gambier and black pepper, and yet evidently did not forget his early Hindu origin for till late in his life he remained a practising *tantric*. In fact, as family hearsay goes, he had placed on his house in Muar a red tantric figurine as a protective talisman from wandering spirits. And then years later, as a part of ET's sense of the religious there was Aunty Hannah, who unlike her *tantric* Father, used Christian science to heal her son Vincent Hoisington when a full toss hit him squarely in the mouth, and his Taoist maternal grandfather who was said to possess psychic powers and often entered into a trance. The links that could be forged seemed endless and even within a single religion there seemed infinite mutated forms which ET became increasingly aware of as he grew older.

This early awareness of connections which essentially came from his Tamil-Christian father and Teochew-Taoist mother, later developed into a more objective, structured study of syncretic religions, what Ludwig Wittgenstein calls the 'family resemblances' between religions that includes elements of both universal validity and contextual relevance.[15] When asked what triggered the study, ET mentions Taoism, the religion of his Peranakan mother. Taoism that derives from *Tao*, one of the most basic and comprehensive words of the Chinese language which means *the way* and is said to be the

---

[14] *Return to Origins*, p. 28.
[15] *Religions of the World*, ed. Niels C. Nielsen (NY: St Martin's Press, 1988), introduction.

guiding light of all of art and science, is by its very nature syncretic, more inclusive than Confucianism or Buddhism.

Perhaps added to this is also his family inheritance that lends itself to syncretism. His grandfather was a recent convert, ostracized by his family and compelled to stay outside the main house because of his marriage to the girl from the 'convent' and perhaps like other converts his Christian roots were not deep enough. It allowed for enduring religious syncretism. On his mother's side, migration to Nanyang had happened in three successive waves from China, the first as early as in the 1780s. Part of the family had drifted to Thailand and the Maluccas, then better known as the 'Spice Islands', under Dutch possession,[16] while the others turned up on the shores of Singapore. The connections between the Singapore branch and Swatow (now Shantou, on the eastern coast of Guangdong), their ancestral home, remained strong while over the years the bond with the Spice Islands withered with cross-marriage. It was a family where 'cults' or ecosystems of beliefs naturally came together and fused with little conflict.

But the more obvious and immediate reason of his interest is the country of his birth, Singapore; an island, a free port, an *entrepôt*, an artificial construct of British colonialism where previously independent cultural and religious systems came into sustained contact, no matter what their individual levels of sophistication. It was a country where population growth had been fuelled by migration since Raffles' landing in 1819, where escape from multi-racialism was impossible. As he puts it, it was this rich panoply that would help convert his syncretic religious consciousness into an acceptance of the inherent multiracialism of Singapore. He would understand early that if the fledgling country was to survive there was need to move from tolerance (a negative word implying sufferance, according to him) and understanding to fusion and harmony.[17] There was need

---

[16]   *Return to Origins*, p. 29.
[17]   Interview 07 August 2017.

to move from understanding the commonalities between cultures to actually arriving at a common culture.

But all this would happen much later, as his public role as a poet and professor of English Literature grew and so did his *weltanschauung*. It was born of an early awareness of connections from a racially symbiotic family. But was infinitely sharpened when as a boy of seventeen he witnessed the tumult and destructiveness of the Maria Hertogh Riots of December 1950. He was in his Uncle's dispensary in Arab Street, called New Surgery, when one of the bloodiest racial riots of Singapore broke out over a custody battle of a Dutch-Catholic child raised by Muslim parents. 'You don't need instructions after that,' he says with characteristic brusqueness.[18] And then, in 1953, he joined the University of Malaya and met others (he knew the likes of Beda Lim and Wang Gungwu even before) and felt first-hand the racial divide there. But perhaps the final step forward was in 1957 when he joined the Singapore Civil Service and realized he needed to read in areas neglected at the university to stave off the monotony of his job in the Income Tax Department. His eventual adult viewpoint of a Singapore of synthesized identity strengthened through his structured reading of religious and cultural syncretism during the civil service years. As he says, 'Consciousness was always there but the need to synthesize wasn't there as urgently,' and it is this sense of urgency that would propel him towards a new path of shaping a 'softer vocabulary' of poetic expression for a potentially implosive nation.[19]

Still Travelling

The doors Ah Kong opened in that curve
On Mandai Road those years ago, still serve.
True to themselves, thus true to me, they
Are my wide beyond. What enters, tints me,

---

[18]   Ibid.
[19]   Ibid.

Incessantly. Light bent and rinsed, reveals,
Offers names; up-dates my GSP; paints my
Seasons. Yellow, red, purple-white frame
Asphalt, sides and sky. Travelling with my
Passing days, contending nights, it plucks
Basic chords, tests the new against ancient
Regiment. On this road I am ungarnished.

Child of many mansions, lactating confluence:
I want to hear your history to know mine, then
Above the theories, complicities, post-colony,
Find and keep tradition, feed as its hunger feeds
Individual talent. That is you, my friend. You.
Here is knowing and renewal, a deep nurturing
That turns questions into answers. It is inland
Grammar making our speech distinct. We are
New and multiracial; go meet our longings.
Others inherit, we assemble. Put in migrations;
Forebear's bloody sweat that prospered rulers.
They took, and left finely judged remainders.
So, roll out the drums; pick your commission.
Recharge the canon, doubly with our voices;
The recent one; some older have done their work.
Distil our narrative; insert metaphor and icon.
Speak that all may see us. Our needs are similar,
Masuri, Yoon Wah, Kannabiran, Alvin, Lynette
And others of our tribe. The rose blooms equal;
The wind gathering, travelling in regular waves
Across lallang or bamboos has a rough music.
Long silence ends in simple speech, and silence.

'Surely, faint hearts never wrote fair poetry.'

A menagerie in the backyard

If not for the timely intervention of friendly neighbours, ET would have been born while his mother was watching *wayang*, so fond was she of the opera—the noble generals, the beautiful princesses in their two-foot long water sleeves, the orchestra music.[20] And particularly since the early 1930s were the golden years of Chinese opera in Singapore. What with the rapid expansion of the *entrepôt* line dominated by the Cantonese, Teochews and Hokkiens, *wayang* troupes performed not only in town centres but also in villages and on plantations, including at Mandai.[21] ET recalls the village at the junction of Mandai Road and Woodlands where there was a Chinese temple with a *wayang* stage in its courtyard which his mother used to visit.

ET was born on 22 November 1933 in his Mandai home, surrounded by the familiar sights and sounds he would grow up with. It was a large family of eleven siblings, born of his father, Jabez Thumboo's two marriages. This means the two sides of his family were rather different, held together by the common thread of spoken English. Since his grandfather had converted to Christianity and so been ostracized before he left India, the Indian side was small and English-educated. It was also anglicized—ET speaks of tea and scones served in the second set of silverware in his Aunty Hannah's home (and also remembers she was slightly patronizing to Mama who knew far less English). The Chinese side was even more mixed—some carried the pure bloodline from Swatow, some were 'sepia' tinted, and others had darker lips and skin, obviously born of mixed marriages. His maternal grandmother for example wore the long Peranakan *baju* dress and yet was quite dark-skinned, presumably with connections with the local community of Indonesia. She was

---

[20] NAS interview transcript, reel 19.01.
[21] *Wayang: A History of Chinese Opera in Singapore* (Singapore: The National Archives, Singapore, 1988), p. 25.

in the habit of going out in the evenings to 'take the air'—not a common practice in other Teochew homes.[22]

In a country of transient, migrant communities like Singapore (then Malaya), having such a wide-ranging assemblage within a family was perhaps not uncommon. What is extraordinary is ET's easy acceptance of these multiple cultural strands. Was it a part of his socialization? Perhaps so. But it is apparent that with ET, quirks and foibles of family members are easily accepted, examined with a bit of indulgent good humour and then set aside with little moral judgement on display. Thus, there is Papa's eldest sister, Aunty Grace who married a Sri Lankan, and Aunty Hannah who married twice. And then there was *makcik*, his grandfather's caregiver who was Japanese and who visited them every two years from Nagasaki. The family called her 'aunty' and ET remembers the swish of her silk kimono as she walked up the driveway of their home.

The ability to put the best possible construction to a tricky situation is an endearing trait in ET. Thus, he speaks of the three and a half years of Japanese Occupation, 1942-45. It was, as he writes, a time of 'seemingly long sadness', 'a stretch of suffering' when his family was banished from his childhood Eden, Mandai, they left with all they could manage to fit into a single car, never to return.[23] Afterwards they were split in three—his grandmother and his sisters in Geylang, his uncle and brother in Minto Road and his parents with him and one sister in SGH. (Singapore General Hospital)[24] His father volunteered for a job with the Medical Auxiliary Services and they evacuated, living in the Chemistry Building in SGH. ET still remembers the acrid smell of chemicals that floated in the air along with the penury of the time. Suddenly from a very comfortable middle-class life that they could afford with the $300 salary that his

---

[22]   This and later family details from interviews 29 May to 06 June 2017

[23]   *1st April '45, 42 Monk's Hill Terrace, Newton.*

[24]   After a while, until they would move to Monk's Hill Terrace, while the uncles continued to live in Minto Road.

father earned as a teacher, they were plunged into wartime poverty. Papa sold off his car and instead cycled to office, Mama could never again save the $1000 she was salting away to buy her Peranakan jewellery, the whole set complete with a *kerogsang rentai* of a phoenix design, ET did various odd jobs—growing tapioca and tending ducks and goats. Eventually, he would land up at the Yarl Store on North Bridge Road where the Jubilee Cinema used to be. Run by a bachelor uncle of an old school mate, it sold razors and soaps and other things men needed where ET attended to 'Thai sailors in Teochew, INA officers in English, Jap NCOs in bows.'[25]

The war would change their lives forever, his father would never be able to afford a car again and would struggle to keep the family afloat and together. Yet, ET speaks rather poignantly of the family bonds he noticed during the difficult times: Mama would give the best portions of food to Papa because he had to go out to work, but Papa would merely set them aside for the children.[26] Or, while speaking of the cruelty of Japanese soldiers with their infamous habit of slapping passing pedestrians at will, he does not forget to mention the birthday celebrations of the Japanese Emperor when the army headquarters close to their home in Newton would be thrown open for all. There would be free *makan* of Japanese *yakitori* and it would not escape ET's notice how the Japanese soldiers enjoyed playing with the little children—they obviously missed their own![27]

When he was young ET faced some amount of racial slur. He was called a half-caste or *chap cheng* in Hokkien and the words hurt more because Papa, always his closest confidante, heard and soothed but did little to help.[28] Possibly he knew ET would have to learn to cope with the unkind moniker. Sure enough, it returned to haunt him—he experienced the prejudice in Victoria School

---

[25] *Government Quarters Monks' Hill Terrace, Newton, Singapore.*
[26] *Interlogue* (2005), p. 58.
[27] Interview 29 May 2017.
[28] NAS interview transcript, reel 19.01.

and again, once, at the University of Malaya, and ET learnt to devise ways to deal with it. The easiest way was to learn to excel both in academics and sports so that his friends needed his help and he could challenge those who denigrated him. But a more permanent solution presented itself when his senior and the future librarian, Beda Lim and those similarly broad-minded, advised that the humiliation needed a good rebuttal. So next time anyone called him a half-caste, Beda told ET, he should reply, *he was the first of the Malayans.*[29] Things then seemed to start to fall into place and ET felt a strong sense of belonging and pride at his new identity. There was a fair number of them and soon they started calling each other 'countrymen'.

So, ET experienced early such pains of being marginalized hurtfully and this lent him an inherent sensitivity to the excluded 'other'. It was this need for fairness, for being treated equally for what one is, rather than for one's racial or family background that fuelled his eventual inclusive poetic vision in the same way that friction with the bedrock causes a river to flow. It pushed him to understand better the cultural cohesions of multi-racial Singapore, composed as it was of the Chinese, Malay, Tamil and Eurasians, and attempt a deeper fusion in his poems to arrive at a common identity. Later, though the hurt disappeared, the sensitivities lingered. And though a baptised Christian now when he accepts unhesitatingly the biblical code of ethics, for much of his adult years he was conflicted over religious and secular scales of morality. For many years he felt, one needs a set of values that is sufficient to answer the demands of life; that enables one to function. And even today when asked if he would reject a friend for doing something morally doubtful, he replies after some thought, in a voice a shade lower than customary, 'I will accept it and respect it. If there is any chance of influencing him, I will try. Otherwise I will keep quiet and maintain my friendship.' But then, how will he explain it to his religion? 'Sometimes it is borderline . . .

---

[29] Interview 07 August 2017.

and that is when it gets difficult.'[30] As usual, it is the nuances of the grey that bother the thinking mind.

It is also this easy tolerance of differences which perhaps disallows him from making religious or cultural syncretism into a compulsive theme in his poems, it remains merely implied for the more discerning. Thus, in *Wat Arun*, written in late 1954 after his first visit to Thailand when he was marginally Christian, the Buddha and Christ come together in their compassion and yet there is no compulsive fusion of the two symbols,

> You my fathers made—
> Left wheat and incense.
> I, vestigial of that line,
> Despite the buffeting of days,
> Still quicken in your gaze.

> Lord Buddha, shaman with the wheel
> Was in the loaves of Christ.[31]

A traveller in a connected world
You went to teach far, far away, at times returning late.
Anxious for your company, I often watched the gate.
I still do, despite the years, in times of double stress.
Or when I think of words like grace, or graciousness.
Or when Sarah talks to *Kong Kong* as she walks with me,
As our little birds start singing, mine in the memory tree.[32]

ET wrote the lines years after his father had passed away. According to him, Papa, who was a Christian in his 'own, quiet way' and spent his lifetime teaching at various schools of Singapore—Serangoon

---

[30] Interview 15 June 2017.
[31] *Wat Arun*.
[32] *Father-5*.

English School, Outram Road School, Pasir Panjang Primary School and then at Bedok Primary School before he retired, was his best friend till around when ET turned fifteen. As he speaks of his father, it is apparent that there are many shades to what he feels for him. Besides the customary love and need to emulate, there is anguish at the wartime difficulties he faced, a restrained sadness at a life spent fulfilling the dreams of others.[33]

According to ET, Jabez was good at his teacher's job because of his strong sense of responsibility and yet he yearned daily to return to the workshop he had built in his garage in Mandai.[34] It was in the workshop with its ordinary tools in Newton and a whole row of batteries attached to a Delco generator that ET assisted his father and together they built, first, a single-acting and then a double-acting steam engine. Jabez loved the rhythmical, low-pitched sound of the steam engine and they would put the miniatures to test—sometimes in a boat they sailed in their neighbour's (the country house of a Chinese *towkay*) abandoned swimming pool or in the pond close to the smoke house in the Mandai-Tekong Estate run by his granduncle, Kang Chiang Hock. But amidst all the excitement of experimentation, what ET remembers is the way Papa used to wash his hands afterwards. There was a certain rhythm, a pattern to it, like when one ties shoelaces or combs hair—a pattern born of long habit.

This habit of noticing patterns, a chain of events that came together in a unifying connection would remain with ET. In the future it would determine his choice of subjects in university—literature, history and philosophy; the subjects he would read with obsessive passion when a civil servant in need of cerebral stimulation—anthropology, ancient religion and mythology; and maybe to an extent it would even determine the kind of poems he would write—poems that seek spatial and temporal connections. From very early, with the keen eye of a detective, he would search out connecting

---

[33]   Interview 06 June 2017.
[34]   Details of workshop, Interviews 29 May to 06 June 2017.

patterns that underscore events, read life as a gestalt collective of individual incidents. Just as he had read in the rhythm of his father washing his hands the nature of the man—meticulous, disciplined, someone who lived life by its simplest rules—he, ET, would see in historical events a causal sequence, distant correspondences that brought all of humanity together in a unifying permanence.

When he joined the University of Malaya in 1953, ET had taken history as his second major for his graduation course but felt exasperated soon enough as they were taught only colonial history— Indian history was only the story of Cornwallis and Hastings and Chinese history was finished off in half a lecture by the fresh-from-Oxford lecturer. The whole course was structured around modern colonialisms, i.e., European expansions—the Portuguese, the Spanish, the Dutch, the French and the British. That was when he started reading on his own—the immense span that begins with the Stone Age, the great early civilizations of the Near East, then moves to the glory that was Greece and the grandeur that was Rome and ends with the advent of modernity in the eighteenth century. He noticed the first connections very soon—how, for instance, agricultural societies formalized the ownership of land and this led to an allegiance to military organizations or the existential anxiety of early religions. But the finer nuances came to him gradually as he combed the second-hand bookstores of Bras Basah, the original educational hub of Singapore with its cluster of schools—Raffles Institution, St Joseph's Institution, Raffles Girls' School, the Convent of Holy Jesus and St Anthony's Convent & Boys' School.

Lingual Roots

After WWII, English drove my crescive world.
Palgrave's *The Golden Treasury*, leather bound,
gripped my hand. I began to see our time, our place,
our 'untrodden ways'. Some were pruned by Uncle's
patriotic sprit and Ken Owen's Welsh yearnings.

English grew: relentless,
kay poh-ish, capacious, confident, unlocking worlds.
It helped digest more of India, China and Nusantara;
the great mythologies. Oxygenated by this fabulous
collective, my tribe of words still grows. It purloins SG
parlance for extra potency. Prepared for any-all seasons.
On the trot, they read continents and the madding globe.
BT Campus then was colonial hash tag, with dollops of
Anglo-Europe. We studied histories, since depleted: Brit
expansion overseas. Then Dutch and French. Saw how
their narratives could cleverly distort.

A massive turning point.

I started to redress, raise antes; unfurl traditions, trysts;
growl and sing, remembering, inter alia, that 'there is
nothing either good or bad but thinking makes it so',
as I unpacked colonial residue, mischievous remnant echoes.
They subvert, out of habit, now low cunning, even as we
enlist compatriots, who loved and laboured, to help undo.

Literature, the mother of all telling, was my main learning.
She still takes me places. Apart from William S, a great
talker in my journey from Chaucer on, I had Kalidasa, Li
Bai, the *Kuruntokai*, the *Mabinogion*, the Hikkatats as boon
companions. Meditate, analyse, judge; re-visit and re-think.

Within that were further awakenings. I scoured areas
much disfigured, suppressed, reduced, to recover
and restore. Nerve by nerve, word by word. In late '59
when labouring between tax and employers' returns,
a neat tweet formed:
Truth re-tunes hope, and hope turns
anger positive. After all a prodigious, grand language had

found me. Transplanted in a corner of our Little Red Dot,
our Earth, Water, Fire and Air added roots, compelling a
hot osmosis, singular passion, and that thermal rising to the
sun. Openly reflexive, words make and multiply journeys.
In their beginnings are our ends;
our ends equally in their beginnings.
These are just for starters.

He recalls there were around six or eight shops, starting from after the
present Rendezvous Hotel (that time Rendezvous Restaurant), most
of them run by Indian Muslims with books pegged to clotheslines.[35]
In the corner was Graham Brash, a *pucca* English and a lovely man
who allowed him generous discounts and then there was the Victory
Bookshop, run by a Chinese man whose brother was a trishaw driver.
Eventually ET would get to know the shop-owner so well that he was
allowed access even on holidays. He would enter through the small
door on the side and spend entire days browsing. It was here that he
stumbled upon the writing of Maurice Walsh, a minor Irish author
and nationalist who spent much of his working life in Scotland and
cultivated a deep love for Celtic legend and folklore. ET read two of
his books, *Green Rushes* and *The Key above the Door* and it was Walsh
who initiated him not only to the world of Celtic mythology with
its fairly discernible commonalities with Gaelic and pan-European
mythological cultures, but also to the Irish nationalist movement,
particularly the Black and Tan War after WWI.

By 1953, Singapore was held in a tumult of political ferment.
Communist insurgency launched in 1948 and the declaration
of emergency had been followed by a spate of racial riots. On the
anvil was the possibility of constitutional reform under the Rendell
Commission but nationalists were doubtful if Singapore would be
allowed complete self-government because of its size and dependence
on its hinterland. ET's family too continued to maintain a declining

---

[35]   Details of Bras Basah, Interviews 29 May to 06 June 2017.

middleclass lifestyle. Jabez had retired and with his small pension bought an *attap* and wood house in Lorong Melayu. But the Malay Kampong with its unpaved roads and puddles of dirty water did not make for comfortable living. Added to the privations of the time and the political unrest in his mind came musings on the Black and Tan, an army in motley uniform put together by Churchill to supplement British power and put down the Irish Republican Army. Walsh's stories offered an insider's view into Irish village life under these ex-Captains and Majors appointed by the British with powers to kill and resonated deeply with ET. It brought to mind not only the day of Colonel Dyer's madness at Jallianwala Bagh but the more recent Batang Kali massacres of 1948 when unarmed villagers were rounded up by the British at a plantation near Rawang, Selangor and shot down. So obviously history depended on who wrote it. If it was the British, it was but natural they would make themselves 'smell like roses' and it was important to read alternative sources, ET concluded.[36] One such was *The White Sahibs in India* by Reginald

---

[36] ET's reading list on history: *Egypt and Middle East—History of Egypt* by James Henry Breasted; *History of the Persian Empire* by A.T. Olmstead; *The Legacy of the Ancient World* by W.G. de Burgh; *Ancient Egyptian Religion: An Interpretation* by Henry Frankfort; *The Birth of Civilization in the Near East* by Henry Frankfort; *From Savagery to Civilization* by Grahame Clark; *India a Short Cultural History* by H.G. Rawlinson; *The Indus Civilization* by Mortimer Wheeler; *An Advance History of India* by R.C. Majumdar; *The White Sahibs in India* by Reginald Reynolds; *A History of Southeast Asia* by D.G.E. Hall; *Far Eastern Government and Politics: China and Japan* by Paul Linebarger; *A History of Japan* by James Murdoch; *A History of Japan to 1334* by George Sansom; *The History of Japan* by Kenneth Latourette; *A Short History of the Far East* by Kenneth Latourette; *China, a Short Cultural History* by Charles Patrick Fitzgerald; *The Indianized State of Southeast Asia* by G. Coedes; *History of the World* by H. G. Wells; *The Story of Civilization* by Will and Ariel Durant (the first four of eleven volumes); *A Study of History* by Arnold Toynbee (selective reading); *The Dawn of European Civilization* by V. Gordon Childe; *The Most Ancient East: The Oriental Prelude to European Prehistory* by V. Gordon Childe; *Ancient History* by Michael Grant; *The World of Rome* by Michael Grant; *The Ancient Historians* by Michael Grant; *Cleopatra* by Michael Grant.

Reynolds which, written by the left-wing anti-colonialist, proved to be a revelation.

Other formulations followed. One of the key ideas which would be a powerful carrier and shape his future writing came from his reading of mythology. He first read Charles Kingsley's book on classical Greece, *The Heroes*. But the finely-etched pantheon of valour soon expanded—to the Greek names were added the Anglo-Saxon Beowulf, the Sumerian Gilgamesh or the Indian Ram or the Scottish Lug and Morrigan and the other sovereign gods and goddesses of Celtic, Welsh, Nordic, Gaelic, Middle Eastern, Aztec, Inca mythology. ET's reading of myths through his university and civil service years was important because it told him myths extended the history of a country, gave it roots and that his own country Singapore had no indigenous, supportive structures in terms of myths. But more important in those early years was perhaps his discovery that myths connected cultures. They were the basic narratives, as fundamental as religion, that gave a culture its values and the values remained universal. If a mythological hero was a distillation of the culture of a country—its thirst for adventure, heroism, endurance and morality, then the template would remain the same across borders—whether he was called Apollo, Achilles or Arjun.[37]

This understanding of commonalities, be it mythological, religious or historical patterns which hold the world together, would change ET forever. He would see there was a fundamental egalitarianism in the construct of the universe—in the religious parables and culture-specific aphorisms which no future radical

---

[37]   ET's reading list on religion and mythology: *Mythology* by Thomas Bulfinch; *Religions of the Greeks and Romans* by Carl Kerenyi; *Archetypal Patterns of Poetry: Psychological Studies of Imagination* by Maud Bodkin; *Studies of Type-Images in Poetry, Religion and Philosophy* by Maud Bodkin; *Mysticism: Sacred and Profane* by R.C. Zaehner; *Hinduism* by R.C. Zaehner; *The Dawn and Twilight of Zoroastrianism* by R.C. Zaehner; *A Test of Time: The Bible–from Myth to History* by David Rohl; *The Lost Testament: From Eden to Exile–The Five-Thousand-Year History of the People of the Bible* by David Rohl.

movement or revolution could hope to surpass. And hence his yet another formulation: the distinction between form and substance. As he says, 'Forms can differ, but substance cannot. It's the forms that make us quarrel. Once we go behind the form and see the substance it is all the same. Religious rituals may differ but no faith allows one to kill without good reason . . .'[38]

It is this philosophy which has elements of both universal validity and contextual relevance, which is not so much about 'moral sharing' as about 'moral commonality', that forms the crux of ET's poems and it is this underpinning thought that makes his writing so relevant to multi-racial Singapore. It is because of this journey of discovery which started in the scruffy bookstores of Bras Basah and continues even today as he struggles to complete his paean to Brother Joe, the Irish master of arts of Singapore, that the motif of the traveller is a reiterated one in his poems. Because it is the traveller who knows the world best, it is the traveller who moves away from the lure of insularity and crosses boundaries, treads on the holy grounds of other cultures and makes them his own. It is because of this that ET's eyes light up when he speaks of Celtic graves found in the interiors of Central Asia or the lady, a café owner he met in Alexandria, who shared his love for Cavafy's poems. It is this fascination with the figure of the traveller that made him read Viking history, that makes him speak of Thomas as the greatest of apostles, that makes him so fond of Cavafy, that made him choose Ulysses as the central character of one of his most significant poems, *Ulysses by the Merlion*.

Thus he writes of Brother Joseph McNally, the La Sallian brother of the small farming community of County Mayo who came to Singapore via Malaysia to teach at the St Joseph's Institution when he was twenty-three and made Malaya (and Singapore) his own, who was so deeply integrated with the local culture that he could inspire many generations of Singapore artists and whose magnificent sculptures still dot Singapore's college of arts,

---

[38] Interview 15 June 2017.

I am of this Island too.
So you were.
Remote sensing compacted time and distance as you
Adapted, as it rearranged Irish memories which inspired
And fed your final SG mission. More equinox, less solstice.
Here trees burnt green, your ancestral shade.[39]

It is only in the heart of the traveller that Ireland's sweeping landscapes
and Celtic motifs can come to live together in harmony with HDB
estates and the buzz of infrastructure of a fast-growing city-state.

A fragmented world: The psychology of colonization

Among the theorists of colonialism, Partha Chatterjee is a significant
name. With some bravado he sets out to challenge the pioneer in the
field, Anderson, and turning around the Westerner's notion of an
'imagined community', posits that anticolonial nationalism is not
entirely a political movement. Rather it is a sociological phenomenon
that fragments the colonized world into two domains—the
Westernized 'outer' world of the economy, statecraft and science and
the 'inner' spiritual world containing the essential markers of cultural
identity.[40] Fieldhouse of Cambridge takes this a step forward and
holds accountable for the 'quirk' of colonialism a remote abstraction
and says it was as if the ability to decide a country's destiny, its
collective mind had been surgically removed and placed in another
mind in London, Paris or Brussels.[41]

ET, growing up as he did in that crucial interregnum between
colonialism and Asian nationalism that Singapore knew, felt this
sense of inner fragmentation as he grew up—subliminally at first and

---

[39]   *Brother Joseph McNally.*
[40]   *The Nation and its Fragments*, Partha Chatterjee (NJ: Princeton University
       Press, 1993), p. 6.
[41]   *The West and the Third World*, D.K. Fieldhouse (UK: Blackwell Pub, 1999), p. 71.

more consciously later as he entered the University of Malaya and was firmly ensconced in the group of budding nationalists there.[42] It is interesting to note how almost all his tales of childhood—told with a sprightly air and twinkle in the eye, grind to a rude halt with the mention of the British. Mention of his father leads to a reference to the trouble Jabez ran into with the English Sports Inspector, Strickland, at Pasir Panjang Primary School and so never got his promotion. ET bemoans the 'terrible' family trait of speaking the mind and adds, 'That's why we all ended up as teachers you see!'[43] Then there was his Doctor Uncle, a bit of a 'freak' who knew the Gita and Virgil by heart in their original languages, was good at Mathematics (Tripos from Cambridge), and who when he said, 'Eddie, I feel like a bit of Milton' ET knew he was in trouble! Or his Uncle Hoisington who would eventually be the author of the ACS (Anglo-Chinese School) school song, who never got that chief engineer's job with the municipality because of the colour of his skin.

ET who had grown up straddling the multiple worlds inhabited by his parents and grandparents, could see there was a difference when it came to the twin worlds of the colonized and the colonizer—there was no possibility of easy assimilation. His Teochew mother could very easily take his Tamil half-brother to a Teochew opera house or visit a Malay shaman, but this was different. When the world of the British came in proximity to their own, it created ripples of unrest and disturbed the harmony. And this ET grew increasingly conscious of as he read. Though ET himself does not claim the time he spent in those bookstores of Bras Basah to be a turning point in his life, but undeniably it was. For it was there, sitting on the floor, with his back resting against rickety bookshelves, that he realized the full extent of temporal and spatial displacement that colonialism involves as he stumbled onto a single fact, stunning in its unalloyed ruthlessness,

---

[42] *Perceiving other Worlds*, p. 277.
[43] Interviews 29 May to 06 June 2017.

'The major movements of the history we studied excluded us.'[44] It was his first confrontation with what Spivak calls the 'imperialist narrativization of history' and perhaps because of the clarity of this realization the poem he wrote during this period (in 1954) is one of the most direct and hard-hitting,

We do but merely ask, No more, no less,
This much: that you white man,
. . . restore this place,
This sun to us . . . and the waiting generations.

Depart white man.[45]

ET writes of a Commonwealth Literature Conference he attended in 1968 in the University of Queensland, Brisbane, where the participants jointly made the discovery that irrespective of whether they were Indians, West Indians, Pacific Islanders, Singaporeans, Malaysians, Maltese or Africans, they had learnt the same nursery rhymes, read the same grammar, debated the same topics, read the same history, geography or hygiene texts and in most cases knew *God save the Queen* better than their recently adopted national anthems.[46] But they also knew, this empire-wide homogeneity that stretched from Aden to Zanzibar was an artificial one, did not run as deep as the older connections of religion—be it Hinduism, Buddhism, Christianity or Islam; culture—be it dance-drama, *wayang* or gamelan; and language—be it Bahasa, Chinese or Tamil. Such deeper exchanges of the mind and culture had made the Southeast Asian region for instance into a 'literary region' or as ET puts it, '. . . there are constructs and processes suggesting a deep sharing in

---

[44]   *Literature and Liberation*, ed. ET (Philippines: Solidaridad Pub. House, 1988), p. 132.

[45]   *May 1954.*

[46]   *Literature and Liberation*, p. 131.

Southeast Asia. Not to suggest a mind for the region, but strong
common elements. There is a *rasa* that makes us *sayang*.'[47]

This realization of alienation in his own country, a manipulated
depersonalization of the bond that linked him to his own history
would leave ET with two aching needs in his character, a persistent
longing that is hard to ignore in his poems. Firstly, a yearning
nostalgia for all that had passed, the world of deeply shared intimacies
where differences were a variation but never a disadvantage. As he
himself acknowledges, 'History gets necessarily rewritten by the
spirit moving a new generation's irredentist impulses, longing not
for lost territory but the completeness of earlier selves.'[48] In later years
one would hear him vociferously demanding for old street names and
the topographical spread of Singapore to be maintained and see him
sitting in a room at the National University of Singapore where he
is surrounded by mementoes from old travel and souvenirs from old
friends. History would forever claim him for its own.

1959 + Fifty

I
Our City that
They half-returned, Raffles founded with precision.
He commandeered slick arrangements to oversee his
Island's cross-straits growth, firmly staving off spicy
Interlopers, then tapped migrant energies to build.

Let's credit the old colonial foresight, grip, tenacity.
They made a notable place, a link in their global grid.
No lonely outpost this. In truth, a posh equator-haven
That never questioned fun so long its form was pakka.

---

[47]   *Anglophone Cultures in Southeast Asia*, ed. Rudiger Ahrens, etc. (Heidelberg:
       Universitatsverlag Winter, 2003), p. 21.
[48]   *Literature and Liberation*, p. 126.

Scan old maps, prints, club traditions, pleasance,
For pulsating tropic therapy. List names now slightly
Tanned: Mt Sophia, Mt Faber, Mt Echo. Little, high
Exclusive places to catch airy melor and champaka
Undulations, while below, variously, were daily lives
Of sweaty heave-and-ho of multi-racial labourings.

They branded Imperial Comfort, kept up ritual till
Worn down, without remit, by a great Depression,
WW2, to a limping victory. Then Batang Kali, Hidup
Negara, and Merdeka, began to stalk the aging itsy-
Bitsy Lion shedding her colonies reluctantly, turning
Pre-National.

II

This our City-State,
Rose above withdrawal-symptoms creeping home from
East of Suez, black-white bungalows, Nee Soon bars.
Plant and renovate according to our leaders who muster,
Deploy and assess; chew, cogitate; rotate dreams, inspect
Possibilities including base conversion; calculate the way
Ahead; split racist infinitives; re-dress, re-vive decaying
Precincts; re-place Old Lobb and farm; learn to re-learn;
Keep tradition, yet change, move, do. Lick trade unions
Into shape. Lance the *Barisan* boil, as ten million sing
Malaysia forever, a brief sojourn, a painful parting for
Our island in the sun.

There is no Paradise; only KPIs:
Labour, Capital, Government; Meritocracy, Equality;
Integrity, Commitment, Skills Development Fund;
And more, to mix and match into a Pledge, a Unity.

Singapore aga aga sudah jadi

Walk down the years between ever taller buildings, cross
Cleaner streets following a small green man who never tires.
Past Copthorne, to that notorious bend which slows our river.
No sulfide air. There are fish. Then backtrack past bridges
Whose names sound our history. See the Merlion, Durian,
Floating Platform, and emerging Double Helix bridge:
Art and design enhance function as in the newer HDBs.

Stroll Marina Barrage. Stop. Hear the waters on either side:
One composed, one rough, two signifiers for our boundaries.

Guard one; watch the other, so sanctify life within our skyline,
As twilight starts to hum, stretch its limbs, as colours move.
This new lake will gradually re-fresh, sweeten, fill sails, sms,
Accost the rising sun, pleasure lovers who hug its shores then

See the evening set in a pair of eyes, gently foreclosing.
Soon moonlight will start to heap.
Guardian hours that pass will come again,
As I remember what fifty years of vision
Un-did and did,
As what was and is, and may have been,
I place in the fifty years to come.

The second need that would remain in him was of order. Memory
of that scene when he had seen a single rifle resting against a coconut
tree in Mandai would stay with him as a symbol of lost innocence
and of the old order disintegrating. He would in the future be on
a continuous search for orders of society which were inherent,
organic, deep-rooted and not artificially imposed for purposes of
political dominance or economic advantage. Hence his interest in

archaeology and ancient religions. Or when he speaks of the ancient civilizations which had spread horizontally from west to east which was subsequently sliced up vertically from north to south for the convenience of colonialists, 'And so we have Cameroon for instance, divided into the French Cameroon, the British Cameroon and the German Cameroon . . . and then there is a bit that is Portuguese and Fulani in the north that was returned later . . .'[49] Colonialism and the pleasures of a lost childhood would sensitize him to the orders that lie behind apparent urban landscapes across the world.

But this order that ET so obsessively seeks also translates into an intuitive scepticism for abstraction. In searching for organic connections his mind delves into history, archaeology and extends itself into myths and legends but scarcely does it allow itself to travel beyond that. So unlike Tagore who had read in raindrops on forest leaves the metaphysical unity of the universe, ET is conscious of his distance from the mystics and theologians. He is aware that he is not a Rumi or an Ibn Arabi or a Lao Tze, that he lacks the discipline of the mystics—the isolation, the sense of purpose, of responsibility, the dedication to religion.[50] And even accedes of his daily struggle with his religious belief, the sense of self-reproof that he knows when he realizes unlike his children or his wife, at eighty-seven he is yet to experience an epiphanic moment. 'The mind will not let go, you know,' he says with earnest concern, 'complete surrender is impossible.' It is a continuation of the same trajectory which made him address the younger generations of Singapore in a voice slightly sententious, a tone which perhaps is reflective of his teacher's genes, while explaining the need for order, '. . . both a people and any dedicated, intelligent government generally know, though the abstractions should be remembered—and given voice—for their holistic, reminding power. But, equally, we should not ignore the realities—initially the political, economic and social sets—that hedge

---

[49]   Interview 07 August 2017.
[50]   Ibid.

the translation of the abstract into *real politic*, into national life.'[51] It is perhaps because of this that, rather than abstract metaphysics, ever-familiar Singapore with its gently flowing rivers and shimmering seas would remain in his line of vision.

Passage O Soul to India[52]

ET has remained an ardent admirer of E.M. Forster, particularly of his last novel (except the one published posthumously), *A Passage to India*. His personal collection holds at least a couple of dozen books of analytical essays on the novel and one wonders why this fervent need to understand the British author so completely. Forster who was the eternal itinerant, who hungered to feel the continuity of things, who remained intensely uncomfortable in England with its heart of a public school and instead found his holy unity in Cambridge where there is no intellectual picking and choosing among traditions, where the point of origin of individual thought remains private and natural.

When asked, ET says it is because the novel dwells on form and substance like no other, i.e., the difference is only in form while the essential substance or cosmic truth remains firmly united.[53] *A Passage to India* is a story of stumbling onto this truth in the echoing, claustrophobic Marabar Caves, an experience which would touch the different characters in different ways yet leave none of them unchanged. ET's attraction is also for Forster in general because he remained an intellectual traveller. In Cambridge, Forster studied the classical culture of Greece and afterwards plunged into the passionate liberalism of Italy where he lived for a while. While in service in Alexandria. he befriended Cavafy and took his poems back to England.[54] But it was perhaps in India that his journey came to

---

[51] *Literature and Liberation*, pp. 127–8.

[52] Walt Whitman's poem from which Forster took his title.

[53] Interview 26 June 2017.

[54] *Selected Letters of E.M. Forster*, Vol. 2, ed. Mary Lago and P.N. Furbank; Letter no. 232 to C.P. Cavafy (London: Collins, 1983–85).

an end because after *A Passage to India* he decided to write no more fiction. Like Kurtz's vision in Conrad's *Heart of Darkness,* the echoing Marabar Caves where 'Whatever is said, the same monotonous noise replies and quivers up and down the walls until it is absorbed into the roof—Boum' was perhaps a life-changing experience for Forster too.[55] Afterwards he needed to seek no more.

The novel, set in British-India of the 1920s, is essentially about building connections. When, for instance, Aziz, the doctor from Chandrapore, strikes up conversation with Mrs Moore, an elderly visiting Briton, they feel an instant connection as they speak animatedly about their children and yet the spark fades fast. Such a flash occurs again when the Brahmin professor, Godbole sings a song about Krishna at Fielding's tea party. But it is in the Caves that everything reaches a climax. The Marabar Caves, marked by a vacuum, sealed off before human evolution really began, which possess nothing but a quintessential nothingness older than creation, where words are reduced to incommunicable echoes, that the characters see reality, the truth within themselves and in so doing understand the outer world better. It is in the Caves that Aziz feels a connection with Fielding beyond their racial differences and yet he knows the political condition of their respective countries will not allow a friendship.

So, *A Passage to India* is about finding a unity that does not really unify. As Forster put it, 'I have acquired a feeling that people must go away from each other (spiritually) every now and then, and improve themselves if the relationship is to develop or even endure. *A Passage to India* describes such a going away . . .'[56] For ET the novel remains significant for two reasons. At a personal level, it is the spirituality of the book, the way in which it points towards the essence of every religion, though it might do so in the garb of the oldest of faiths— Hinduism. As he says, 'The Marabar Caves merely amplifies all that

---

[55]   Ibid; Vol. 1; letter no. 49.
[56]   Ibid; Vol. 2; letter no. 248.

is inside you and that is what religion does, isn't it? Like reflections on a polished glass you see all these images and the worst is when you see the evil in you.'[57] ET speaks of Godbole who sees no difference in substance between a wasp and an old lady and knows good and evil are both aspects of 'my Lord. He is present in the one, absent in the other.' Yet absence does not mean non-existence, but rather implies presence—goodness that waits to be invoked.

As a thinker and a poet, what appealed to ET was Forster's delving into an alien culture, the restlessness that Forster knew when he wrote, 'How I wish I knew what India is after' or as he tells English fellow writer, J.R. Ackerley, that he will first need to get used to Indian boredom before he sees India, not its Anglo-Indian years but its years of reality.[58] It is this crossing of boundaries, exploring beyond the foreground of cultural landscapes that appealed to ET and that he attempted in poems like *Ancestral Houses, Goa,* the hybrid town where an Indian Maria Miranda Flores feels the stirrings of her mixed genes and waits for her Portuguese lover:

> Maria Miranda Flores, a great
> Beauty, intact. Honed by horse and stirrup, her thighs
> Wait endlessly to grip his flanks. Lonely. Hungry. He
> Knows. She ignores tempting surrogates. In helpless
> Ache and agony, that bare moment, green priestly eyes
> Enter her to reappear, like Gor-gor's single nipple. Gene
> Magic. Perhaps they transmit racial memories as well.

This search for an underlying unity is a skill that ET would hone and sharpen over the years to envision and realize the common culture for the newly formed city-state of Singapore, post- the increasing levels of self-government granted by the British and eventually as it stepped away from its merger with the Federation of Malaya in 1965,

---

[57] Interview 26 June 2017.
[58] *Selected Letters of E.M. Forster*, Vol. 2, letter no. 238.

to become an independent republic. Like the polished glass of the
Marabar Caves his poems would try to amplify and articulate what
is inherent in the cultural fabric of Singapore, move away from the
enforced, artificial control of colonization. It was the brewing racial
tensions of Singapore that ET had witnessed and the independent
PAP (People's Action Party) government's edict of multi-racial unity
that would water the aquifer of ET's poetic imagination.

Max Havelaar: Exploring a deeper unity

It is D.H. Lawrence who led ET to Multatuli's classic, *Max
Havelaar*. While he read Lawrence through his university days, he
came upon the Dutch writer only after joining NUS as a lecturer in
the Department of English in 1966. It was while writing an essay on
Conrad's short stories that he came across Lawrence's reference to the
book—*a real book that doesn't pall, though as far as composition goes,
it is the greatest mess possible.*[59] As ET puts it, 'I felt, if Lawrence had
taken an interest in Multatuli then he must be worth it. So I followed
up—and oh man!'[60] As he speaks, the excitement of that discovery
still glitters in his eyes, the realization that as a book of satire on
colonial administration, *Max Havelaar* was a first of the firsts, even
outstripping Conrad: 'Multatuli writes from inside the colonial
system while Conrad could only write from outside.'[61] *Max Havelaar*
would lead ET to other colonial writers of Dutch Indonesian, the
Philippines and eventually of the region—the Henri Fauconnier and
Maurice Collins of the time.

Like *A Passage to India*, the Dutch classic written by Multatuli,
Max Havelaar, is also about a journey. But while in the former the
travellers to the Marabar Caves stumble upon a truth as old as time,

---

[59] Multatuli, *Max Havelaar or the Coffee Auctions of the Dutch Trading Company*
      (London: Heinemann, 1967), introduction by D.H. Lawrence.
[60] Interview 29 May 2017.
[61] Ibid.

in this, Max Havellar, the somewhat naïve, romantic revolutionary hero in his journey to the heartland of colonized Indonesia sees the failings of the Dutch bureaucracy and through him the reader sees the deadly systemic flaws of colonialism at large. As Edward Said noted, Multatuli did not share the prevailing imperialist vision that colonialism was a 'mission civilisatrice' of the West for the non-Western world, a grand design by which a colossal poem in granite like the Cologne Cathedral could be built.[62]

What struck ET about the book was its narrative structure, in the way it is built on a series of flashbacks while the characters invent a set of characters who in turn invent yet other characters. It is as compelling as de-stacking a set of Matryoshka dolls as one is first introduced to Droogstoppel, the Dutch coffee broker who is so pious and bigoted as to appear a caricature and yet represents the Dutch society as a whole, caught as it was in the doldrums of an economic slowdown. He leads one to the second narrator, the idealistic German, Stern, who is greatly admiring of Havelaar's poetic and fiery soul and contemptuous of everything that Droogstoppel stands for. At the centre of the novel in the midst of famine-stricken, miserable Lepak which grows the rich harvest of coffee and opium that feed the Dutch ships, are two couples placed opposite each other—the Dutch Havelaar and his Tina and the Indonesian Saijah and his Adinda. What is remarkable is that despite belonging to opposing sides of the colonial power structure, the same fate of utter misery and destitution awaits them. And yet cutting through this inherent and very humane sense of unity is the essentially exploitative structure on which colonialism pegs itself, the shrewd political use that is made of the ancient feudal system of Asia by which a native chief is appointed as officer of the Crown, thereby creating a hierarchy where brother is turned against brother

---

[62] Edward Said, *Culture & Imperialism* (NY: Knopf, 1993), p. 240. *Max Havelaar*, pp. 64–5.

and at the summit stands colonial authority exercised by the Dutch colonial Governor General.[63]

Max Havelaar as a literary text held ET's attention primarily because of the perpetuation of the remarkable traveller motif. Like *A Passage to India*, it tells the story of a traveller who looks beyond cultural boundaries and discovers connecting bedrocks of universal human values and human bonds that stand the test of time. ET would try, very consciously to do the same, keep Singapore in mind, its myriad religious and cultural sects and subsects and provide the newly-minted republic with symbols of cultural unity that would hold it together. The next section discusses some of his Sino-Indian poems as a curtain-raiser to the kind of poetry he would write in the future with an aim to provide Singapore with symbols that transcend borders. From *Max Havelaar* would come his understanding of the importance of the governance structure that post-independent Singapore was trying to build, one built on mutual correlation and interdependence of religious and cultural groups rather than on mutual exploitation that was prevalent in the colonial times.

Hanuman: Unity in Sino-Indian poems

ET grew up in the shadows of two intimidatingly large and overwhelmingly ancient cultures—that of India and China. Part of the assimilation of the two cultures was subliminal by dint of his Tamil and Chinese parentage, part of it was conscious as he grew older and had the opportunity to study and travel. In writing of his friend, the Indian philosopher and scholar, Raja Rao, ET noted, 'Rao's circles of understanding enlarge as he absorbs and fills out his possession of the Indian tradition . . . That long odyssey commences with his discovery of India, leading to the increasingly confident projection of her and the taking of her with him as he visits or lives in and seeks to

---

[63] *Max Havelaar*, p. 67.

understand other societies and cultures . . .'[64] The lines can very easily be used to describe ET himself once India is replaced with India *and* China. If the phenomenon of the 'expanding form' is a recurring symbol of both Hindu and Buddhist civilizations, wherein gods as well as the Buddha expand themselves at will into cosmic giants, then in ET's case it is safe to say the proverbial 'expansion' happened over time as he immersed in and understood the root cultures of Singapore. Among the three dominant races of Singapore (Chinese, Malay and Tamil), though he admits of an intense admiration of the Malay culture, which according to him is present in its fully-extended range in Singapore, self-confessedly his understanding of China and India run deeper.[65] As he writes while describing his ancestral home in Swatow, a house that he never really saw, yet to which he belonged by blood, 'it was part of an inheritance . . . ensuring a sense of continuity' and he needed to belong to it in spirit because it was part of a larger culture, a larger history, a larger continuity, which was China.[66] And though his early exposure to India was more limited because his Tamil grandfather had emigrated alone and was ostracized as a newly-converted Christian, the urge he felt to understand India was equally intense because the complex, introspective, monistic mass of Indian civilization was also a part of his identity. The need to know the 'other' half would continue to haunt him.

ET entered China, as many do, through stories of djinns and noble ministers and shamanistic spirit journeys heard on the knees of grandmother and mother under the mysterious half-light of a mosquito net. And India came to him in the pleasurable though perplexing Tamil words of church hymns. But perhaps it was fortunate for him that when in adulthood he set out to explore the two cultures, he did so through the highest possible routes of

---

[64] *Interlogue*, Vol. 7, ed. Peter Nazareth (Singapore: Ethos Books, 2008), p. 129.
[65] Interview 26 June 2017.
[66] *Return to Origins*, p. 33.

instructive, liberating scholarship. Though he had visited Delhi in 1967, when his teacher and academic, Maurice Baker, became Singapore's first High Commissioner to India, his 'real' visits started with his acquaintance with C.D. Narasimhaiah, the very erudite writer and principal of the college of Mysore.[67] This friendship would lead him to the metaphysical dwellings of Raja Rao and ET's connections with Mysore would continue with Dhvanyaloka, the centre for Indian studies founded by Narasimhaiah. And as far as China was concerned, his first official visit was at the same time when the Chinese government was re-establishing the Xi'an Jiaotong University of Shanghai.[68] ET travelled there with a group of poets and witnessed first-hand the pride of the residents of this city considered to be the poetic capital of China. But his love for Chinese poetry started much earlier, in the early 1950s, when he read the poets of the Tang Dynasty—the poetry of Li Po for instance, tales of the Yangtze Valley and the An Lushan Rebellion and the way Li squandered away an Emperor's gift in gold on a single evening's drinking pleasure.

Through the years, ET's understanding of India and China has been cumulatively extended as he has first looked at real histories and then mythological histories of the two countries, followed the strain as it fades from the legendary past to the mythical past. But what is interesting to note is how seamlessly the two cultures come together in his poems. As he says in the context of the bilingual policy of Singapore, the purpose of his poems remain to move out of the root cultures and grow aware of a second, perhaps even a third culture which is unique to Singapore.[69] If he admires Forster or Multatuli for their exploration of cultural common ground, of shared experiences in the echoing caves of Marabar or the mud tracts of Lepak, he tries to do the same in his poems.

---

[67]   Interview 15 June 2017.

[68]   Ibid.

[69]   Ee Tiang Hong *Responsibility & Commitment: The Poetry of Edwin Thumboo* (Singapore: SUP, 1997), p. 7.

Thus, there is his quintessentially Indian poem *Krishna*, dedicated to Raja Rao and said to present in a microcosm ET's understanding of India. Yet, it is difficult to miss its unmistakeable Chinese elements as the poet explores the sensuality of Krishna and his radiant Radha in Vrindavan where they cavorted by the dark waters of the Yamuna. In describing the sublime union of Krishna's unstirring eternal divinity with the activating energy and dynamic creative impulse of Radha, he brings into play the male and female duality and interdependence of the *yin* and *yang*. Right from the outset it is a poem that works on opposites—the expanse of a thousand years with the effulgent beauty of a single face or the great inclines of Krishna's noble heart with the timorous eyes and nimble fingers of his consort. And then the immediately following lines:

> She gazed upon him
> With a look of morning lotus,
> Till each stood within the other.
> So the blue god, his votive flute
> Multiplying his love, the gopis,
> Sporting with them all,
> He sported with but one.

Not only is there a contrast of opposites here with Krishna's singularity juxtaposed with the multiplicity of the *gopis,* there is also a distinct parallel drawn with the poet with his *votive flute* or pen as a tool of expression and his audience, in whose multiple minds is reflected his own thoughts. And in the final union of the two gods, as

> The world revives, quickens,
> Renews itself, turns whole,

there is reflected the perfect balance of the *yin* and *yang* which when brought together represents an interactive, dynamic composite whole much greater in potency than its assembled parts.

On the other hand, is a poem like *Uncle Never Knew* on his Chinese Uncle, who was a part of the extended family, a Lee, though ET cannot recall his full name. He was around a decade older to ET and with him ET developed a close bond in the late 40s. Uncle was very much a misfit—anti-business, an intellectual and an ardent follower of Mao—the stereotypical Communist of Asia who despite his radical political beliefs, was very much a traditionalist.[70] He was anxious to go back to Swatow, but the politics of China, the civil war after the defeat of the Japanese prevented him and it was through his nostalgic recollections that ET was initiated into his Chinese inheritance. Yet in telling the story of this Uncle, who lived in a state of suspended reality, in a home that was a fantastical recreation of his memory of China:

> At his table. Preparing
> Ink and brush; fingering his father's piece of jade

ET takes us through many of the *rasas* of the ancient Indian *Natya Sashtra*. If there is something gently humorous in this lonely, homesick man who waits for his *drinking friend,* stroking his *undernourished beard,* speaking *to clouds, not people,* the pathos of the situation is underscored as the poet helps one see the man who is *always alone but never lonely.* There is something also faintly heroic in Uncle's unwavering allegiance to the old way of life *which brooks no breaking of fidelity.* But even more interesting is the way ET brings into play the response of the Singaporean reader, who in all probability would be a migrant like Uncle and would feel the diasporic desire for his lost heritage, the emotional wrench of moving from the *great houses* which *are history* to this *island so little that the migrant reader barely noticed.* As in the ancient theory of *rasa,* ET places together on the same platform his own creative process as well as the aesthetic gratification that the reader is to experience from the poem.

---

70   *Return to Origins,* pp. 28–33.

But perhaps the coming together of China and India is nowhere more obvious than in his choice of the cultural symbol of Hanuman, the faithful follower of Ram who finds his way into the Chinese pantheon as the legendary Wu Kong on a journey to the Western Paradise to get Buddhist scriptures for the Monk Xuanzang. When asked about symbols of cultural integration, ET unhesitatingly points to this mythological figure who he says is the perfect traveller because he changes in character as he crosses borders to remain culturally relevant to the two countries.[71] In India he knows nothing but unswerving loyalty to Ram, a loyalty that springs from the great love in his heart for his master. If he errs at all and sets fire to the Lanka where Sita is held prisoner, he does so in his eagerness to save her. But in China, as it often happens in adapted tales, his character is stretched and simplified. He is the errant, boisterous *monkey mind* symbolical of human nature prone to folly and if he finally turns over a new leaf after a series of adventures in the Cypress Grove and Lotus Cave, it is out of fear of the Head-splitting Helmet that the Buddha has placed on his head which tightens every time he commits a misdeed. But as ET points out, whether he is the beautiful rebel of China or the resolute devotee of India, the Monkey God is one person who knows his position in the power hierarchy and struggles to restore order.[72] And eventually if he is guaranteed a place in the pantheon it is because he has done his duty to his master, often at great personal risk.

Conversation with my Friend Kwang Min at Loong Kwang of Outram Park

Among
Sensitive vases,
Silk birds

---

[71]   Interview 26 June 2017.
[72]   Ibid.

Lamenting sullen, fading flowers;
And those delicate golden statues
Caught in some potent gesture . . .
You are captured by serenity:
Kuan Yin upon the lotus.

Conversation fades—
Time splits itself.

There are centuries here,
In these images.
Many generations left
These signs of contemplation,
Embodiments of hope, despair—
In art. The art of living;
Of mounting better worlds.
Man emerging from the dark
Made dreams, tamed nightmares
Into lovely moving monuments,
Each a voice stealing
Upon you, conversing softly
Out of its secret heart.

This jade pomegranate
Is succulent; that ivory boat
Will always sail to Mogadishu,
Taking Cheng Ho by our city. In that
Corner, intimidating himself,
A cutish lion glares.
Half-way up the wall,
In porcelain, a rare Hanuman.
He ravished the gardens of Heaven,
Cowered the gods one week-end,
Was tamed and sinonised,

Absorbed, given a role, then
Adventured home to India
In search of texts.
He scratches still, in kungfu fashion.

On a plinth,
Li of the Iron Staff
Whose gentle heart belies
The terror of his face,
Remains a comfort.
What better lesson is there
Than to suffer because
You helped another?

Empires wax and wane
States cleave asunder,
Coalesce in this carved panel.
Kun Ming deceives his enemy
By playing his favourite tune
While perched
Upon the city gate. He smiles,
Who faithfully served a cause
He knew was lost;
He, who ruled the winds,
Understood the stars,
The very hand of fate,
Kept true unto the last.

As you move into
Presences of the past
Little things emerge:
Tea-pots, a cracked,
Perky cup; incense-burners
Heavy with prayer; brush stands,

Wine jugs . . .

All looking contented
In a Singapore afternoon.

On to Singapore

This chapter has been rather adventurous in the period it covers. Like
the proverbial Hanuman, it has taken giant leaps in time and space—
from pre-war Singapore to post-Mao China or from the dirt-tracks
of Lepak to the mists of pre-Christian Ireland. All this to understand
the makings of a single scholarly mind. What has been achieved is
clarity on the reasons why the traveller motif with implications of
shared borders and a deeper cultural unity, finds pride of place on the
altar of ET's poetic imagination. What remains to be achieved is to
see how he deploys it to carve an evolving multiracial identity for his
nation. On the way, colour will be filled in and requiems composed
to give the reader a fuller understanding of this journey.

So far what emerges is a highly curious mind which constantly
peers over borders—be they geographical, historical, logical or
metaphysical. To him two things remain of highest value—the
individual, whether it is the 'I' or the 'You', and the essential
connections to be made—be it the connection of the moment with
time or the near with the far between cultures—in order to achieve a
unified, continuous whole. His is also a voice that remains steeped in
empathy. If Multatuli had written of Max Havellar, '. . . he was gentle
by nature, in complete contrast to his powers of penetration, which
the reader will by now have discovered to be uncommonly keen . . .
he could not see sorrow without suffering personally,' he could have
very easily been speaking of ET.[73] Combined with this empathy and
an uncanny power to perceive, there is a hint of obduracy, a digging in
of heels so to say, which does not augur well for someone who would

---

[73]   *Max Havelaar*, p. 216.

spend much of his life working within a system or establishment. It would be interesting to observe how he recast himself (if at all) to be able to 'fit in'. One thing is for certain, whether during his civil service days or his time with the university, it was his own relentless scholarly pursuits that gave him the motivation to carry on. It was this and also the sense of mission that drove his entire generation. Or as ET puts it, 'It was the challenges of that historical moment after independence that provided the opportunities.'[74]

This chapter stops short of university. The year was 1953 when he had taken the University of Malaya Entrance Examination in mid-March 1953 and was expected to go up to the university in September of the same year. It was a time when he started to see Singapore's racial inheritance, 'All our groups—Malay, Chinese, Indians and Eurasians—had sub-groups. The Malaya had Bugis, Bataks, Achenese, Javanese and others. The Chinese had Hokkiens, Teochews, Cantonese, Hainanese and so on. The Indians were far more complicated.'[75]

What emerges from this period are the two clear streams of his thinking on the multiracialism of his country. Firstly, that this sensitivity towards the social 'other' came to him as much by nature, by dint of his own family background, as nurture as he witnessed first-hand the racial tensions in his school and university and the racial riots of the 1950s. The awareness of the first two decades of his life was merely honed into structured understanding and firm conviction as he studied the syncretic cultures of the world during his civil service days. So, according to him, multiracialism was an urgent part of the country's cultural fabric and had little to do with the PAP (People's Action Party of Singapore) mooting the issue after it was institutionalized in 1954. 'There were many like us at the university—Wang Gungwu, Lim Thean Soo, Goh Sin Tub, Beda Lim or I for whom the subject was already top of the

---

[74] Interview 18 September 2017.
[75] See ET's comments in Appendix I.

mind,' he says, 'the PAP shared and amplified what was there in the environment.'[76]

The second part of his thoughts on multiracialism is his understanding of the relevance of the Indian and Chinese cultures to Singapore (Malay too, though self-confessedly, his understanding of the Malay culture does not run deep). He feels, for a true Singaporean culture to evolve which is unique to the country, there is no escaping the root cultures—equally important are the majestically instructive, liberating power of the *Mahabharata* and *Ramayana* as of the *Li Sao* and *I-Ching*.[77] His own poetry was born from a spontaneous fusion of the two—if the classic Sangam poetry of the *Kuruntokai* taught him poetic structure, convention and the objective correlative, then the first translations of Chinese poetry from Arthur Waley's books taught him to feel the texture of words, to listen to their voice and hear what they say when they fall silent.[78] And so, eventually the magic of his poetry would be forged in his personal smithy.

But the same scholarly mind that assimilates with ease the dynamics of multiracial Singapore and seeks an overarching homogeneity—of which *Satu Bangsa, Satu Agama, Satu Bahasa* and *Satu Negara* (One Race, One Religion, One Language, one Nation) would be a good example—could also prove to be his undoing. As he himself confesses, even at a considerably advanced age, he knows daily struggle with his spiritual practice, finds it difficult to surrender his fully awakened mind to the dictates of the heart. Faith does not come easily to him. A consciousness always remains, or rather the deeper, more intuitive consciousness that awakened Tagore as a child, does not emerge. For the same reason he reads the theologians and mystics but knows he cannot be one of them. Or as he puts it, 'You see the connections like the mystics but adapt them to your situation

---

[76] Interview 18 September 2017.
[77] *Interlogue* (2008), p. 190.
[78] Interview 18 September 2017.

or country,' and even when he writes on Moses, it is a political and not a religious exercise.[79]

Hence ET's preoccupation with poetry with a purpose, and the purpose very clearly remains to move from tolerance and understanding to fusion and harmony in the Singaporean context— chiefly its active pursuit of multi-culturalism for all. The quest appeared more exciting for ET as he witnessed the gradual dissolving of divisive barriers after independence, the gradual emergence of the hyphenated identity, the coming together of for instance, the Teochew with the Hokkien and then as second stage the Chinese-educated Chinese and English-educated Chinese. For him his poetic life was an opportunity to look at race more closely, especially the dismantling of its barriers, and discover a host of other issues: language, customs, taste, nuances of family structures, management of colour and shape, literature, music, dance, painting, sculpture, religion, and their histories and traditions. And as he says, 'From this a Singaporean Identity would emerge.'[80] If the Chinese literary critic, Chou Tso-jen, wrote of humanitarian literature that does not reconcile the individual's right to liberty with the survival of the race or Tagore wrote of poetry, 'But does one write poetry to explain something? . . . if someone smells a flower and says he does not understand, the reply to him is: there is nothing to understand, it is only a scent,' then such writing is not for ET.[81]

But then maybe such a conclusion that ET is all pragmatism and purpose with his transcendental instincts running thin, is a bit too hasty for is it not said that writers and poets who combine their idealism with social commentary are perhaps the 'neo-romantics' for whom 'real' is more than 'realism' and 'romantic' is more than 'romanticism' as they doggedly continue to believe in the power of

---

[79] Interview 07 August 2017.

[80] See ET's comments in Appendix I.

[81] *Search for Identity: Modern Literature and the Creative Arts in Asia*, ed. A.R. Davis (Sydney: Angus & Robertson, 1974), pp. 235–6. *My Life in My Words*, p. xiv.

literature to change the world? It would be wise to find out and to do so it would be necessary to take a closer look at the intervening years before he wrote his pièce de résistance, *Ulysses by the Merlion*: the exact colour and texture of nationalism that surrounded him as he entered university and the literary circles of Singapore, the modification of sensibility as he dwelled on African literature.

At this point, if a single lingering doubt remains, it is about his need to turn to Christianity and a formal worship of the church after nearly a lifetime of religious struggle and belief in the syncretic similarities of the faiths of the worlds. One wonders if it is only the compulsions of the firmness of faith that runs in his family or has something to do with his mention of the sanctity of social order and his obvious admiration for the iconic Hanuman. Such conjectures gain in further resonance when he is placed against his homeland—Singapore—a country known for its Confucian predilection for the state and society over individual will.

Such assumptions warrant a closer examination and so for now, it is on to Singapore.

2

THE ISLE IS FULL OF NOISES

Nationality is the summary name of many things. It seeks a
literature made by Irishmen, and coloured by our scenery,
manners and character. It desires to see art applied to
express Irish thoughts and belief. It would make our music
sound in every parish at twilight, our pictures sprinkle
the walls of every house, and our poetry and history sit at
every hearth.

—Thomas Davis, *Language & Nationality*

Our Japanese soldiers who came back from overseas were a
pitiful sight. They looked thin, weak, and exhausted. And
some of them were invalids, drained of colour and borne
on stretchers. But among them there was one company of
colourful men. They were always singing, even difficult
pieces in several parts, and they sang very well . . . Everyone
asked if they had received extra rations, since they seemed
so happy.

—Michio Takeyama, *Harp of Burma*

And the idea of the Nation is one of the most powerful
anaesthetics that man has invented. Under the influence of its
fumes the whole people can carry out its systematic programme

of the most virulent self-seeking without being in the least aware of its moral perversion—in fact feeling dangerously resentful if it is pointed out.

—Rabindranath Tagore, *Nationalism*

The Cough of Albuquerque

Unlike most of his poems, ET is able to 'almost' date *The Cough of Albuquerque*.[1] He remembers well the September 1954 trip with Kenneth Tregonning to Wat Arun on the banks of the Chao Praya River that finds mention in the poem. Tregonning, later to become the Raffles Professor of History, was then with the Department of History at the University of Malaya. Going by his memory, ET pegs this long poem to 1955 or at most 1956, when he was still in university, reading history and literature with a minor in philosophy.

Part I of *The Cough of Albuquerque*

Time is a parabolic creep
With soft cat-paws
Scratching the pitch of night.
Haze unspun, forgotten by the moon
Lines my cold heart.
Quick the east shafted
Spring of seed
Tilt the hills.

The temple,
Cabalistic eye, old guardian of the door
Links the lotus and its doom,
Dido and her pyre, infinitesimal love and hate.

---

[1] Details *The Cough of Albuquerque* from interview 30 October 2017.

I learn to wait the loss of old masks:
But near, dew dying into morning
Of fresh flowers.

Corded by that eye
Living and dead are two ends of a dream;
Roots of a tree, desire unadorned,
Life in the touch of teats,
Are kin to thoughts in the peepal shade
Where passion has played truant
And silence everything.

What colours have the blind
In the brightest hour?

These thoughts dredge:
The slow inevitable move of habit
Unwinding into routine
Gather my limbs, shave, breakfast of cereal
Stair spiralling a web
'O what a beautiful morning
O What a beautiful day . . .'
With no redemption.
I've heard wound from spool to spool
Yesterdays and all tomorrow:
With this ghost wear thin.

Punctuality, slow destruction from abacus,
Death through skill:
Cold gathers, rends the trembling veil.
Plumb depths,
Labyrinth and layer—
But hero, fisher of men will not bite.
Nor image, the strength of loneliness,
Cling together.

What we have heard till the spirit rebels at hearing
Blood imperious pushed aside,
Will pulse and seed surprise, filling itself.

In the beginning was the word
Made flesh. I'm still there,
Still and forever near
Stations of the Cross;
Cock crew thrice;
I changed my clothes—
Lord made me worthy.

Do I have to wait till
Flesh, primordial out of fear
As the mind sneaks off
Do I have to know
How man made up the whole
From one moment in the garden?
See faces when sleep is ridden by a beast,
Where Adam falls again
Find a sight beyond the eye
To straighten doubt
That bubbles in the soul.

ET also remembers that he had just started reading Eliot more extensively and intimately and like many in his time, could not resist the influence. The title is taken from the line '*The goat coughs at night in the field overhead*' from Eliot's *Gerontion* and though like Eliot, the poem is heavy with allusions and uses the same style of stringing together polaroid shots of fragmented images to create a sense of tensed movement towards a new reality, the central protagonist is anything but similar to the 'gerontion' in question. Unlike the latter, who lives out the futility of his final years and at best is charmingly pathetic and at worst, tiringly pessimistic, the character in *The*

Cough of Albuquerque undeniably carries a stamp of the poet's own personality. He is unceasingly a seeker—a seeker who is endearing because he is not affected or gratuitous.

Spread across the five long sections of the poem, ET goes through an internal journey which begins with the restless vitality of youth and ends with a somewhat mature resolution to start yet another journey. The poem is a coming together of his many interests—history, geography, art, philosophy, myth and religion. It is almost as if his many minds flow into one as the borders of his memory shift to reveal a new mind of single purpose. Some of the images and themes do remain incomplete or stop short of being fully developed perhaps because the poet was then in his early twenties and maybe given to some impetuosity. In the review, C.J. Francis does not mince words, 'The introductory pieces, moreover, do not, in image or otherwise, forecast well the content of the poem; the end does not well recall the rest; there is a distinct lack of the feeling that a basic idea is being throughout churned over . . .'[2]

However, the poem definitely is a reflection of its time. 1954 was when the Rendel Report was passed, casting Singapore into a flurry of political debate. By 1955, the schools of nationalist thought were getting clearer—ranging from the conservative right to the radical left, with the socialist moderates of PAP (People's Action Party) trying to wrench themselves away from those with communist leanings and carve a place closer to the centre point of the political continuum. It was a time of awakening nationalism when, as Philip Jeyaretnam puts it, the youth of Singapore felt the need of a certain defiant shrug of the shoulder in the face of all threats.[3] They felt it marked them from the general mass of mediocrity. It was a time when Meira Chand's Moon from

---

2   Review appears with the poem in *Write*, October 1958, pp. 7–8. *Write* is an independent student publication of the University of Malaya.

3   Philip Jeyaretnam, *Abraham's Promise. Written Country: The History of Singapore through Literature*, ed. Gwee Li Sui (Singapore: Landmark Books, 2016), pp. 65–7.

A Different Sky loses his way among a crowd of strikers and his girlfriend Greta soon discovers, Moon's death was of greater use to the cheering mob than his life.[4] In short, it was a time of turbulence and a compulsive need to sacrifice, when some lost their way and some found their life's mission.

Almost ten years later, ET at a conference on the teaching of English in Singapore would say, 'Generally, the more sensitive the poet, the more likely will he be characteristic of his age. I do not mean dated, but rather more likely would reflect the material and spiritual temper of his time.'[5] And this is exactly true for *The Cough of Albuquerque*. Apart from the fact that in all probability it is the first long poem in English to be published from Singapore, what is interesting is that it perfectly bridges ET's childhood with his youth and is a portrayal of the time in which and with which ET had grown up.[6] The initial sections have no unifying theme and instead read like a handful of symbols that signify the contradictions that was such a noticeable feature of his childhood. The binary arrangements of different cultures, different faiths, different sets of values and understanding make their way into this poem and seek a sort of resolution or unity. And it is this unity that has to be sought which propels him beyond youth to a life of new purpose.

Some of the contrary emotions are reflected in the title of the poem with its reference to Afonso de Albuquerque—the Portuguese General, the Great Conqueror and empire-builder and also the archetypal explorer. Here held up to scrutiny is the figure of an explorer, a leitmotif of ET's later poems. Albuquerque—the first colonizer from the west to establish an Asian Empire, the first Duke of Goa, the one to have established a colony in Malacca in 1511, but

---

[4] Ibid. Meira Chand, *A Different Sky*, pp. 68–73.

[5] *Report of the Conference on the Teaching of English in English Medium Primary and Secondary Schools Singapore, 10th to 18th August 1966* (Singapore: Government Printing Office, 1966), p. 180

[6] The poem was first published in *Write*, October 1958, pp. 6–8.

also the one who fathered a bastard son born at a considerable age. Hence the reference to Eliot's *Gerontion*—the old man with a latent sexuality that he finds hard to vent or to control. Thus, Albuquerque is an explorer who goes beyond the role of an ordinary traveller—he decides to overpower a foreign culture with or without understanding it and bastardize it with a third culture that lacks legitimacy. Hence while a traveller can bring about a happy union of cultures, he can also dominate and subjugate and thereby makes the archetypal figure a manifestation of opposing themes.

The poem opens with some of the inherent contradictions ET sees around him—the 'soft cat-paws' which can also scratch, the lotus which wilts and yet is a symbol of renewal, the cross that reminds one of the great compassion of Christ but also of the lethal malice of the Roman people, the figure of Dido out of whose hatred for her brother Pygmalion was born Carthage, the city of great antiquity. The list gradually leads him to Adam's fall but then comes the puzzling thought that it was because Adam 'made flesh' that 'I'm still there.' So is there a need of a certain transforming force, a certain severity that will change the pattern of the slow inevitable move of habit and lead to new creation? Or is creation born of an interdependence between opposing forces? And to answer this question comes up the line that holds the central thought of the poem, 'two ends of a dream'—that every cause almost always is bifurcated into multiple outcomes and man's destiny is to be suspended in between, faced with the difficult prospect of choice.

But before he moves to the answer, the young poet must stumble through other experiences—for instance sexuality, that inevitable part of youth. But like everything else that has its hidden shades and nuances, sexual gratification comes with its share of guilt, the 'turmoil in a savaged garden.' Then there are the pleasures of an intellectual life 'with Plato as a prop' and yet there too, as in the original *Gerontion*, falls the shadow of the weariness of knowledge, the slow agonizing drying up of emotions which leaves ET wishing for

. . . a simple night, when knees are kept apart
And the breathing of her womb
Is the secret of her heart . . .

So tormented, his mind 'bunched', he peels within, till his mind
returns to the memories of

. . . a stupa-templed grace
Cleansed by the ash of Kings . . .

—the temple of the Sun God on the banks of the Chao Phraya River
that he had recently visited. To him it returns as a living monument
that portrays how seamlessly Buddhism had sprung from Hinduism,
without any rupture or loss in continuity. And suddenly ET sees it
all, the underlying bedrock of grace that supports every faith,

Lord Buddha, shaman with the wheel
Was in the loaves of Christ.

From here, as if on cue, the poet turns an inward eye with little
reference to European or classical traditions of poetry. It is almost as
if he wakes from torturous thought and looks around him and in that
moment of illumination sees his own surroundings—the country of
his birth. He sees the chempaka flower that blooms, the blue flash of
colour of the kingfisher, the oriel's golden rise to the sky. Here what
he needs to seek is Mount Tahan, the highest point of Peninsular
Malaysia, what he needs to understand is the folklore of Mount
Ophir where once resided a princess of magical powers. And once
he sees these visual images where his very marrow calls out, *this is my
country,* his tongue is stripped of its 'false choir' and with new-found
confidence and pride he turns to acknowledge his identity—it is here
that 'I'll plant my feet.'

This self-discovery and rooting brings its own gratification—
there is no guilt associated with the act of sex anymore, it is a now

a beautiful self-sealing act of love. There is also acceptance of the colonizing cough of Albuquerque—after all it is the cough from where sprang his identity, the making of his colonized nation. Just as there is acceptance of the humdrum flow of local life—the tuakow stuffed with pilfering of copra, wholesale retail rice, the mah-jong addict who dreams of a virgin. The poet has finally found the unity that the diverse elements of his multicultural life sought—he has found it in his country. Yet the calm is splintered almost as soon as it is reached. But now if there is any restlessness still left, it is the 'anxious aching for birth'—the birth of a new nation. There is finally 'shanti' on the lotus.

The final section pulsates with new intent as he turns a full circle and returns to the cat-paws. Yet there is nothing that disturbs him anymore as he calmly takes in the beat of the beetles' wings, the fall of the dead leaves. If there are contradictions and change in the landscape around him, then it is all a part of his inheritance,

> The road forks
> Take both, each path and bleeding
> No separate peace
> But the dissolution of turmoil
> At the edge of being.

Individual and cultural borders come together seamlessly and at the edges of being, scattered among the little things of a hybrid life which transcends difference, he discovers a new identity and a new sense of purpose. At this point he almost rejects religion, deciding to keep the 'great book shut'. And instead settles

> . . . for a patch of green
> Tea upon a mat . . .

Nothing is more sacred than his own land.

The Isle is Full of Noises

In a 1955 issue of the *New Cauldron*, (Michaelmas Term), selling at an astonishing thirty-five cents, appears one of ET's early poems from what was to be his first anthology, *Rib of Earth* (1956). The *New Cauldron* was the in-house magazine of the University of Malaya which was established in Singapore in 1949 and continued un-bifurcated for the first fifteen years or so. The magazine, first published in 1950, would soon become one of the key carriers of the first English writings of Singapore and Malaysia.

In the 1955 issue, among rather solemn literary articles written by the two young associate editors (the editor was Thomas Varkey), Ee Tiang Hong and Edwin Thumboo, appears ET's poem, *For Peter Wee*. The poem would re-appear in *Rib of Earth* with two more sections appended and is perhaps one which on hindsight appears 'weepy/moany' to the poet as it dwells on the futility of human existence in a Hamlet-like reverie. But what does not escape the reader is the genuine note of sadness that it strikes in the opening lines,

> Is it the wind or tomorrow
> Prying at the door or
> Peter home with the answer?

It is the same warm touch of authentic feeling that C.J. Francis refers to when he says in his review, 'Thumboo's Malayan background, themes, imagery, are pervasive and convincing, because not artificial or pretentious; because, I think his ideas are not "elevated" but natural.'[7] And it is the same 'natural' love that is evident when ET now, at considerable advanced age, speaks of Peter Wee or the group of friends he made in university. There are many on the list and in fact, when asked if there was anybody he didn't like, he thinks hard

---

[7] Ibid.

and does come up with the name of an impatient Maths teacher or a bullying senior in school but adds, 'But I could understand why they did it, you know . . . you just have to work it out.'[8]

Peter Wee was a senior in University, a gentle Peranakan who spared ET from ragging when he as a new entrant was picked on by others.[9] So a friendship was forged. They lived not far from each other and would cycle over to each other's house during summer vacation. And then Peter went to Malaysia, driving pillion on a bike with yet another friend, Megat, and never returned. ET heard the story later: Peter was in hospital after the road accident and had asked for cigarettes. Megat went out to fetch them but when he returned, their friend was no more, dead from a haemorrhage in the brain. ET still regrets losing the one poem that Peter had written, a poem that he placed on the mirror in his hostel room. It was cleaned away during summer and the only thing that remains with ET is the beauty of a single phrase, *Pacific pools.*

Peter was one among a large group of undergraduates. ET went to university in 1953 after spending two years in Post-School Certificate Class, presumably the equivalent of the 'A' levels, for which he signed up but did not take.[10] Instead he spent the two years of unexpected freedom reading literature, history and mythology—subjects for which he had developed a fondness even in school. When joining University, his strongest subjects were science and maths and yet he opted to study humanities because that meant attending only two lectures and a couple of tutorials in a week. His decision met with little resistance at home because his parents scarcely if ever interfered in his decisions.

ET's group of friends were largely from his peer group but included some seniors and with time, extended to his juniors as

---

8   Interview 5 October 2017

9   Ibid.

10 *Peninsular Muse*, ed. Mohammad A. Quayum (Bern, Oxford: Peter Lang, 2007), pp. 36–7. Interview 5 October 2017.

well.[11] Though Wang Gungwu, later a reputed scholar of the Chinese diaspora, or future authors, Beda Lim and Goh Sin Tub, had by then moved on from the university, it was an intimate circle of similar-thinking youth and they would have enough occasions to meet. Among his 'literary' friends were poets Ee Tiang Hong, Wong Phui Nam, Tan Han Hoe, Oliver Seet and Lloyd Fernando. But the 'non-literary' were also many and with each ET shared an individual and close bond. He recalls Victor Gopal, P. Arudsothy, or Goh Soon Khing, Henry Chia who were not writers, yet very perceptive readers. There was Agos Salem or K.J. Ratnam or Leem Teong Quee or Herman Hochstadt or Mahadeva or Zainuddin Hashim later to be commandant of the Malayan police training school and guitarist. With them he could have a discussion on anything that caught their attention. The entire group of around ten would land up in his home. Afterwards they would travel to Batu Pahat and Malacca and Seramban and finally land up in KL for a longish stay before going further north to Ipoh, Taiping and Penang. At each stop the group would get smaller as the friend whose house they stayed in dropped off from the group. He recalls the pub near Zainuddin's digs in Circular Road where he met Phui Nam and Zainuddin. Whoever reached first ordered three rums and three gins. Zainuddin abstained because of his faith but would arrive, put his police pistol on the table and they would reminisce till late in the night.[12]

Friends

Friends who have read
With steady eye, my verse:
Friends, yet I sitting in dread
Of my uncertain selves, tense

---

[11]   Friends' details: Ibid. *Peninsular Muse*, pp. 39–41, 55–6. *Looking Back*, ET. *Solidarity* (1991), pp. 11–4.

[12]   Interview 5 October 2017.

To know if rumination
Planted in my most certain ground
Was laboured or found
In true equation.

Out of the silent seventh year
I do not walk unscarred.
Words left alone to die
Lose their heart in clear
Official use, disorganized, marred,
Reduced to explicate and tie.

Each made comment
Deduced a pun, focussed a flaw
Suggested that the government
In some had too much metaphor;
Like the language of the hills
Without a fracture in the lines;
How an image there distils,
Tentative, sought Malaysian eyes;
One verse portentous. Even then
I knew that words would
breathe again.

It was an exhilarating time when their young minds were in a constant ferment. And underneath the picnics and jungle-trail walks and drinking binges, there were two rather significant things happening—one, a more conscious coming together of feelings for a distinct Malayan identity and the other, the need of this identity to find expression in English writing. As ET says of the time, 'We wrote, published, discussed, started or took over magazines and edited collections.'[13] He had been in

---

[13] *Peninsular Muse*, p. 57.

touch with a group that had spontaneously sprung up around
Sin Tub who ran a poetry circle in St Joseph's Institution and
through this contact started contributing poems and serving on
the board of *Youth*, the combined Singapore Secondary Schools'
magazine, while even in school.[14] And it was perhaps under
Sin Tub's mentorship that ET famously wrote in the *Youth*
about the need of a genuinely original Malayan literature, a
startlingly mature reflection from someone very young. If while
at the Victoria School, ET was mentored by James Frazer,
the Scotsman from Devon who was warm and generous in
helping ET find his own style and introduce him to the beauty
of English literature, it was Sin Tub who helped him make
connections between poetry and the real, distinctive, middle-
class, English-educated life of Singapore. And occasionally
Beda Lim, then a librarian remained a sensitive critic—quick,
and alert and as ET says, he was best able to enunciate the spirit
of this particular literary movement that was spontaneous,
touched by nationalism and yet emphatically English. He
has no compunctions in admitting their influence in his life,
'Meeting them and listening to them discuss literature within
the larger context of an independent sovereign in Malaya that
included Singapore, helped me crystallise my own feelings and
thoughts about these large issues.'[15]

While with the country placed under Japanese Occupation
and then self-governance (full internal self-government 1959–63)
which proved to the world the fallibility of the British, it is easy
to understand the emerging sense of Malayan nationalism (it was
Beda Lim who advised ET to say he was the first of the Malayans
when called a half-caste), one wonders why the emphasis on English,
the colonizing language? While countries like Burma and the more
right-wing Malaysians complained of becoming strangers in their

---

[14]   Ibid, pp. 36–41.
[15]   Ibid, p. 39.

own country, why this need to explore a new hybrid culture that had naturally emerged in colonies?

To understand, one needs to look at two incidents described by two poets of the time. The first is a memory of Sin Tub when he was living in Emerald Hill just after the war.[16] That was a period of racial unrest and there was a rumour that the Malays were coming down from Johor Bahru with *parangs* and they were about to kill the Chinese. Sin Tub who was a teenager then came out to the street to join the crowd, ready to defend his home and says, 'And if a Malay had come along, he might have been slaughtered by us. That was the psychology of the nation, the mob mentality.' It was a time when racial sensitivities ran high and there was need to explore the neutral grounds offered by English.

The second story is narrated by ET about his dear friend Tiang Hong.[17] In an issue of the *Solidarity Magazine* started in 1966 by yet another friend, Frankie Jose, from the Philippines, ET speaks of Malaysia where with the predominance of *Bahasa*, English was being written as a sectional literature. This meant the imaginative writing of a significant part of the population was reduced to a secondary status. In this context he referred to Tiang Hong who would agonize over the plight of older writers like him, brought up under a solid English-oriented education system who shared strong emotional links to Malaysia and yet were made to feel like outsiders in their own country. Eventually, Tiang Hong would of course decide to migrate to Australia and continue to write of his loss of country and continuity. But his story helped ET to prove the criticality of English as an effective channel of expression for those who were not inwardly bilingual and who did not enjoy the same manipulative reach and confidence in *Bahasa* or any other regional language as in English.

---

[16] *Interlogue*, Vol. 4, ed. Ronald D. Klein (Singapore: Ethos Books, 2005). Interview with Goh Sin Tub.

[17] *Looking Back*, p. 12.

Apart from these two reasons, what is self-evident is the genuine love which writers like Sin Tub or ET had for the English literature that had been a part of their childhood—the copy of *Golden Treasury* that they all possessed. Added to this was their love for their country—the need to write about what they encountered every day. The result was a feverish desire to create a new idiolect. As ET puts it, 'I realised first-hand that English was a fabulously, creatively available language. It was there for the re-making . . . You begin to replace the ordinary, the borrowed with your own way of saying . . . Gradually, you had a language of your own; your idiolect.'[18]

On the flip side of this argument which is a powerful alchemy of love for nation and language, there is the darker story that Singapore still labours under—the loss of dialects. Dialects like Hakka, Hokkien or ET's own Teochew or even Malayalam or Gujarati which have been lost from popular parlance under the domineering shadows of English and the other nationally recognized languages. But at that point in the late 1950s, with the rejection of a multi-racial Malaysia not far down the road, there was only a need for a maximum oneness: 'The wish to be one people was extremely widespread and strong, circulated as an idea that muted the potential disharmonies, sharply ethnic in origin . . . It was the moment of *fajar*, of an integrated society, of unity out of a diverse society . . .'[19] Unity seemed like the only answer.

Reading Yeats

ET is unequivocal in acknowledging his debt to Yeats. According to him, just as Yeats had to consciously shake-off Shelley's 'Italian light', he too had to gradually rub away the influence Yeats had on him.[20] It was from the Irish poet that ET learnt to understand the power of language—the wave of storm it can evoke, the messiness,

---

[18]   *Peninsular Muse*, p. 41.
[19]   *Looking Back*, p. 11.
[20]   Interview 15 June 2017.

the edginess, the wildness of words and at the same time the sweet tranquillity of it. He read Eliot obsessively too but for ET, Eliot remained a bit too cerebral, his lines did not hold the music that he sought in poetry.

In conjunction with this obvious adulation for Yeats, when one looks at Yeats' own work in reviving Irish literary traditions, it is tempting to think that Ireland had something to do with Singapore's early development of local literature written in English. For after all, it was Yeats who turned away from interpreting Irish nationalism as a mindless revival of everything that was Gaelic and instead decided to write about everything that was Gaelic but in the more widely accessible English tongue. Ireland had the longest colonial history. It taught many lessons. As he said, 'Can we not build up a national tradition, a national literature, which shall be none the less Irish in spirit from being English in language?'[21] But as ET points out, when he or his predecessors like Gungwu or Sin Tub turned to English, it was more of an organic decision, born of the environment of racial unrest in Singapore. In fact, ET was first introduced to his thoughts on 'de-Anglicizing' the Irish people and yet nesting the movement within the English language when he stumbled upon the first volume of uncollected prose by Yeats published in 1970.[22] To the Malayan youngsters English was a more intuitive choice as a means to achieve a cultural bridge. In addition, ET was also significantly different from Yeats or Samuel Ferguson or Thomas Davis of the Irish nationalist movement because he, taking a leaf out of their book, did not attempt only to delve into Malay anecdotes or antiquities which were readily available as the Irish did when they took to writing histories or romances about great Gaelic men of the past, from the son of Nessa to Owen Roe.[23] Instead when he did indulge in myth-

---

[21] *Uncollected Prose by W.B. Yeats: First Reviews and Articles*, Vol.1, ed. John P. Frayne (London: Macmillan, 1970), p. 255.

[22] Interview 7 August 2017.

[23] *Uncollected Prose by W.B. Yeats*, p. 255.

making in his poems for the *Ulysses by the Merlion* anthology, it was a renewal of history, keeping in mind the unfolding modern character of Singapore.

ET says the Yeats they knew in school and university was a rather 'sanitised' one, shorn of his rebellious anti-British character— he was more of an Anglo-Irish poet rather than just an Irish poet. He first heard of the Irish aspect of Yeats from Frank James who taught at the St Joseph's Institution and was an important member of the Catholic community who returned to Ireland regularly.[24] The Irish experience as instruction came when he joined the editorial board of *Youth* where James was a senior adviser. It was in his home in Capitol Flats, Stamford Road, that ET first heard of the tragic history of Ireland, the first of Britain's colonies. During one of these sessions a nostalgic James recited Yeats' *The Lake Isle of Innisfree* and according to ET, it was because of James' own Irish background that he allowed ET to write the editorial for *Youth* in which he spoke of creating a Malayan literature.

In university ET read Yeats with Alan B. Painter. A person who has never forgotten his gratitude to teachers, he writes of them, 'They made knowledge alive, teased out significances, connected fact and fact, uncovered patterns, made us curious and hungry, showed us how the mind could travel and the imagination leap.'[25] This was certainly true for Painter who had a starred Double First from Cambridge and who, unlike Frazer, did not look at ET's poems and yet taught much through his poetry criticism classes.[26] According to ET, Painter was not one of the best-prepared lecturers and yet in every one of his classes there were a couple of ideas which really made ET think. It was Painter who taught him to unpack every word in a poem and from him ET learnt that 'everything is language.'[27]

---

[24]　*Peninsular Muse*, p. 55.
[25]　*If Not for My Teacher: A Nation's Tribute to Teachers in Singapore*, (Singapore: Compass), p. 52.
[26]　*Interlogue* (2005). Interview with ET.
[27]　Interview 15 June 2017.

So what was it that ET took away from Yeats? Yeats, who from an Anglo-Irish had become an Irish nationalist, whose poetic psyche was shaped by an evolving sense of Ireland, taught ET the power of the connection between country and language. In one of his early poems, the *Song of the Happy Shepherd*, Yeats had written, 'For words alone are certain good.' For him the spiritual renewal of his country lay in the creative use of language, in the making of a language that reflected the undefinable Irish quality of rhythm and style.[28] And it was this thought that held and stimulated ET for many years to come. From Yeats he learnt also the use of symbols and one of the themes that was particularly relevant to him in his college days and subsequently evolved and took the form of the traveller motif—the theme of unity.

When asked about his favourite Yeatsian poems, ET, among the many others, speaks of the *Tower* and the *Winding Stair* volumes. The *Tower* with its poems of bitter, sterile images of a crumbling tower which are carefully balanced against the more optimistic poems with themes of regeneration and sexuality of the *Winding Stair*. It is not a coincidence that the first focuses on everything political while the second with the circling stair, which is enclosed by and yet gives form to the masculine tower, concerns itself with everything feminine and aesthetic.[29] It is important to remember at this point that Yeats as a poet was a firm believer in contrariness, that his poetic genius grew out of a sensitive engagement with extremities, in which commitment to either extremity is avoided and the poem grows out of the tension between the two.[30] His poetic practice is based to an extent in straightening these contraries; that consciousness for him is identified with conflict and the greater the distance between extremities, the greater the excitement of having them bridged. As

---

[28]   *Uncollected Prose by W.B. Yeats*, p. 255.

[29]   John Unterecker, *W.B. Yeats: A Poem by Poem Analysis*, (NJ: Prentice Hall, 1963), p. 169.

[30]   B. Rajan, *W.B. Yeats: A Critical Introduction* (London: Hutchinson University Library, 1965), p. 124.

Yeats put it, 'the greater the tension, the greater my self-knowledge.'[31] And perhaps, apart from the beauty of words that so beguiled the young ET, he was intuitively so strongly drawn to Yeats because of the extremities of his own situation—the extremities of his own country's culture which to an extent he embodied with his Teochew/Taoist mother and Tamil/Christian father. That insight was further strengthened when he came across William Blake's famous quote, 'Without contraries is no progression. Attraction and repulsion, reason and energy, love and hate are necessary to human existence.' (*The Marriage of Heaven and Hell,* Plate #3).

To take a closer look at Yeats' theme of unity, one could turn to two poems—*Sailing to Byzantium* from the *Tower* volume and *Byzantium* from *Stair.* In both, the ancient city of Byzantium about which Yeats wrote, '. . . never before or since in recorded history, religious, aesthetic and practical life were one,' provides a deep sense of organic continuity between worlds of flesh and spirit. It is a place where the great contraries of youth and age, life and death, change and the changeless are reconciled as nature and art disclose themselves in a creative interdependence where each demands the other for its completion.[32] Before writing the poems, Yeats had devoted himself to a systematic study of Byzantine art and history and concluded that it was a place where the painter, the mosaic worker, the workers in gold and silver, the illuminator of sacred books, almost impersonally, without any consciousness of individual design had produced an art that was so integrated so as to have the impact of a single image. It was an artistic integrity that held together the pictures in a gospel book as well as the building, the pattern in a mosaic, the metal work of rail and lamp—it was as though all was a single image.[33]

---

[31]   *W.B. Yeats: A Critical Introduction,* pp. 145–7.
[32]   Ibid, p. 125.
[33]   *W.B. Yeats: A Poem by Poem Analysis,* p. 171.

Yet there was a difference in the Byzantium of the two poems. Perhaps the difference is nowhere more emphasized than in the last lines of the two poems.

In *Sailing to Byzantium* Yeats writes:

> Once out of nature I shall never take
> My bodily form from any natural thing,
> But such a form as Grecian goldsmiths make
> Of hammered gold and gold enamelling
> To keep a drowsy Emperor awake;
> Or set upon a golden bough to sing
> To lords and ladies of Byzantium
> Of what is past, or passing, or to come.

Whereas *Byzantium* ends with:

> Astraddle on the dolphin's mire and blood,
> Spirit after spirit! The smithies break the flood,
> The golden smithies of the Emperor!
> Marbles of the dancing floor
> Break bitter furies of complexity,
> Those images that yet
> Fresh images beget,
> That dolphin-torn, that gong-tormented sea.

The Byzantium of the first instance is a place of stillness, of unageing monuments, of fire frozen into golden mosaic, where the bird sits on a golden bough with the equilibrium of a purified spirit that sings of eternity. Yet it is an eternity of artifice, for the golden bird is made of hammered gold in a smithy. But in the second, the city becomes a place of intense, tormented energy where dance is the climactic image. The tension builds up in the writhing movement of the spirits, their fury and agony, till the final release in the images that fresh images beget and the return to the original 'Cathedral gong' of the first lines. The vision of a perfect unity is but momentary peace, not really a permanent unification. One can force it into categories of body or spirit as per one's inclination, but the experience remains transitory. What is permanent is the opposites—the opposites that need each other to complete each other in an act consummated in love—bodily or spiritual.

The Cough of Albuquerque is one of ET's earliest poems which show strong influences of Yeats in phrase and line. In it are many of the symbols reminiscent of the Irish poet. Along with the more Eliotesque rain as symbol of renewal, there is the compulsive ascent up the winding purgatorial staircase, the flight of the golden oriel bright as day, the call of the merbak that sits for once mateless on the branch, the moon of the haze unspun reminiscent of feminine beauty. He finds a Byzantium-like stillness in Wat Arun:[34]

> Chao Phya, broad belly of the day
> Turned the corner—feet dipped –
> Washed away pregnancies of hate.
> Ears of mango, eyes of agate
> Germinating in the sky
> With hands that calmed waters.

As he peels away layers of history, he finds his own *daimon* in the heart of Asian living—the Temple of Dawn, seeded by India, with bits of porcelain as embellishment which were used before as ballast by boats from China, with Khmer-style elongated *prangs,* where the inner sanctuary once held the celebrated Emerald Buddha, moulded by the hands of the king himself—a breathing monument as testimony to the process of adaption by which imported ideologies and cultures find a local home.

---

[34] Parts of the *Cough of Albuquerque* has been used in other poems of ET, particularly *Wat Arun* and *Lines.*

But before the vision of a reality that is brought into existence by powerful forces of history, comes the Yeats-like awareness of the inner contraries of life—the death of the creative mind that comes with a growing skill on the abacus, the image that clings to the mind even in moments of intense loneliness, the real sight that lies just beyond the human eye. Like in Yeats, there is momentary peace as he sits in all humility before the Lord Buddha who speaks to him of the compassion of Christ, before the calm is shattered by a return of minute, iridescent images, like the fires that dance on Byzantium's marble floor. Yet, in the second coming, the inherently diverse images do not add to his poetic tension because he is been through the purifying purgatory of Wat Arun and the vision he sees is of his own country where he firmly plants his feet. There is a calmness in accepting his own roots where he can clutch at a drift of leaves and yet miss some voices because he does not understand all the spoken languages, where superstition burns as bright as the sunlight marching through, where the cliff cuts out the vision and yet gives his veins the compulsion to start a difficult hike. And the last line holds his final humanizing call—*Two ends of a dream*—a unity that is achieved by understanding the inherent contrariness of the human experience without which man ceases to be man and is reduced to a golden singing bird fashioned in a smithy.

Harp of Burma

ET read *Harp of Burma* long before actually visiting the country, as he did *A Passage to India* much before he visited India for the first time.[35] But the books left a deep imprint on him not only because of the stories they narrated, but because they showed him how to enter the soul of a culture different from one's own. While he read *A Passage to India* when still in university, he discovered the English translation of the Japanese *Harp of Burma* while he was in the Civil

---

[35]   Michio Takeyama, *Harp of Burma* (Tokyo: Charles E. Tuttle Co. Inc., 1966).

Service and yet the second book helped consolidate his thinking on the first. It is relevant here because in it he found fruition of thoughts seeded in his university days—how an idea can take over one's life with such vigour that one surrenders to it completely, at the cost of every other priority.

The slim volume of Japanese story-telling, originally meant for a juvenile audience, was first published in 1946, though translated into English almost two decades later. It tells the story of a brief period of history about a company of Japanese soldiers stranded in a village in Burma after the close of war. The lines of division are sharply drawn—the British army with its turbaned Sikhs and green-clad Gurkhas, the insurgent Burmese army, once allies of the Japanese who had now turned coat and the Japanese themselves—who when they dressed in a *longyi* and carried a Burmese harp of native bamboo, looked not very different from the Burmese.

The book opens with a Burmese scene:

> We had been on a long march down a valley through dense forests. Suddenly a lake came into view . . . clusters of white-walled houses on a small bay stood half submerged, meeting their reflections in the water . . . During the three days we were stationed in that village we practised singing every day. We sang hymns, nostalgic old favourites like 'The moon over the Ruined Castle' . . . even difficult German and Italian songs. There beside that picturesque lake the captain waved his baton happily, while we soldiers, carried away by the sound of our own voices, sang from the very depths of our beings.[36]

And so the story continues, lucid with the flow of life, and the character of Mizushima unfolds. He is a Japanese corporal, a lean, sinewy man of medium height with big, crystal-clear, deeply recessed eyes who finds himself in a company of singing soldiers. The soldiers

---

[36]   Ibid, p. 12.

with their improvised instruments made from a simple reed or
a tambourine of stretched dog hide, sing under the threat of war
perhaps because they want to do one last thing before they die and
Mizushima joins them. He has no formal training and yet he learns
extraordinarily fast and soon is a master of the Burmese harp. When
he plays, tones halfway between a piano and a Japanese lute hang
in the air and a lasting image of him is as he is silhouetted against a
starlit sky, climbing the face of the ravine all alone carrying his harp
as he lures the enemy away with his music.

On the face of it *Harp of Burma* is a story of war and of renouncing
the ways of violence for a spiritual life in a Buddhist monastery. For
that is what Mizushima eventually does. He is enamoured by the
Burmese way of life right from the beginning, taking pride in wearing
the *longyi* like a native and looking wistfully at travelling Burmese
musicians who come to perform in their village. In the course of
events he is left injured and close to death in a cave that has been
bombarded by the last of a contingent of Japanese soldiers after war
has ended. He is nursed back to health by a monk and later decides
to don the monk's yellow robe and shave his head. He starts back
on his journey, searching for his own friends but on the way finds
mutilated bodies of the Japanese war-dead and decides to bury them.
With time this becomes his life's mission and even when the Japanese
army leaves Burma, he decides to stay behind in the land where men
wore *longyis* and where instead of business or engineering, priests
teach *sutras* in temple schools.

But the simple, linear text is underpinned by several important
themes. One is of course ET's old favourite—the coming together
of cultures. It is a book of twin identities—the Japanese soldier who
is mistaken for a Burmese musician when he wears a dirty *longyi*
and plays a harp and the Buddhist monk who seems to look like a
lost Japanese corporal when he stands silently observing a Japanese
contingent of men singing songs they have learnt from British
soldiers. When he leaves the village, he has two jade green parakeets
perched on either shoulder—they are brothers hunted down from

the same tree and yet one speaks Burmese and the other replies in
Japanese. The central figure of Mizushima is important because he
holds in him the best of both cultures, just as he wears a Burmese
ruby in a Japanese pill-box around his neck.

In a book rich in symbols, the harp appears as a symbol of the soft
power of art. When Mizushima and his men take shelter in a Burmese
village, deep in a tropical forest, at first the song of the villagers
appears harsh. But as they listen carefully, they can hear the plaintive
undertone and then they see the pictures—the clouds gleaming on
the Himalayas, the streams of molten snows. The Burmese have never
seen the Himalayas, only heard of it from the *sutras* as the place where
Gautama Buddha meditated, and yet the mountain range becomes
true to them because they sing of it as it does to the Japanese.[37] This is
exactly what ET achieves when he writes:

> No—just durian-hot,
> Lalang trimmed by fire
> Iguana far from ooze
> Creepers loose their coil
> Merbak, mateless on the branch
> Nonya bought her fan
> To milk the little shade.[38]

Little details of a torpid summer afternoon that make an entire land
come alive.

But for ET, perhaps more important than the cultural themes, is
the theme of a singular purpose that is so overwhelmingly present in
the book—a purpose that preoccupies one completely and overtakes
all else in life. Mizushima, when he decides to enter the monastery,
leaves behind his earlier identity of a Japanese corporal though he
knows that in the future there will be days of intense loneliness

---

[37]   Ibid, pp. 22–3.
[38]   *Cough of Albuquerque.*

when he will have nothing but his harp for company. As ET puts it, 'Yes, *Harp of Burma* was important to me because it gave me ideas about how I could create a vocabulary for Singapore. But it was more important because it told me that an idea can have so much power that you can forget all else and dedicate your life to it. When in our college days we thought of serving the nation, we knew it would come at a cost but for those in my generation particularly there was no escaping from the fundamental requirements of the founding phase.'[39] When quizzed about the very first steps in creating a new vocabulary for Singapore, he speaks of adding nuance and complexity to existing words, teasing them open to accommodate larger webs of connotation. Thus, he speaks of the word *race* which denotes a primary identity but in the local context, as a first step, includes the Chinese, Tamil and Malay and as a step further, the Indians are divided into Tamil, Punjabi, Bengali, Gujarati, etc., and similarly for the other predominant races.

ET's university experience was important because it gave the nationalist sensitivities awakened earlier a sharper focus as he came in touch with similarly driven intellectual minds, both of fellow students and teachers. And as he became more active in literary circles, it was clear that his future lay in serving the nation through its literature. That would be the all-consuming passion for many years to come, sometimes at the cost of personal art.

A New Dawn

Running college publications to meet the cultural aspirations of literary-minded students was a long tradition of Malaya, one of the first being the Raffles College magazine, in existence since before the war.[40] Later, in 1947 came the *Cauldron*. However, it was with

---

[39] Interview 30 October 2017.
[40] Rajeev S. Patke and Philip Hoden, *The Routledge Concise History of Southeast Asian Writing in English* (Oxon: Routledge, 2010), p. 49.

the formation of the University of Malaya in 1949 and the post-war rise of Malayan nationalism that such publications became part of a significant movement—the demand for a democratic, multi-racial Malaya for Malayans expressed through writing in English. The *New Cauldron* came in 1950 and *Write* in 1957 to both of which ET contributed.[41] In fact, he had been drawn into writing while in school when he was on the editorial board of *Youth,* the combined Singapore Secondary Schools' magazine. It was in *Youth* in 1952, when he was nineteen, that he had contributed an editorial on the need of youngsters to submerge racial identities and Malayanize themselves: 'A way to begin with is to destroy or banish the world of illusion they have created for themselves through the reading of subversive publications that masquerade under the name of modern literature, and to take a keen interest in their immediate surroundings.' Subsequently, when the University Socialist Club (USC) started in 1953, followed soon by a new monthly publication called *Fajar* or Dawn, it was but natural that ET would be—in a minor way—on its editorial board too.

However, from the outset the USC and by extension *Fajar,* started with a clear political purpose.[42] The objective was to bring under its radar every shade of political opinion with the common platforms of anti-colonialism and a Malayan consciousness as the basis for unity among races. The Club had an inclusive multiracial, socialist vision that would later be shared by the People's Action Party (PAP) as its founding principles when it was formed in November 1954. In fact, the connection between USC and the PAP went far beyond a common ground of ideas. Many of the student leaders of the Club including James Puthucheary, Lim Hock Sew, Poh Soo

---

[41]   *Sharing Borders: Studies in Contemporary Singaporean-Malaysian Literature,* Vol. 2, ed. Mohammad A. Quayum and Wong Phui Nam (Singapore: National Library Board, 2009), pp. 79–81.

[42]   *The Fajar Generation: The University Socialist Club & the Politics of Post-war Malaya & Singapore,* ed. Poh Soo Kai, Tan Jing Quee and Koh Kay Yew (Petaling Jaya: SIRD, 2010), pp. 7–9.

Kai, M.K. Rajakumar, Jamit Singh and Sydney Woodhull would
become founding members of the PAP and a young Lee Kuan Yew,
Singapore's future Prime Minister, would be the students' junior
defence lawyer for the *Fajar* Sedition Trial of August 1954.

May 1954

We do but merely ask,
No more, no less, this much:
That you white man,
Boasting of many parts,
Some talk of Alexander, some of Hercules.
Some broken not long ago
By little yellow soldiers
Out of the Rising Sun . . .
We ask you see
The bitter, curving tide of history,
See well enough, relinquish,
Restore this place, this sun
To us . . . and the waiting generations.

Depart white man.

Your minions riot among
Our young in Penang Road
Their officers, un-Britannic,
Full of service, look
Angry and short of breath.

You whored on milk and honey
Tried our spirit, spent our muscle,
Extracted from our earth;
Gave yourselves superior ways
At our expense, in our midst.

Depart:
You knew when to come;
Surely know when to go.

Do not ignore, dismiss,
Pretending we are foolish;
Harbour contempt in eloquence.
We know your language.

My father felt his master's voice,
Obeyed, but hid his grievous, wounded self.
I have learnt:
There is an Asian tide
That sings such power
Into my dreaming side:
My father's anger turns my cause.

Depart Tom, Dick and Harry.
Gently, with ceremony;
We may still be friends,
Even love you . . . from a distance.

Speaking of the *Fajar* Trial, ET says, 'I was just a small fry at the time, a first-year student. There was nothing heroic about me, unlike Puthucheary and the others.'[43] In fact, he was not present in the university hostel at all when on the morning of 28 May the entire eight-member editorial team (seven without ET) was arrested and charged with sedition for having published an editorial entitled, 'Aggression in Asia'. Published in issue number seven of *Fajar,* the editorial did not really attack specific colonial policies in Malaya or Singapore but instead criticized the global Cold War strategy of the

---

43   Interview 22 July 2017.

US which under the garb of attacking communism appeared to be keen on perpetuating Western colonial control over Asia.[44]

ET was away from the hostel on the day of the arrest because that day he had a terminal exam to take.[45] He being a good student, was often stopped on the way to the examination hall by friends who wanted to clarify doubts. Of late he had found such last minute discussions often confused him during the writing of the paper and so had taken to staying with his friend Henry Chia, one year his junior and like him a 'magazine-activist', the night before the exam. Henry Chia's home was in Kampong Java Road from where ET could take a Green bus, pay the ten cents fare and be back in the hostel in no time at all.

He was the last of the group to be arrested when he returned to his hostel room in the afternoon.[46] According to him, his role in the editorial was limited to proof-reading the magazine. An important correction that he recalls—the writer had inadvertently mentioned the 'sceptre' of communism rather than the 'spectre' of communism—a small change which if left unrectified could have perhaps vexed the British even more!

All eight students would eventually be acquitted but the trials would gain some notoriety as evidence of the growing repression of Malayan nationalists by the British. Politically it would bring anti-colonial sentiments in sharper focus in Singapore and for ET personally, it would prove to be a turning point. Once he was released, his father extracted a promise that he would never indulge in politics again. ET would find it impossible to refuse a father who had never before asked him for anything, though subsequently it would be difficult explaining his decision to his friends.[47] He never did. Yet afterwards politics would always

---

[44] *The Fajar Generation*, pp. 123–4.

[45] Interview 22 July 2017. Later details of Henry Chia from interview and *Peninsular Muse*, p. 54.

[46] *The Fajar Generation*, pp. 135–6.

[47] Interview 05 October 2017.

remain in his broader line of vision and he would gradually carve
out a path for himself by which he could continue to serve his
nation—through its literature.

The Trial would sensitize him to the fragility of human
destiny. Years later, as part of the anthology, *Gods Can Die,* he
would write an important poem, *The Interview,* on Tan Jing
Quee, who was first arrested in 1962, though involved in politics
from earlier. ET had known him personally as a friend of his
sister's former husband. While in 1954 Jing Quee was the hero
of the day, by 1966 there was a cloud of doubt hovering over him
after he was released from prison on the basis of a compulsory
confession of his Marxist leanings which was then broadcast on
national television. In the intervening decade the mainstream
PAP leaders had drifted away from the more radical minded,
the *Barisan Sosialis* had been formed as an important voice
of opposition and finally in 1963, under security operations
undertaken by PAP and the British, the leftist group had been
imprisoned. Jing Quee later spoke about how the ISD (Internal
Security Department) of Singapore slowly wore him down to
accepting their humiliating terms and also about how his friends
doubted him as a traitor to their cause after he was released.[48]

What ET objected to was not the destruction of Jing Quee's
political capital, but the destruction of the man himself,

> The state above all else,
> Above extremes of personal liberty.
> But it should not break,
> So alienate painfully a man.

There were other ways to deplete his political capital.

---

[48]   https://www.theonlinecitizen.com/2014/06/14/in-memory-of-tan-jing-quee/
       retrieved on 06 December 2017.

The Colour of Nationalism

According to historians, nationalism came to Singapore in 1945; what followed after 1965 was chiefly economic development.[49] In fact with the end of war, it appeared to be globally accepted that nationalism would be the dominant political credo. Yet faced with the prospect of the Cold War, it was a very different kind of nationalism than what was prevalent before. As the US and Soviet Union faced each other and China emerged from centuries of imperial mismanagement, the world appeared to pursue a course of a more state conscious, aggressive nationalism. Gone was the relative innocence and idealism of the past with its focus on individualism, liberalism and reform. Instead nationalist movements were more of a means to ensure the country's security, led by charismatic and often militant leaders like Sukarno, Mao or Ho Chi Minh and pivoted around surrendering the individual will to the power of the state.

Thus, this was the kind of nationalism that ET encountered as he stepped into university. There was an urgency to it, a need to make a difference and also a sense of lingering threat that political events could take a violent turn at short notice. When asked about nationalism, ET points to various sources.[50] Like his other life experiences, his sense of nationalism too is finely layered with observations drawn from inherited as well as lived history.

He speaks first of Subhas Chandra Bose and the Indian National Army (INA) that Bose spearheaded from Singapore. ET during the war while living in Newton, would see the uniformed soldiers of the INA marching down Armenian Street and particularly the women of the Rani of Jhansi Regiment in front of the St Joseph's Institution. Tamil women wearing trousers was a rare sight and the image and

---

[49]   Eddie Tay, *Colony, Nation & Globalisation: Not at Home in Singaporean and Malaysian Literature* (Singapore: NUS Press, 2011), p. 79.

[50]   Interview 09–30 October 2017.

the rhythm of their march remained in his memory. He would write of them in a yet unpublished poem, *Cry Freedom:*

> Down the road from here, the Padang shone with bayonets.
> Women stood equal to battalions ready to do or die. Steeled
> By faith, hope, love, colonial memories, they travelled north,
> Across Arakan hill, ravine, jungle, river, battling hard into
> The motherland, Kohima and Imphal, capturing cantonment
> And fort . . .

The other strand would come from his Chinese uncle of whom he wrote in *Uncle Never Knew.* From the uncle he would not only receive his first lessons on communism and Maoist China, but also feel first-hand the yearning for a lost motherland. It was a time of revival of nationalism in China, the time for recovering their nationalism and lost national identity. As ET puts it, 'The paradigm was very different in China. They did not have to fight for their independence, but merely to restore their lost glory.'[51] It was a time when nationalism in China was torn between the growth and economic prospects of its urban borderlands and the maintenance of its traditional mandarin values and literati in its rural interiors.[52] ET, spending his evenings with his uncle in the house that held as living companions Marx, Engels and Mao, Lu Shun, the *Li Sao* and T'ao Ch'ien, could feel the longing of the exile to return home so he could be in the midst of all the action. It seemed his uncle had never really allowed himself to know the surrounding Singapore and yet his true national identity eluded him—it was an existence as fragile and tentative as a half-formed wish.

Plus there was his literature teacher from school, K.C. Owen, a Welshman who sang Welsh songs full of nostalgia, who knew of

---

[51] Interview 09 October 2017.

[52] Wang Gungwu, *The Revival of Chinese Nationalism* (Leiden: IIAS, 1996), pp. 9–12.

ET's interest in literature, often read his poems and made helpful suggestions.[53] And yet ET noticed him deferring to Frazer, the Scot. That was the internal hierarchy, he realized, even among fellow educationists, under the dictates of colonial structures. As he says, he knew Frazer was a nice man and treated Owen as an esteemed colleague and yet the difference remained, 'I started to sense a hierarchy, a class system among the British and gradually saw a pattern. The top posts, Director of Education, the Principals of Raffles Institution and Victoria School and the subject-specialists were all Oxbridge types. Next came those from provincial universities, followed by Asians. I reflected a little, recalling the British history learnt from Standard One to Standard Eight.'[54] It was not too hard to make the connection—the Scots and Welsh were conquered by Edward I who had proclaimed his son the first Prince of Wales. So, the Scots and Welsh had remained the 'subject' people and only some families like Frazer's had been able to make the transition by dint of their own merit. The roots that colonialism had let down into the society were deep and could be reversed not only by securing the independence of their country but by considerable amount of hard work.

ET's understanding of nationalism boils down to the inspiration he drew from three countries: China where he realized nationalism was a great unifying force that made it a strong monolithic culture, India with its diverse richness which could accommodate the pacifism of Gandhi and the more confrontational Subhas Chandra Bose, and Japan where nationalism had unleashed such energy that they could be the first Asians to think of pan-Asianism. His own brand of nationalism is emotional like that of the Indians, fed by the sentiments of sacrificial patriotism and mother worship that he had encountered in the INA. Thus his poetry can carry lines like:

---

[53] *Peninsular Muse*, p. 54.
[54] Ibid, pp. 54–5.

> To the sky my last look; to the earth my last touch;
> To my beloved, and our children, my last prayer.[55]

His nationalism also contains a healthy dose of pragmatism that he learnt from his Chinese ancestors. As he says at the cost of making a fair generalization, 'We cannot forget that in India Brahmins ruled, while in China the mandarins ruled.'[56] So by extension, spirituality was of utmost importance in India while in China it was a pragmatic understanding of statecraft, the sentiments of loyalty and dutiful service which were valued. It is this pragmatism that helps him accept without hesitation Singapore's unapologetic need for economic success, its constant need to modernize and stay ahead of the curve. There is little inner conflict between his imagination and the social vision of the state when he admits,

> They make, they serve,
> They buy, they sell.
> Despite unequal ways,
> Together they mutate,[57]

From Japanese nationalism, he borrows the energy. Self-confessedly he would never be a political animal and his chosen nationalistic path would be that of an intellectual's. This was also the trend among the English-educated middleclass. According to him, they, the students of English-medium schools, always lacked the courage and discipline of the students of Chinese schools who rioted against the British.[58] Instead, he along with his compatriots from the University would decide to use the energy released by nationalism to fuse together the multiple, community-centric nostalgic literatures of the past to form a new literature of nation building written in a more widely

---

[55] *Cry Freedom.*
[56] Interview 09 October 2017.
[57] *Ulysses by the Merlion.*
[58] Interview 22 July 2017.

accessible English. It would be clear to him quite early that there were four kinds of independence required to recover from colonialism—political, economic, intellectual and psychological.[59] He knew he would not be able to contribute towards the first two and instead would focus his energies on the remaining.

If there is something missing in ET's sense of nationalism, then it is the lack of need to look at how negative or how restrictive a force it can be. He merely speaks of it as a tremendous positive energy. This could be because, unlike in countries like India where nationalism had the leisure to evolve over a century or China where there was a heritage-filled past to fall back on when it came to national restoration, nationalism was thrust upon Singapore as a bit of a surprise that needed to be dealt with. It neither had a long history of communal living nor after the separation from Malaysia, would it have a thriving hinterland. Thus, unlike Rabindranath Tagore for instance who had been consistently critical of nationhood which according to him merely created a political and commercial man—a man of limited purpose—and had said nationalism was a menace that focussed on efficiency at the cost of morality, for ET nationalism remains a power needed to create a nation.[60] In nationality he sees the vision of a unifying harmony while Tagore sees in it the negative benefits of peace and order that gradually loses the benefits of expansion and movement.

Rib of Earth

When asked what kind of a person was he when he wrote the poems of *Rib of Earth* (1956), ET is prompt in his reply—*terrible*! When prodded a bit further, he appears a bit pensive and adds after some thought, 'Restless, very active . . . hard to describe.'[61] It is exactly this

---

[59] ET, 'Conversion of the Tribes: Societal Antecedents & the Growth of Singapore Poetry', *World Englishes*, 9(2) (1990), p. 155.

[60] Rabindranath Tagore, *Nationalism* (ND: Fingerprint Classics, 2016), pp. 99–104.

[61] Interview 30 October 2017.

'hard-to-describe' persona that comes through in his first anthology for it contains the expressions of a mind on a quest—a quest not only to find himself but to find a fulfilling theme to which his mind can latch itself without guilt or self-consciousness. At this point of creativity what he can attempt is maximum lyrical intensity, a complete capturing of the nuances—those threads of nebulous, inchoate thought that occupy the peripheries of the mind. The ideas that surface here will be quarried later to form consistent themes. But this collection is successful too for it gives him several of his most important images and symbols, tells him about some of his abiding preoccupations and lends him a unique poetic voice. There is a photograph of his from this time, sitting straight-backed on the floor of his hostel room with his feet firmly planted on the ground, reading a copy of the *Four Quartet*—the same firmness of confidence and controlled vigour comes through in the poems. It is the voice of a confident seeker, a seeker who knows he has the intellectual energy to find and in finding continue his search.

Yesterday

Silence growing on a stem;
touch of rustic life:
a thin twig of smoke
following a dead creeper
among old branches
and both twisting
old thoughts to new ideas,
betrays a habitation.

Yet walk to the shadow
Of Mandai mountain
I will show you a
sleeping secret stream.

Perhaps it is this confidence which helps him delve into himself, his real self, his real feelings with very little that he borrows from other personalities. Singapore made a unique beginning as a nation of migrants. As Wang Gungwu has pointed out, among the traditional Chinese there was no concept equivalent to immigration.[62] The original Chinese term which is roughly equal to this very Western concept, is *qiaoju* meaning sojourners or birds of trade who intend to return to their homeland. In a country where the many communities, from the Tamils and Chinese to the minority Jews, Parsees or Armenians came with the intention of return, it is but natural that early vernacular literature was marked by nostalgia for a lost homeland. And even when Gungwu writes the opening verse, *Moon Thoughts* for the first English anthology, *Pulse* (1950), despite a distinct Malayan imagery at work in being able to see the moon through *drooping leaves of rubber trees,* the overriding theme remains a Chinese one of homesickness in an alien land. Or in 1954, when Ee Tiang Hong writes *Alien Shrine,*

> here who cares to lament us
> in this sort of tomb—
> O, of course, there's the tree
> And insects in the gloom.[63]

while the shrine is definitely Malayan, the Muse who sits within is of the English Romantics who in a very classical refrain bemoans the ephemerality of human life. Yet when ET writes of the waters of Ayer Biru, a picnic spot desolate of campsters and muses on the stillness of an 'unthought symphony', the moment of emptiness that comes before reflection is all his own,

---

62 Leo Suryadinata, *Chinese Adaptation and Diversity: Essays on Society and Literature in Indonesia, Malaysia & Singapore* (Singapore: Singapore University Press, 1993), p. 121.

63 *Sharing Borders*, p. 82.

> Blue waters, I mutter,
> Blue waters:
> A stray drop of sand
> In a mangrove pattern.[64]

Unlike other anthologies too, it is difficult to find a single unifying theme in *Rib of Earth*. Instead there is often a uniform pattern in the poems—in the course of a poem one comes across a single line, stronger than others, which contains the young poet's central thought. And this central thought is more often than not unique or different from the others present in the volume for as ET says, in these poems he merely tries to find his own voice. Thus in the opening poem, *Emergence* is the emphatic closing line, 'I too was part of the story', corresponding to his incipient thought of the time that much of the colonial history that they read excluded the Asians. Or in *Moments*, when he says, 'I'll trade the moon for a dream' as he is torn between a life of approving-complacence and a life of purpose. Or yet again the unease that he feels as he turns to look at himself and wonders what the search will unearth, will it be the 'sea-snake' that he had found swimming in his own image, when he writes in *Reflections*,

> Do not lift the settled stone
> To expose the bloated worm

At this point it is wise to remember that ET has always admired Ben Jonson's virtuosity in his craft, the width of his range which can include a merciless satire like *Volpone* and have nesting within it a tender love song, *To Celia*.[65] It is this diversity that ET tries to emulate in his attempt to extend his own craft. And so there is ET's own heart-achingly beautiful love poem that he wrote to his first girlfriend, Louise. Critics have commented on how it rises from

---

[64]   *Ayer Biru.*
[65]   Interview 29 May 2017.

the dredges of the poet's heart, contains the direct utterance of the Muse.[66] Yet in the second stanza the rising curve of lyricism falls as he wonders in a more rational frame of mind what he would do if Louise 'should sleep and never wake'. And as one hears of his resolution to wait for a God's hand to clear the way so he can

Being shall sing and singing give

one realizes that under the exuberance of youthful romance, this is actually a poem about his thoughts on the legacy he can leave behind. Running under the palpable grief at the thought of losing his beloved is a quieter acknowledgement of his own vocation as a poet which the gods have destined for him and which he needs to refine and with which he needs to push forward.

If there is something that keeps this volume together then it is his experience of reading Chinese and Japanese poems. It was in the early 1950s, when university was still two years away that he strengthened his contact with year mates who had a strong Chinese background through activities organized by the Literary Society.[67] He had already started reading Arthur Waley's translations of Chinese poems, *A Hundred and Seventy Chinese Poems* and *Japanese Poems: The Uta*. After doing a few translations himself with his Chinese friends, ET managed to absorb the special idiom developed by Waley and this impact of Eastern minimalism is apparent in the poems of *Rib of Earth*. If there is something *haiku*-like in the way Waley draws the reader into the experience of the poet in lines such as,

The white aspens how they murmur, murmur;
Pines and cypresses flank the broad path.[68]

---

[66] *Sharing Borders*, p. 83–4.
[67] *Peninsular Muse*, p. 37.
[68] *A Hundred and Seventy Chinese Poems*, translated by Arthur Waley (London: Constable & Co., 1918), p. 46.

Then ET does much the same in the simplicity of his images, yet create an incisive, clear picture,

> Weak showers of light
> Drip through the thick foliage.
> Knotted mangrove-roots are grey.[69]

But more important than poetic style are two ideas that he derives from Waley, both of which are emphatically Confucian and perhaps already lay dormant in ET as part of his Chinese inheritance. The first is the image of the poet as a thinker and the second, the insistence on a life of public service, often at the cost of personal time spent with the lady love. Thus, in poem after poem the picture that Waley paints is of the poet, neat and tranquil, sometimes even a timid recluse, given to candid reflection and self-analysis. Reflection emerges also as an important preoccupation of the poet in *Rib of Earth*—whether by the quiet waters of Ayer Biru or when he muses on the silence of Mandai as a thin twig of smoke follows a dead creeper.[70]

Along with the poet as thinker, there is also a certain Asian sense of guilt that pulls him away from a life of loving. If in *East Wind* he writes of living out old age with a lasting sense of regret for having ignored the Confucian analects,

> Yet those who sip the Analects
> mix regret with lotus water

in the final poem of the volume, the poet's bend of mind becomes clearer,

> Leave the Rose
> drinking dew of dew

---

[69] *Ayer Biru.*
[70] *Yesterday.*

> not to touch the blossom
> to find instead
> her thorns touch you.[71]

This poem, entitled *Philosophy,* the young poet would have placed at the end of the volume with a clear purpose—it actually holds his closing thought that has gradually crystallized as he wrote the other poems of the volume. Unlike the usual originality of his imagery, here it is the clichéd twin of a rose and its thorns. Perhaps his use is intentional because he wants to invoke thoughts of feminine beauty classically associated with the flower as he decides that not for him is the gentle fragrance of rose petals but rather the sharp, incisive competence of thorns. And there is no regret in this conscious turning away because it is the thorns which 'touch' him. The last line is clever in its play on the dual meaning of touch to mean tactile contact as well as something that arouses feelings.

It is this underpinning realization that makes ET correctly conclude that he carried the experience of *Rib of Earth* to *The Cough of Albuquerque,* unlike critics who comment on the difference in style between the minimalism of one and the forced artificiality of the other.[72] For along with symbols of the merbak, the shadow and the moon, he carries with him this sense of duty and service without which he knows now a simple life of love or intellectualism cannot satiate him. *Rib of Earth* also makes him aware of his inner dualities—the way even when he looks in front, his past pulls him back or when he breathes a casual whisper into his lover's sleeve he stops to wonder of the legacy he will leave behind. It is through the energy released by the 'cough' that these dualities will find a home in his own land.

---

[71] *Philosophy.*
[72] Interview 30 October 2017.

Prospero and Caliban

This chapter, deriving its title from *The Tempest* as it does, dwells on the nascent sense of nationalism that stirred Singapore from after the war. ET is at its centre with his range of response to British colonialism, the archetypal Caliban who feels resentment for his colonizers and at the same time cannot help a spark of admiring gratefulness towards them.

The period covered is his college days from around the mid-1950s—a time when the proverbial butterfly emerged from its chrysalis. His father retired from his teacher's job and though he did take up odd assignments as substitute teacher, it did not amount to much.[73] The family continued to stay in Lorong Melayu but it was the first time when ET moved away from his family, metaphorically if not physically, though he carried the family ties with him. It was also the time when he first fell in love, decided to explore some of his Chinese heritage as he was swept away by the beauty of Waley's translated Chinese verse and most importantly, emerged as a poet. He was all of twenty and already learning his craft fast and through his first poems would also glimpse the first threshold a budding poet stumbles on—an abiding theme. His first anthology would bring him the awareness that a sense of duty towards his country and a very Confucian sense of public service was what moved him and perhaps subsequently, this would be one of the reasons for his taking up a job in the Singapore Civil Service.

Fingers of the Cape

I rise in a phantom city
where a dark veil hangs careless,
merging with star-whispers.
Miracles of moonlight dart,
choke the shadows.

---

[73] Interview 05 October 2017.

Sprawled on oozing fingers of the Cape,
the City,
(a child's unfinished jigsaw puzzle)
is cast-about, dishevelled.

Open the petals of night,
drink from the nectaries;
poppy-juice meanders through the brain
singing

Only the moon is real.
We are perpetual shadows
of giants and old gods.
Even the owls hooting
are sounds and shadows,
dew-drops sleeping
are thoughts and shadows:
only the moon is real.

Where the dark veil hangs careless
merging with star-whispers
the sum-total is a phantom city.

That he was keenly aware that this period of his life was very different
from his younger days is clear in the epigraph to the *Rib of Earth*
where he writes,

We met at the Second Circle of the moon
Above some dry corner of Asia.

The 'Second Circle' is of course a reference to the Yeatsian idea of
the twenty-eight phases of the moon, the second circle referring to
the second phase of life. It is a phase very distinct from the first
and he, subliminally aware of this, dedicated the book to Shamus

Frazer, his mentor and the English Master of Victoria School, little realizing how much it would hurt his father. The surprising reference to the wetlands of Singapore as a 'dry corner of Asia' indicates some of the ongoing banter in his mind: there is perhaps a tongue-in-cheek reference to the Indian influences he had recently discovered in Yeats and Eliot, a burgeoning consciousness of Asian literature from the Chinese and Japanese poems he had been reading and perhaps also an awareness of the awakening in him as a voice from Asia. 'Dry' is perhaps a reference to the tautness of his own mind which reflects on these connections with some amount of railing sardonicism as he understands the relationship of interdependence between the colonized and the colonizer and yet with the bitterness of personal experience still fresh, finds it difficult to accept the same.

ET's poetry from this period is interesting because not only are they of his coming of age but like an unfolding origami, they reveal the peeling layers of his mind. The single phrase of *Cough of Albuquerque* for instance, *Two ends of a dream*, which holds the multiple streams of thought that preoccupied him at the time. There is of course the influence he found difficult to shake off of Western poetry but there is also a twenty-year-old's taunting sneer at an old man's sexuality, the hauteur of the seriously gifted who knows he can adopt a foreign tongue and return it better, as well as his conflicting thoughts on the colonizing Portuguese, Afonso de Albuquerque, who in capturing Malacca opened up a whole network of commercial exchange between India and China, of critical maritime importance in the future. In a way it was Albuquerque's invasion that eventually shaped Singapore as a trading hub of Asia.

This period is also important because after experiencing first-hand the racial riots of the 1950s and the racial discrimination he faced in school and college as a half-caste, he was left in little doubt that racial unity was the only answer for Singapore and this unity could be found in a common usage of English. Of course, his own multi-racial background and the rupturing experience of war would leave him with a recurring sense of inner fragmentation and consequently, duality, and a resolution thereof would be the leitmotif of his poetry. And what is interesting is, whether in the *Cough of Albuquerque* or in the later anthology, *Ulysses by the Merlion,* he would repeatedly seek the answer to the inner yearning for a restoration of order in his own country. Thus is *Kelong,* the first poem he ever wrote from 1950, where he watches the waves from the offshore wooden pier and notices the daily union of the sun and moon in Singapore's waters:

> Unbroken, joyful lines that ride,
> See them rush towards the shore,
> In lovely, daily flow of ebb and tide
> With Sun and Moon forevermore.[74]

If in ancient Byzantium, Yeats found a deeper unity of practical and aesthetic life, where each became the extension of the other, ET seeks it in Singapore where each race needs the other to complete itself and thereby ties Singapore as a unifying whole.

Yet the question remains, if ET's unifying vision is unifying enough, as after all, it is born of an individual perspective, shaped by his own socialization and not to forget, a highly scholarly mind. For instance, when he speaks of the government quarters of Monk's Hill Terrace where he spent a large part of his childhood.[75] It is a wonderful mind-map that he still recalls—a line-up of houses inhabited by a Jaffna surveyor or veterinary surgeon, a Christian teacher from Goa, an Eurasian clerk or executive officer, a Peranakan inspector of schools—warm memories of homes similar to his own where the boys were often his life-long friends and the girls at times the object of conjecture. But is this truly an English-educated microcosm of Singapore, as he calls it? Isn't it more of the English-speaking, middle-class elite world, privileged with government jobs, with the promise

---

[74] Ee Tiang Hong, *Responsibility & Commitment: The Poetry of Edwin Thumboo* (Singapore: SUP, 1997), p. 93.
[75] Interview 26 June 2017.

of an equally steady future career for their children? There were some Malay boys who would come over to fly kites from the neighbouring Javanese village but with only one house in Monk's Hill belonging to a Malay, the latter were an anomaly. Later in college when he would make a number of Malay friends, and the foundation of their friendship would be their English education, they could no longer form a part of his socialization. As a result perhaps, though there is definitely no anti-Malay shades (as distinct from anti-Malaysian) to his vision, his poems on Malay themes remain restricted to very few.

Perhaps the more worrying bit about his vision which evolves from his socialization is his focus on English as a medium of artistic expression, particularly keeping in mind his otherwise broad-minded acceptance of difference. While there is no denying the need of a single language to hold together the multi-racial potential turmoil of Singapore, it comes with its own set of problems, not to mention the sense of cultural colonization that the non-English speaking majority of Singapore would continue to labour under after independence. That he is not unaware of this is apparent in an article from 1991 entitled, *Looking Back*, where he speaks of the extensive use of English in Singapore which has led to a lower level of subtlety in its literature, or the loss of reading habit that has been caused by not only the focus on science, technology and management but maybe because the denotative implications of the English language has proven threatening to the general populace, not as accustomed to the Queen's tongue as the English-speaking middle-class.[76] Limitations in the command over the language also meant filtering out or leaving unexpressed much of the rich patina of the nation's life.

As an extension of his stress on English is the unquestioning acceptance of the British system of governance. According to him, though he admits that he has not dwelt much on the theology of state craft, British nationalism is the best for while encouraging

---

[76] *Looking Back*, pp. 11–3.

love for the country, it allows for political criticism.[77] And yet there are thinkers like Rabindranath Tagore who have spoken out against British nationalism saying the dense perfection of the British nation is like a hydraulic press, whose pressure is impersonal and on that account completely effective.[78] Or that the British nation in continually turning the wheel of power for its own sake, has created a state that seeks a political and economic union of its people, at the cost of dehumanizing society.

At this point, it would be easy to gloss over this entire period and conclude that there was no shade of doubt that ever marred ET's vision. The exuberance with which he has embraced his new role of a poet and the buoyant optimism with which he looks forward to the next phase of life—they all point to that direction. Yet, all this would be true if only it were not for the closing lines from *The Cough of Albuquerque*,

> There eyeless in the sun
> Incubates the plot of man
> Two ends of a dream.

Even after appearing to resolve all dualities, the possibility of perfection does not delude him even for a moment—if the birth of a new nation is self-sealing and complete, then it also brings with it the loss of innocence, the loss of an earlier way of life where,

> We found our earth ourselves
> Uncovered.

What the independent nation would bring only time could unravel but before that he would spend almost a decade with the Singapore Civil Service, a period when he hardly wrote poetry, but spent time

---

[77]   Interview 18 September 2017.
[78]   *Nationalism*, pp. 52–60.

on reading history, mythology, anthropology—connected social sciences which would lend colour and structure to his writing and a post-colonial accuracy.

III

TRIBES

For beyond the blare of sirened afternoons, beyond
the motorcades;
Beyond the voices and days, echoing highways; beyond
the latescence
. . . The glimpse of a dream lies smouldering in a cave,
together with the mortally wounded birds.
Earth, unbind me; let me be the prodigal; let this be
the ram's ultimate prayer to the tether . . .

—Christopher Okigbo, *Elegy for Alto*

Cast your net to the right side
Nothing?
Nothing
Cast it to the left side
Nothing?
Nothing.
Then cast it to the back of the canoe
And draw gently and carefully . . .
It's only the Back caught
in the meshes of Today

—Gabriel Okara, *The Fisherman's Invocation*

Demoke: *I work with fire. Carving and smelting. Sometimes I merely trace patterns on wood. With fire. I live by the forge and often hold the cinders in my hands. So you see I am not afraid of fire. But I wish to be saved from death by burning. Living, I would rather not watch my body dissolve like alloy. There must be happier deaths.*

Rola: *Like what?* . . .

Demoke: *A fall from a great height.*

> —Wole Soyinka, *A Dance of the Forests*

Gathering of the Tribes

C. Day-Lewis, the Anglo-Irish poet and teacher of poetry from Oxford, in conveying the struggles of reconciling the demands of the past and the present wrote,

> In me two worlds at war
> Trample the patient flesh,
> Their lighted ring of sense where clinch
> Heir and ancestor.

What Day-Lewis celebrates is that tremulous moment which stands between the past that cannot be altered and a future that is yet to be formed, a single moment that holds a quiet acknowledgement of one's history and some uneasy trepidation about what is imminent. And it is in this moment that one cannot deny the power of the past in fabricating the future, for it is the past that is the only tangible thing that one takes with oneself as one journeys into the unknown. It is the same insight that is expounded and recast in terms of anthropology and structuralism in Claude Levi-Strauss's masterpiece of 1962, *The Savage Mind*, a book that speaks of the tempering of civilization by that savage mind, i.e., the old 'drumbeats' of the tribal self that continue to be a part of and fashion civilizations. Or how the traditional, which in particular cases is also the preliterate society, remains as the undeniable bedrock even as tribalism moves through city-states and small nations, through empire, feudalism and the industrial revolution to reach a state of fragile open democracy.[1]

As it emerged from its two years of merger with the Federation 'of Malaya and eventually achieved independence on 9 August 1965, Singapore had a society that was somewhat similar to Day-Lewis's vision, with old and new elements jostling for recognition and a future that awaited discovery. Many of the colonized countries in Asia and Africa during this part of the century were going through a similar moment of moulting. But perhaps the situation in Singapore was a bit different. India, for instance, was at a different level of social development when it was finally decolonized. For it had many years of living with its rich diversity before the British took over and even under the British for over a century nationalism had moulded the country into some semblance of unity. But in Singapore, a colony artificially created by the British of migrants drawn from different countries, living in clans was still the overriding credo. Even as late as in July 1955, a small incident near the Kallang gasworks was enough to spark a riot which eventually killed 223 and had 454 injured, even as Chinese villagers fled from Malay-dominant estates and Malays bolted their doors against the Chinese. And if one moved a bit further back to the 1950s when Singapore first experimented with indigenous parties being made a part of the Legislative Assembly in its attempt to transit from colonial rule to self-government, then as the definitive *Men in White* recounts, 'Vote-buying was inextricably linked to gangsterism and secret societies in a still largely immigrant society whose welfare needs were ignored by the colonial government

---

[1]   Robin Fox, *The Tribal Imagination* (UK, USA: Harvard University Press, 2011), pp. 69–70.

and whose impoverished masses had to fend for themselves. Often the lines between clans, guilds, self-help societies, trade unions and secret societies overlapped.'[2] Thus, there were these various pockets of societies, guilds and community life which waited to be drawn into a unifying web.

As a result of the above scenario, when ET speaks of tribalism in the context of Singapore it has three implications. First and perhaps the most important, is the residue of distrust between the communities that the racial riots left in their wake. It was to remain in the subconscious mind of the nation for a long time to come. The second consists of the traces of the pre-independence society—the gangsterism and buying of votes, the pig and poultry farms, secret societies and clans which formed powerful networks of nepotism— the 'drumbeats' of a pre-civilized, tribal way of living that would continue to echo. Lastly, the culture that was actually prevalent in the city-state belonged to two outside and overwhelmingly large worlds—India and China. If Chinese settlements of Singapore had the three figures from the period of the Three Kingdoms—Liu Bei, Guan Yu and Zhang Fei and a secret armoury of *parangs* and bicycle chains in their honour, then the Indian community too only but recently had marched to the rousing tunes of the INA, singing '*Kadam kadam badaye jaa*', inciting the patriotic platoon to move towards *Hind* or India. It was only the Malays who had the advantage of enjoying a complete trajectory of home-grown culture but that could not be adopted in entirety in exclusion of the others. Thus, in 1965 when Singapore set about establishing a new 'Singaporean' identity, it meant not only forging a new self which went beyond the overriding native cultures but also understanding inter-community dynamics and determining how much and in what mutated form the old would remain as part of the new.

---

[2]   *Men in White: The Untold Story of Singapore's Ruling Political Party* (Singapore: SPH, 2009), pp. 61–2.

National Language Class:
Oil on Canvas by Chua Mai Tee

Because history and geo-politics sustained
One irredentist Nusantara pulse, especially
Its lingual nerve, we sing our national anthem
In Bahasa which has bits of other tongues some
Fifty generations took, ingesting script, word,
Grammar and poetics to enrich shairs, pantuns,
Proverbs. It can be swift as Hang Tuah's blade,
Yet ululate *dongdang sayang's* rare sweet-
Sadness, lift court and kampong; grace adat.
Satu Bangsa, Satu Agama, *Satu Bahasa.* Add
Satu Negara.

So we schooled. See the dark left canvas patch
Light towards multi-racial faces, each intently
Focussed on this brown Nanyang voice that still
Harangues regional moments, neighbourly loud;
Yet it raised ringing slogans for 12 million hopes.
Spot Jawi etched faintly on the blackboard. Note
Chegu, text in hand, encouraging his pupils
Testing each the other on what's just learnt.
But
All this changed, in post-Merger anger, angsts,
Unfriendly gestures. That grinding aftermath
Marred it all.

Our prodigal Little Red Dot and all in her—cut off
And cast upon bitter tides, turbulent seas—lived
Precariously. We re-started bare, small and mixed;
Mitigated; sought moorings for our migrant peoples,
Cultures, orthodoxies, prejudices.
So our founding

Fathers strategized: three pillars, best free marketing,
Socio-economic growing; rising GDP and Surpluses;
Semi-socialist means of sharing gains; educate; unite;
Shift mentalities; our languages for roots, English
To bridge, its spurs to globalise, as we, advancing,
Sing and celebrate
Majulah Singapura.

ET was more than aware of the nuances of this background but
could take the first proactive steps only after a few years when in
1966 he joined the National University of Singapore as an Assistant
Lecturer and subsequently in 1967 set off for Africa on a mission of
doing a thesis on Commonwealth Literature for a master's degree.
The decade in between, since *Rib of Earth* had been published in
1956, was spent working with the Singapore Civil Service—first
as a part of the Income Tax Department, later with the Central
Provident Fund Board, and nine months with the Singapore
Telephone Board. When asked about these ten years which are all
but missing in most accounts of his life, if he is in an unusually
bitter mood, he confesses it was a daunting period for him when
he learnt new ways to say yes and no and kept his sanity only by
keeping up with his reading. But more often than not he brushes
it off with his staple sardonic humour, 'Well, the services did teach
me to do things which I didn't like and do them well—so that was
a good enough discipline I learnt!'[3] So under good or bad weather,
the dislike for bureaucratic work remains, and that despite knowing
its importance.

Once a part of the faculty at NUS, a dream that he had harboured
for long, ET found it was necessary that he add a master's degree to
his credentials (it was a different matter that later the thesis would be
upgraded to a PhD by the University) and decided to study African
Literature. When asked the reason, he says he was aware of the

---

[3]   Interview 19 December 2017.

similarities and the differences between the cultural experiences of Africa and Singapore and knew that with Africa Singapore shared a common cause and a common history of colonialism. But in the same breath he adds, later he would very consciously settle for Southeast Asia and the literature of the region as a 'hinterland' closer home and perhaps closer in culture too with similar Indian and Chinese markings that he found in his homeland.[4]

ET discovered Africa in the mid-1960s. By then *Négritude* as an assertion of African values in the face of French and Portuguese assimilation was all but over.[5] Yet the lessons remained. As a literary movement in African nationalism against colonialism, it brought to light a new genre of literature that believed awareness begins with history. Certainly, among the mission-educated intellectual elite of the continent it was important to show Negro values as culture markers. But at the same time the movement threw up the conflict between authorial ideology and aesthetic ideology that was a hallmark of *Négritude* poetry as it did the possible danger of lapsing into romantic idealism. It had declined into a kind of reverse conservatism which involved an escape to an idyllic pre-rational past and depicted the African Personality as associated with suppleness of limbs, an emotional heart, in whom physiology and psychology found a perfect union. These were pitfalls ET would avoid in the future, particularly the strong element of romanticism he found embedded in the individualistic idealism of *Négritude* poets. But what he would perhaps take away was the difference of intent of public and private poetry that was an inherent part of the movement as also the role of pioneer poets in a newly awakened country. In his thesis he cites the example of Lenrie Peters, the Gambian surgeon, novelist and poet, for whom the poetic idiom was important as a means of communication rather than creation

---

[4]   Interview 02 January 2018.
[5]   Emmanuel Ngara, *Ideology and Form in African Poetry: Implications for Poetry* (Nairobi: Heinemann Kenya, 1990), pp. 22–3.

and for whom an exploration of the inner life was not critical to the creative process.[6]

But of more critical importance than *Négritude*, ET openly confesses, was his exploration of African tribalism. It taught him not only the dangers of tribalism but also how traditions can travel across tribes and how certain awkward traditions of the past can find their way to the present.[7] For this was a time when inter-tribal rivalry was a part of everyday reality in Africa, when monogamy was difficult to consider because of the fundamental tribal gene which dictated the need to outbreed other tribes. It was a low-trust society which struggled to come together under modern bonds of political and economic significance even while the old tribal concepts of kin and kinship remained important. It was also a society that was making a difficult transition from tribe-related nepotism to a modern culture of meritocracy and to a new system of democracy that involved a voluntary ceding of power to the opposition—a practice that was impossible to accede to in a tribal world.

Thus, there was much in common between contemporary Africa and the post-independent, sharply fragmented Singapore and some of these learnings would find their way into ET's next collection of poems, *Gods Can Die*, published in 1977. Back home, the '70s was a decade by when the routes taken by local writing in English for Malaysia and Singapore were clearly differentiated by the language policy of the respective governments.[8] In Malaysia English poetry was afflicted by a decline in publishing outlets and readers while that in Malay was promoted vigorously by Dewan Bahasa dan Pustaka. In contrast, in Singapore, with a quick consolidation of the role of English for the independent nation, English poetry had flourished slowly but steadily. The 1970s saw the publication of almost three

---

[6]   ET, *Personality, Intention and Idiom: A Framework*, pp. 3–4.

[7]   Interview 19 December 2017.

[8]   Rajeev S. Patke and Philip Hoden, *The Routledge Concise History of Southeast Asian Writing in English* (Oxon: Routledge, 2010), p. 115.

dozen volumes of poetry including those by the veterans Lim Thean Soo, Ee Tiang Hong, Wong Phui Nam, Oliver Seet and Goh Poh Seng, as well as new talents like Arthur Yap, Robert Yeo and Chandran Nair. What is interesting is to follow the divergent poetic careers of the two friends—Ee Tiang Hong and Edwin Thumboo. The former as a Peranakan Chinese in Malaysia found his poetic response severely restricted as he lamented the ethnic essentialism of his home country that served the cause of a very narrow kind of nationalism. And surprisingly, perhaps ET too imposed certain restrictions on himself as he travelled from his private to his public self and expressed the voice of the new Singapore—fast changing, self-reliant, meritocratic, multi-racial. It was a government-endorsed space that was responsible, structured, puritanical in its civilized demands, offering a certain bandwidth in which to explore personal relationships and emotions. In 1974 was introduced the Newspaper and Printing Presses Act in Singapore, bringing with it further need for self-censorship and yet both poets would remain true to their vocation and their chosen sense of mission.

Heart of Light

ET has a wonderful capacity for conversation. And while he speaks, he slides at will on a trajectory of complexity, constantly extending the range of conversation. So his narration of his African journey can at various points visit various milestones. It can stop by at Kinshasa where his red Singaporean passport was looked upon with scepticism because of its communist colour and where he confessed to a little man called George, a bystander at the airport who helped him out through the immigration proceedings: 'The only word of French I know is *oui*. What if they ask him if I am a terrorist and I in my confusion say *Oui!*'[9] It can also stop by at Freetown, in Sierra Leone where he met Eldred Jones, O.R. Dathorne and Lenrie Peters. And

---

9   Interview 19 December 2017

Thomas Dekka, a Permanent Secretary, who gave him a manuscript of Shakespeare's *Julius Caesar* which he had freshly translated into Creole. After that the conversation can take various loops and turns, travel through Uganda and Kenya where tribalism was already making a restless assertion, and stop by at Martinique and the Caribbean poet, *Aimé Césaire's* coining of the term *Négritude* and the Nobel Laureate, Soyinka's subsequent rejection of it saying, 'If tigers don't proclaim their tigritude, then there is no rationale for Négritude (my paraphrase).'

Yet if one takes a closer look, all these stories, spoken in self-deprecating humour or in a deep-voiced moment of serious contemplation, lead up to a single point—the issue of language in Africa. When ET joined NUS and realized very quickly that he needed to do a master's degree, it was his intention to do one on a Commonwealth topic and follow it up with a PhD on a classical mainstream subject of English literature, for instance the Romantic poets.[10] At first he toyed with the idea of India as Commonwealth brethren but then it appeared all too familiar and he finally settled for Africa—where he says he found it all. It was an exhilarating world peopled by the Ghanaian Awoonor Williams, later known as Kofi Awoonor, who wrote in English instead of his native Ewe and in whom politics and poetry made strange bedfellows, the Nigerian Wole Soyinka and his exploration of Yoruba literature and a firm understanding of how the past fed into the future, J.P. Clarke or Christopher Okigbo whom he could not meet because of the impending Biafran War and for whom their 'Africanness' was not of such paramount importance and who explored both the English and African worlds with less inhibition or Dennis Brutus of South Africa who like ET was born of mixed parentage and who encountered double isolation as a 'Coloured' rather than 'Black' poet.[11] So it was a literature rich in implication, bringing together the various impulses

---

[10]   Ibid.

[11]   ET, from *Personality, Intention and Idiom: A Framework.*

that overwhelmed decolonized countries—nationalism, skin colour, race, awareness of inheritance and, above all, the need to reconstruct the past while keeping in tune with an ever-shifting present.

In Africa
(Freetown, Sierra Leone)

This airport is nicely rural
But it grows and will get up-to-date
This landing strip where kites circle for prey.
Unlock the sky,
This scar in the earth to which night comes
When glow worms fly,
Will soon be better lit.

The country's flag is new
Unfurled just modestly.
An old colonial cannon sits
Just quietly.
But hear the trucks and tractors, busy with the earth
Pushing the trees quite out of sight,
Dismantle the frame of land
The green-red flowers.

There a nocturnal lizard finds a sudden day,
Moves unnaturally, glaring at the sun,
Displaced into the century.

ET went to Africa on a grant from Asia Foundation and on his first stop, London, he was hosted by the British Council. It was in London that he met the most important of his contacts for African literature, Ulli Beier, the German Jewish scholar, critic, translator, publisher or as ET puts it, the 'catalyst' who played a pioneering role in developing the literature in English of Nigeria and later Papua New

Guinea. It was Ulli who drew ET firmly into the network of African authors and poets whom he met as he subsequently travelled through Sierra Leone, Ghana, Nigeria, Uganda and Kenya. ET also speaks of Ulli's publishing outfits—the Mbari Publications and *Black Orpheus*, the first African literary journal that he founded, which proved to be valuable storehouses of Nigerian literature. Subsequently, while in Uganda, he would also be introduced to Rajat Nyogi, the founding editor of *Transitions*, which would provide him important insights into post-independence African literature so much so that on return to Singapore, ET would be able to put his thoughts together very rapidly and the thesis would be ready in a couple of months' time.

The resultant thesis that ET wrote would be an interesting representation of the rich diversity of African poetry written in English, analysed from a three-point framework of Idiom, Intention and Personality. But underneath the analysis is perhaps something more important, something that would play a key role in deciding the future trajectory of ET's poetic and academic focus—the use of the English language in the cause of Africanization.

What ET found in Africa was that while modern, post-independent African literature was born of anti-colonial struggle and still bore the marks of the same, ironically enough in order to assert their right for self-determination and to have their voice heard, the Africans had had to adopt the language of their colonial masters. Of course the use of English as a medium had led to its own set of problems in literature—there was often a divorce between the substance of this new literature and its linguistic medium.[12] ET noticed the struggle among African authors to convey the whole complexity of African culture in an adopted tongue. There was need to unlock the syntax, disentangle the metaphysics from poetry and proverb, understand social philosophy and habits of moral thought and extract them from the rhythm, the imagery and the very circumlocution of native

---

[12]   Lewis Nkosi, *Tasks & Masks: Themes and Styles of African Literature* (Harlow, Essex: Longman, 1982), pp. 5–7.

African speech. Often it could mean too many stories of fantasy and fable in an attempt to write about what was considered 'authentically' African or as the poet Christopher Okigbo put it, 'Where you have this African feeling summoned for the occasion—put on like Sunday clothing—you have a bastardization of the idea of *Négritude*.'[13]

But beyond such pitfalls of literary quality was the much larger sociological issue which had its hooks firmly embedded in politics, history and economics—language seemed to be in the heart of the rift in African society. While much of the new African literature was written in English, if not European languages and was by far the most influential in developing a national consciousness, it somehow lacked relevance for eighty per cent of the African people who lacked literacy. Even those who could read and could handle with ease vernacular literature, could not be expected to handle the complexity of modern fiction and contemporary verse written in a foreign tongue. Thus, the masses were effectively sealed off from the educated elite who through constant creative and intellectual discourse constituted an 'objectification on African soil of another culture and values.'[14]

ET, after what he witnessed across Africa and more than aware how divided the society of his home country could get over issues of race and language, was in full support of the Singapore government when in 1987 English was officially adopted as the first language of schools and promoted as the common unifying language with no reservations about its colonial origin. If he heard African poets and scholars bemoan the lack of government-backed school programmes to bring larger sections of the African population to reasonable standards of literacy in European languages, particularly English to bypass the issue of the number and variety in native African languages and dialects, then this prompted him to take certain decisions in the future.

There were other elements too that he took away from his African experience and ET is open in acknowledging his debt to his African

---

[13] Ibid, p. 7.
[14] Ibid, pp. 2–3.

friends. According to him, they opened up a whole new world to him of literary connections and confirmed that it was possible to enter a new language and make it his own. It was not something he was unaware of, but because of their similarity of experience, seeing the African poets at work gave him a 'tremendous' amount of confidence. As he says, 'Comparing their literature and their use of the English Language told me we were not alone.'[15] It was an intellectual comradeship that he found among these poets and writers driven by a rare sense of national consciousness who it was said, *did not sleep to dream but dreamt to change the world.*

A Brother
(In Nairobi)

The African can be my brother
When he is most himself.
But some have learnt to mini-laugh,
To adjust their tie before they give a hand,
Or make cold assessment as you stand,
Greeting most efficiently.
These are not themselves,
And are not brothers.

There was a clerk in town
Who dressed himself to death.
So proper, so spruce,
So carefully correct
That he must have felt
Himself most pukka . . .
At home with foreigners.

He knew to put inferiors in their place,
How shade his words to please or growl

---

15   Interview 19 December 2017.

To suit the situation.
A good lad, the Old Colonial said,
Approving such understanding, such service.

He was disliked by some, indulged by others,
And felt superior to protect himself.

I wonder if he takes tie, overcoat,
The crease of his trousers, his new baggage
Into his dreams,
To match them with
The lion, the assagai,
Plains, drums, maidens' breasts and
Bare, simple eyes?

Heavensgate

In 1967, Nigeria lost one of her best poets, sadly enough just as he was said to be entering the prime of his poetic career.

By end-1965 colonial territories of West Africa, both Anglophone and Francophone, seemed well on their way to sovereignty, much to the elation of nationalists. And yet by beginning-1966, the political situation had taken a worrying turn—the first of the army coups occurred in Nigeria and Ghana, tensions gradually escalating between the existing semi-autonomous states and West Africa seemed well on its way to one of its most bloodied periods of Civil War, a loss of innocence that it could not afford. When the peace program was emphatically rejected by the Eastern Nigerian leader Colonel Ojukwu, the secessionist republic of Biafra was established and by July the first skirmish of the Nigerian Civil War occurred.[16] Okigbo, a poet whose works had been heavy with Cassandra-like warnings about the slow emergence of a carnal nightmare, threw in

---

[16] Robert Fraser, *West African Poetry: A Critical History* (Cambridge: CUP, 1986), pp. 251–5.

his lot with the secessionist forces, never to return. It was said the poet of foreboding, dimly discerned himself as a force of destiny and so willingly lunged towards self-destruction.[17] The novelist Chinua Achebe, whose apartment received a direct hit, caught a glimpse of him in the flare of the bombings. He wore his customary white gown and cream trousers and Achebe could scarcely have a word or two with him, before he disappeared like a meteor, forever.[18]

ET, who is unhesitant in calling Okigbo the best craftsman among all the African poets of his thesis, reached Nigeria a bit too late to meet him.[19] He was already in Biafra. Instead he heard stories. Soyinka who told him, 'I speak to Chris very often on the phone and at the end of the conversation I say "hello" to the CIA boys.' He also learnt how important it was for the Igbo people, the ethnic group to which Okigbo belonged, to own land: 'They never move away because their ancestors have been there, they can't desert them. It's like the Chinese in Singapore who carry their tablets [from the burial ground of their ancestors] around.'[20] Yet though they never met, it is interesting how similar the two poets are—both in the plurality of their beginnings and the syncretic thoughts that this duality bred in them.

Okigbo is a poet in whom the rhythmical oral traditions of West Africa came together beautifully with the musical compositions of Europe. As an undergraduate at University College, Ibadan, he was well known for being a jazz player on clarinet and piano and later constructed his poems on the analogy of European musical compositions, 'in a sequence of movements with themes, developments, variations, repeats and reminiscences.'[21] As he

---

[17] Ibid, pp. 254–5.

[18] Ibid.

[19] ET, *Personality, Intention and Idiom: A Framework*, pp. 244–5; Interview 19 December 2017.

[20] Interview 19 December 2017.

[21] K.L. Goodwin *Understanding African Poets: A Study of Ten Poets* (USA: Heinemann, 1982), p. 30.

confessed himself, that while writing *Heavensgate,* the first part of his final anthology *Labyrinths,* he was working under the spell of Impressionist composers Debussy, Caesar Frank and Ravel and unknowingly their watery, shadowy, nebulous world seeped into his writing.[22] And yet Okigbo's feet remain firmly planted in his native village of Ojoto, among the Igbo people and his poetry is of the Ashanti drum invocations, notes of the *udu* and *ekwe,* the hand bell of forged iron and the mongoose and elephant and panther that inhabited their forests. Such combinations do bring to mind ET's poems on Indian or Chinese themes—stories of his lonely Chinese Uncle, the pathos of which reaches us through the sensuous gratification of the Indian *rasa* or the amorously entwined image of *Radha-Krishna* whose inseparability is conveyed as the unified serenity of the *yin* and *yang.*[23]

Yet the similarity does not end there. Both poets draw their beliefs from two religions which are different in ilk and yet between which they see little cause for conflict or disharmony. If ET sang Tamil hymns at Christian churches, sought the blessings of Mazu, the Taoist Sea Goddess when setting off on journeys or found in his grandfather's house remains of an old Tantric belief lurking behind Christian ones, then Okigbo was no different. He was born into Christianity and yet was believed to be a reincarnation of his grandfather who was the high priest at the shrine of Ajani where Idoto, the River Goddess was worshipped. Okigbo was expected to carry on the duties of his grandfather and when he started taking poetry seriously he felt it was a call to perform the full functions of the chief priest of Idoto.[24] And like ET too, Okigbo sees no conflict between his native and adopted beliefs—both to him were ceremonies of innocence, different routes for reaching the same place.[25]

---

[22] Ibid, p. 31.
[23] For a fuller analysis, Chapter 1, 'Crossing Boundaries'.
[24] Goodwin, *Understanding African Poets,* p. 33.
[25] Ibid.

The two poets were merely born of a new culture—the hybrid culture of the Commonwealth and they embraced the plurality of their roots with equal amounts of equanimity. It is because of this that ET says his exploration of Africa gave him 'tremendous confidence', that he found the possibility of a creative hinterland in the continent. Thus, if ET, perhaps not even conscious then, vocalized the sentiments of a syncretic heart when he wrote in his early *Cough of Albuquerque*, of Lord Buddha the 'shaman with the wheel' who was 'in the loaves of Christ', then Okigbo too with the same lack of self-consciousness wrote at the end of the *Initiations* section of *Heavensgate*:

> And he said to the ram:
> disarm
> And I said:
> except by rooting,
> who could pluck yam tubers
> from their base?

Written in the tone of story-telling of oral traditions, Okigbo brings together the innocence of the lamb from the Bible with the castrating image of 'disarming' the ram. Yet 'pluck' is not used in the conventional Christian sense of plucking out the eye if it offends, but in the very African sense of digging deep for yam tubers, the staple of the Igbo people.

It is this aspect of convergent cultures that ET repeatedly emphasizes when writing of Okigbo whom he quotes in his thesis on African Literature, 'I belong, integrally, to my own society just as, I believe, I belong also integrally to the other societies than my own.'[26] He writes of not only the assimilation of influences that take place in Okigbo but also of the genuine soul-searching and constant adjustment of the inner life that brought about

---

[26]   ET, *Personality, Intention and Idiom*, p. 196.

such assimilation. For someone who had not met Okigbo, this is remarkably perceptive and perhaps it is so because it is a conclusion born of a shared experience?

Some of this soul-searching is evident in Okigbo's poem *Heavensgate,* a poem that starts with an invocation of Idoto and spreads out into sections—*Passage, Initiation, Watermaid, Lustra,* and *Newcomer*—each functioning as a movement of a musical piece. Paul Theroux, the American novelist, writes of *Heavensgate,* that at the beginning Okigbo finds himself in the 'watery presence' of Idoto and he is naked, a supplicant, offering himself as a sacrifice to his own poetic impulse: preparing to suffer creation.[27] Yet very soon the figure of Idoto gives way to Anna, a Christian equivalent of a Mother Goddess of protection, referring to either Mary or Mary's mother Anna or both:

> Oh Anna at the knobs
> of the panel oblongs,
> hear me at crossroads
> at the great hinges
> where the players of loft pipe-
> organs rehearse old lovely
> fragments, alone—

Interestingly it is ET rather than the other critics who notice that words like 'fragments' and 'alone' point to a correlative of spirituality but a spirituality that is lifeless, indicating a reduction of physical life. Or as he puts it: 'Christianity is attractive to the protagonist; parts of his personality genuinely respond' and yet words like 'fragments' cut Christianity down and 'offer a conspectus of its limitations.'[28] Such a conclusion seems born of a moment of revelation when a

---

27 *Introduction to African Literature: An Anthology of Critical Writing from 'Black Orpheus',* ed. Ulli Beier (London: Longman, 1967), p. 125.

28 ET, *Personality, Intention and Idiom,* p. 209.

Singaporean poet found a Nigerian poet had known the secret undercurrents of his heart.

As Okigbo moves through the sections of *Heavensgate*, his purpose is unmistakeable: he accepts the ordeals of religiosity only to arrive at a new religion of finding himself. At each stage he moves from perception to perception and struggles to accept and understand the religious trappings only to discard them, for otherwise he will lose himself. At the end he stands released, left again on the edge. Here too Okigbo is similar to ET who at the end of *Cough of Albuquerque* had stood at the start of yet another journey but here also lies an important difference. ET had written in his analysis that in order to bring all the divergent parts together, the snake, the mongoose, the elephant, the panther, Okigbo needed rituals but while Eliot or Pound were ET's high priests, ET worked his own salvation.[29] But significantly enough, the salvation that Okigbo worked was of a spiritual kind. Through his journey of opposite faiths what he seeks is a union with divinity. Thus he speaks of this journey in several ways in the introduction to *Labyrinths*—'a ceremony of innocence', 'something like a mass', 'psychic union with the supreme spirit that is both destructive and creative' and as a 'journey to the palace of the white goddess'—a sexual union with whom generates poetry.[30] ET rightly concludes in his introductory paragraph on Okigbo that the latter saw the issue of conflicting experiences and their final assimilation as a poetic problem rather than a cultural one.[31] But while Okigbo sees and in fact suffers this internal journey of assimilation for the possibility of an individual union with the divine, for ET the journey is important for finding a psychic affinity with his multiracial nation.

If one finds in himself a microcosm of the transcendental, the other finds in himself a microcosm of his country. And herein lies an important point of difference.

---

[29]   Ibid, p. 197.
[30]   Goodwin, *Understanding African Poets*, p. 37.
[31]   ET, *Personality, Intention and Idiom*, p. 196.

Poets of the Creeks

Besides J.P. Clark, the other poet of the creeks is Gabriel Okara. Born in the riverine delta of the Niger River, they belong to the tribe of the maritime Ijaw people who made their living from fishing and floodland agriculture. As such it is not surprising that rivers and images of water hold sway over much of their poetic imagination and traditional religion centres around the water spirits of Niger. The creeks not only give them livelihood but the rivers Nun and Niger also take them to the wider, outer world, exposing them to Western influence, making them the first mediators of slave trade. So it is the delta that lends them their identity and with the rivers they share a relationship taut with both love and unease.

Okara is a poet who stands a little apart from the other Anglophone poets of his generation. Almost a decade older than most of them, he is also not a graduate of the University of Ibadan. The war interrupted his studies and much of his eventual erudition was self-taught. He was also a fine artist and learnt watercolour under the tutelage of one of Nigeria's most renowned painter and sculptor, Ben Enwonwu.[32] If a riverine lifestyle inspired him to write, then perhaps it was his training in art that gave him a keen eye for detail in the landscape, the special ability to create an atmosphere. With ET he shares a rather unique quality—the ability to notice a pattern in fragmented movements. If ET in the hand movements of his father when he combed his hair or washed his hands had glimpsed a bit of the man, then Okara, who qualified as a professional book-binder, saw in book-binding the sleight of hand that created a piece of art, 'Book-binding has something to do with creativity—the artistic use of the hands to produce a work of art—that's what book-binding is.'[33]

---

[32] Gabriel Okara, *The Fisherman's Invocation* (London: Heinemann, 1978), p. xi.
[33] Ibid.

ET admits that he learnt 'a bit of language' from Okara, whom he had occasion to meet more than once and came to like.[34] Yet unlike the other Nigerian, Clark, who alert to the need to establish a reputation had co-founded the *Horn* while an undergraduate and become a co-editor of *Black Orpheus* while still in his twenties, Okara was more of a natural. Careless of self-esteem, his first novel, *The Voice*, was published when he was forty-four; content for many years to live a life committed to art, he lost much of his unpublished manuscripts in the Nigerian Civil War, a fact that he lived to regret. But it is of him that ET says, 'To exploit words the way Okara does requires an intimate knowledge of their interior landscape, their poise, and the syntax to coax the maximum out of them.'[35] This understanding of the interiority of words perhaps comes from the fact that Okara is more of a natural, not in the sense of an artless naïveté, but in the sense of being more intuitive, with an intense engagement with his subject. This intensity, the fierce need to communicate his poetic thought makes sure his sophistication does not get in the way of his creativity. Consequently, the many influences, both traditional African and foreign, blend rather than obtrude and as ET concludes, 'There is nothing mechanical in what he aims to do.'[36]

ET speaks with sympathy about Okara's (and the other African poets') struggle to adapt his English to his African-ness, his search for equivalents for proverbs, metaphors and images that would be African in their essence and convey the African experience. From a country himself which had newly started a tradition of English writing, ET knew well the pain and rigour of the process of attempting to replace English or French terms of reference which enjoyed wider acceptance and understanding in common parlance. In this context, he writes of Okara's first novel, *The Voice*, the poet's one sustained experiment in moving the sensibility of one culture into another

---

[34] Interview 19 December 2017.
[35] ET, *Personality, Intention and Idiom*, p. 135.
[36] Ibid, p. 127.

language, while maintaining a 'mobile sensitiveness.'[37] Thus, in a novel which is essentially about a clash of value systems between the young and unbending Okolo and the selfish and less-emotional village elders, Okara uses certain words with great intent. There is the expression, *inside* for instance used to mean the inner hall of a man's integrity wherein he judges and is judged or *chest* which seems to correspond to the outward, visible sign of a man's spirituality. ET speaks of the concept of *shadow* which if not strong seems to indicate an individual's lack of moral integrity.[38] As ET openly acknowledges, all such experimentations might or might not work but point to a valiant effort to create a whole new world of literary imagination, rooted elsewhere than in standard usage. In the case of *The Voice* the expressions work towards building Okolo's world—the ethical impasse between his search for a bigger morality and the elders with their pompous protestations based on vested interest.

ET is quite scathing though in his criticism of similar attempts by Okara in some of his poems. He writes of *The Fisherman's Invocation*, a poem about the organic relationship between the past and the present in which Okara's use of 'back' and 'front' to denote the past and present respectively, was rather unfortunate he says.[39] The two words, smothered by familiar usage, are extremely difficult to coax into a new liveliness and fail to acquire the stature of 'powerful masks.' The past and how to achieve a meaningful relationship with it is a theme that recurs in African poetry, or as ET puts it, is the black poet's 'favourite burden'. And not surprisingly for one who grew up in the Niger delta, for Okara the river is the curve inscribed by history that delineates the relationship between the past and the present, it is also the point of decision, the river that must be crossed before an individual destiny may find fulfilment.

---

[37] Ibid.
[38] Interview 19 December 2017; Fraser, *West African Poetry*, p. 190.
[39] ET, *Personality, Intention and Idiom*, pp. 129–30.

ET analyses yet another river poem by Okara, *The Call of the River Nun* but this time is more complimentary. According to him Okara 'develops' his idiom over time and this is primarily because of his 'abiding interest in words.' Thus, the first lines of the poem,

> I hear your call!
> I hear it far away;
> I hear it break the circle
> of these crouching hills.

According to ET the use of the word 'crouching' is shrewd—it is both descriptive and dynamic, adjective and verb and though oft-used it strikes up a 'hurried and complex energy to counterpoint the hurried repetition of the earlier lines.' Similarly is the word 'circle' emphasizing the poet's isolation and at the same time referring to the hills surrounding Enugu—a single word rich in latent and manifest content.[40]

Okara's skill in using words that connect the inner life with the outer life in the smooth flow of a river wave, comes to fruition in his *One Night at Victoria Beach.* It is a poem about his search for the certitude of faith about which ET comments with the empathy of perhaps a shared experience, 'The failure to retain faith, most elusive when it appears to be within grasp, attest, paradoxically, to his [Okara's] integrity.'[41] The poem opens with,

> The wind comes rushing from the sea
> the waves curling like mambas strike
> the sands and recoiling hiss in rage
> washing the Aladuras' feet pressing hard
> on the sand and with eyes fixed hard
> on what only hearts can see . . .

---

[40]   Ibid, p. 135.
[41]   Ibid, p. 136.

ET writes about the image of the waves—the striking mambas that the readers apprehend sensuously, hear and see them curl and hiss as the line almost traces the curve of the poet's thought and the water's instinct with movement which contrasts dramatically with the 'hard' single-minded concentration of the Aladuras. These Christians, a prophet-led religious sect, impress Okara though in admiring their firmness of religiosity, their ability to penetrate the veil with the sheer power of their prayers, the poet knows he is going against the 'fishermen in dark huts', the 'cowries' and 'Babalawo' (fortune teller) of the indigenous faith. Yet in testament to his honesty, Okara continues to speak of them still praying and it is to his credit that his poetic diction holds up to convey not only his own awakening spiritual consciousness but the Aladuras' absolute contact with the divine. It is the integrity of a sect and the integrity of the poet which find expression in the hard, unflinching firmness of language.

ET similarly analyses the more academically ambitious Clark— his intense response to nature in poems like *Ibadan* or *Night Rain*. In the latter, for instance, he praises Clark's ability to convey the opening up of the mind with increasing rain, the increasing awareness of time and space as the rain drops fall into the 'wooden bowl' like mangoes or oranges. The images of the fruits might be outlandish but they are a part of Clark's reality and as ET points out, the constant presence of the rain in his past and in his present combined with the immediate sharpness of the raindrops represent the poet's attempt at unifying his experience.[42]

So what ET found amidst these poets who grew up in the meandering creeks of the Niger Delta, is a reconfirmation of the need to maintain the magical power of words, the need to neatly sum up the nuances of a situation while remaining firmly entrenched in the reality of immediate experiences. To do this the poets often use words and images from a lexicon different from the Anglophone or the Francophone one so that they can create an alternative reality

---

[42]   Ibid, pp.156–7.

for their readers. But what is more interesting is that, whether it is the duality of Okigbo's poems or the exploration of the stereotypical deltaic situations in the creek poets, the purpose is even larger than creating a foundry of new words. It is to build an African Personality that is charismatic enough to neutralize tribal differences, that sometimes may provide an idealized vision of Africa or be reduced to an oversimplified polarization between the black and the white, but at all times attempts to unify Africa.

ET makes a mention of the African Personality more than once in his thesis, but not so much in the context of the politically and culturally aspirational African Personality Movement that preceded *Négritude* by a couple of generations as an affirmation of African uniqueness in the face of European prejudice. Instead he speaks of the African Personality as a neutral space created by drawing together images and metaphors that work across tribes. Ironically enough, he finds Christianity as a result of colonial acculturation, to be one such recurrent image even though at times the response to it might be hostile. Along with this irreversibility of personal Christian faith, there is the sense of history and homecoming and a certain yearning for unity. Later, in his own way he would adapt the African Personality when back in Singapore, he would write poems on community spaces like the National Library or Botanical Gardens or explore local stereotypes like *Manikam* or *Ibrahim bin Ahmad*—all in an attempt to break through clan loyalties of his own country.

Ibrahim bin Ahmad

We sit in quiet communion.

Like you, we have our sinners
Who are godly.
We fed on courtesy these many years
And had proverbial friendliness.

That Hang Jebat
broke the selfishness of victory
To put such pride in giving
Was counted among us
These three hundred years or so.

We stood for much.

Things . . .
Things have changed.

Like yours, my Elders
Find uneasy times. A sharp concern
Distorts plain living—
They borrowed a great leap forward
You know from where . . .
And now elevate an Asli.
Though well meant
It makes a crescent of the moon.

Perhaps it puts us in arrears,
Or I say too much,
Even to myself . . .

Dance of the Forests

When he stepped on Yoruba land, the first thing ET noticed was the
streets free of stray dogs.[43] They had been sacrificed to the Yoruba
god of iron, war and craftsmanship—Ogun. And yet perhaps then,
when he noticed the streets free of stray dogs, ET would not have
guessed that in Ogun lay the key to understanding much of the
enigma that Soyinka was.

---

[43]   Interview 19 December 2017.

By the time ET met the first future Nobel Laureate of Africa, Wole Soyinka, the latter was thirty-three years old, just slightly younger to ET himself. He was already known as the leading dramatist of Africa and perhaps one of the most talented at work in any part of the English-speaking world, had published several works of import, formed two theatre companies, was a tireless controversialist, had landed himself in prison once and would do so again very soon.[44] With ET he was remarkably affable, dropping him back personally to the airport and ET remembers with regret that he was starting to explain the symbolism of *A Dance of the Forests* when some nuns interrupted and the conversation became polite but non-revelatory.

Soyinka is unmistakeably an author of symbolism. Born in the Yoruba city of Abeokuta in West Nigeria, he was powerfully influenced by the physical and spiritual presence of this city which sits astride the river Ogun. The large elephant-grey boulders of the riverbed and hills loomed over his childhood and a swift, rocky river bridged by the reckless road of man's modernity formed one of the unmistakeable master-images of his writing. The city's guardian deity, Ogun's shrine sat dramatically on Olumo Rock, crowning one of the surrounding hills and was the site of numerous sacrifices. It was here that Soyinka grew up in a sprawling parsonage compound where fervent faith in the revelations of the Bible was as common as the passions and traditions of the Yoruba people, where he roamed freely in the realms of the dead and the living and where it was easy to careen towards the edge of the world and get a glimpse of the supernatural.

Perhaps it is because of the presence of this mystical third dimension in his childhood that Soyinka would find it difficult in the future to describe events without relating them to some abstract idea, some concept that required him to go beyond mere narration. This gave his writing a density of texture and a strong presence of

---

[44] Gerald Moores, *Modern African Writers: Wole Soyinka* (UK: Holmes & Meier, 1971), pp. 3–4.

abstract symbolism. It was a skill that he had honed at Leeds where
he was particularly active in university theatre. There the figure of
George Wilson Knight, one of Britain's most imaginative theatre
critics, looms large. Knight's insistence on always penetrating to
the structure of symbolism underlying dramatic ritual, whether
in Shakespeare or Ibsen, was undoubtedly one of the strongest
influences bearing upon Soyinka.[45]

It was this sensitivity to symbolism that Soyinka used to bridge
the two central parts of his life—his social activism and his aesthetic
posture. And he did so by transposing symbolism into an abiding
concern for mythmaking. For him myth was what made the African
past relevant to its present, it demonstrated how so often social
behaviour was but an unwilling obedience to the subliminal impulse
of ancestral memory.[46] And he used his chosen medium of drama to
communicate the hardly tangible anatomy of ancestral memory and
because of this hardly 'tangible' presence his language is summative,
syntax complex, for with his words he aims to travel beyond the
'sterile limits of particularization.'[47] The way he envisaged his role as
an author in the newly-awakened African society was one who would
expose the senses of his countrymen to the language of myth—myth
not in terms of their 'particular concretions' but in terms of those
experiences of truth which triggered off memory, symbolically and
not rationally, and were shared as a community experience.

It is apparent that in his thesis, it is Soyinka's attitude towards
the writer's role that intrigued ET right from the outset. He writes
about Soyinka, who like Okigbo, rejected the notion of conflict as
a false simplification and for whom insistence on cultural purity,
the idealization of the past and the present was a perpetuation of
dishonesty.[48] Simplistically put, the author's role was to meet rather

---

[45] Ibid, p. 6.
[46] *Critical Perspectives on Wole Soyinka*; ed. James Gibb (Washington DC: Three
      Continents Press, 1980), pp. 200–01.
[47] Ibid, pp. 207–11.
[48] ET, *Personality, Intention and Idiom*, p. 170.

than evade the experiences of life (and hence Soyinka's rejection of *Négritude*). Politics and culture would continue to distract in different but powerful ways, but the writer as a leader of the society was to be able to grasp the 'fundamental truths of his community', truths which would give him a prophetic insight and eventually it was the writer's imagination (rather than the politician's analysis) which would renew society. Incidentally, this idea comes out most strongly perhaps in Soyinka's second novel of 1973, *Season of Anomy* where the supreme moment of a revolution is defined as the moment when a man of ideas ceases to be a mere thinker and becomes actively involved in the process of liberation.

ET, on his part, analyses Soyinka's play, *A Dance of the Forests,* presented as a part of Nigeria's celebration of independence in 1960. It is significant that ET cuts through the structure of this rather complex play to focus on Demoke, the Carver of the tribe, through whom he feels the reader is granted Soyinka's view of the artist in society. Of this ET points out two variations: that the artist must rummage under the surface and not accept appearance as reality and that an artist is never alone but always in the company of his tribe.[49] Thus the representative totem of the tribe when it is eventually made is the conception of Demoke as the tribe's Carver and yet in it resides the 'work of ten generations'. For, as ET comments, the politician is interested in events, but the artist is interested in continuity.

What drew ET so strongly to the play was obviously its message that it is the artist who is the mythmaker for the society. Unlike the three others, Rola the prostitute, Adnebi the court historian or Agboreko the soothsayer, it is Demoke the carver who was a poet in the previous empire of Mata Khribu, who is able to redeem the bloody cycle of history that the play represents by returning the Dead Woman's long unborn child to its mother. The parallel is simple enough, as the town dwellers of the play prepare for a feast, 'The Gathering of the Tribes', very similar to a celebration for the

---

[49]   Ibid, p. 172.

newly independent Nigeria, the town-dwellers want to hear only of their good deeds and past glory. But instead, arrive the Dead Man and the Dead Woman, horrifying pictures of the true past who come to remind the living of the violence inherent in human nature. Amidst the depressing picture of hypocrisy and betrayal that unfolds, it is Demoke who in a simple act of instinctive human warmth, by returning the baby to its mother, completes the cosmic cycle between the living, the dead and the yet-to-be-born, a cycle that lay broken so far. It is worth noting that the new child or the nation is born of the warrior, the one man of integrity from the past. Yet without the artist's protection the child had remained in the danger of being destroyed.

So Demoke is the cosmic unifier and it is so because he enjoys the protection of Ogun, a god from the Yoruba pantheon that Soyinka grew up with. It is significant that it was Ogun who first plunged into the abyss of transition, hacked through primordial chaos and forged a bridge over the abyss, a bridge that connected the humans with their gods, the dead with the unborn. As Soyinka put it, 'To fashion a bridge across it was not only Ogun's task but his very nature, and he had first to experience, to surrender his individuation once again to the fragmenting process, to be absorbed within . . . the deep black whirlpool of mythopoetic forces, . . . understand its nature and yet by the combative value of the will . . . forge a bridge for his companions to follow.'[50]

ET while speaking of *A Dance of the Forests,* says rather abruptly, 'The moment I read Carver, I knew it was the Carver of the nation.'[51] But then he falls silent for a while, immersed in thought. Even his analysis of Soyinka lacks the fresh, often audacious energy that he devotes to the other poets of his thesis. It is even sketchy at places. It is almost as if for ET, Soyinka, like a spiritual faith, threw up

---

[50]   Wole Soyinka, *The Fourth Stage: The Morality of Art,* p.129, quoted by ET in *Personality, Intention and Idiom,* pp. 194–5.

[51]   Interview 19 December 2017.

reflections of him that were too deep to write about, they could only be pondered on. What ET essentially took away from Soyinka was the idea of an author as a myth-maker. Part of it was the language of myths—the way Soyinka with Ogun as his titular deity, uses masonic diction, a language of disjuncture, stress and demonic energy to smelt old Yoruba myths into contemporary drama. But a larger part of it was the role of the myth-maker, the unifier of the cosmological order, Ogun's disciple with his impulse for tragic dare who must undergo the experience of transition himself, only to re-assemble, emerge stronger, wiser and forge a path ahead of his companions. And he does so merely out of an instinct of human warmth!

Gods Can Die

ET's second collection of poems, *Gods Can Die*, was published in 1977 and it is rather remarkable how closely it reflects the contemporary psyche of Singapore. It is almost as if poet and nation are so deeply intertwined that they involuntarily reflect each other, one coming unfurled if the other is fingered ever so slightly, like the skeins of a delicate weave. The 1970s decade was a time when Singapore had left the question of its survival undeniably behind. Separation from Malaysia was a thing of the past and Singapore had already made the herculean leap to join the select club of first-world nations, found its political and economic groove. The *laissez-faire* economy throbbed with the promise of success, an integrated chemical hub and oil refineries dotted the Jurong Island and a slew of Multinational Corporations flourished in the various industrial estates. The ship-repair industry of Keppel and Sembawang had seen unprecedented success and the forays into banking meant Singapore was poised to become the financial capital of the region. It was a time of fearless forging forward, the only pitfall seemed to be of excessive presumption.

Yet, underneath was a whole new story—the other face of the moon. It was of a nation forced to face its destiny: the separation from its hinterland which baldly displayed its vulnerability, the racial riots which forced it to see itself as a gestalt of differing cultures which would perhaps otherwise not have been immediate neighbours. Colonialism, that had yoked it all together was gone and a new culture struggled to be allowed its rightful place. ET in this context speaks of civilizations which on one hand impose and on the other resist.[52] It is in the very nature of civilizations or cultures to control, to dominate, may be even to intimidate and at the same time to resist what is unauthorized, unofficial, unsanctified. In Singapore's case the tensions released by the new post-independent culture was made all the more complex by three factors—the speed at which change had happened, the fear of survival which underscored the change process and the inexorable force of globalization which unleashed fierce competition and a vital need to maintain separate identities. Thus it was a success story which had an undeniable underbelly of pain—the subcultures, subidentities, the hidden ecosystems of comfort and renewal which had been compressed by this bonding trauma as the nation developed its sinews and muscles.

It is exactly this duality that *Gods Can Die* portrays. The splitting of the personal psyche at multiple levels—the public self that lauds progess, the personal self that fears failure, laments the loss of community traditions, is apprehensive about a future which will perhaps change before change has arrived. Thus the poems of the collection are fairly multi-layered, rife with incessant speculation and debate, a relentless catechismic self-questioning. In terms of complexity, if one was to draw a graph from the confounding darkness of ET's fellow-poet Goh Poh Seng when he says:

I am the bird with one wing,
never knowing when to return
from the night shaped with malevolence,
catching the paranoia of the times,

---

52 *Peninsular Muse*, ed. Mohammad A. Quayum (Bern, Oxford: Peter Lang, 2007), pp. 50–1.

to the comparative self-knowing lucidity of Lee Tzu Pheng when she
says:

> We have borne each other's cries
> long enough to have hope
> neither race nor creed could sever
> the bond between us, sisters,

ET's poems are definitely closer to the first than the second.[53] And
it is the complexity and relentless self-questioning which lift the
poems of *Gods Can Die* from being paeans to Singapore. Because
of the intense presence of the self, they give the impression of being
born of real experiences—that sudden moment of precise awareness
that gives one a sharp objectivity about one's surroundings. ET calls
it a part of growing up, 'At some point something happens to you;
it's part of your growing up. As when in your dreams you feel you
are falling.'[54]

As such, the poems of *Gods Can Die* are deceptive. Compared to
the tremulous innocence, the closer directness of *Rib of Earth*, one
notices the strident note of poems like *9th of August* ('A proclamation,
gently colonial: *Singapore shall forever be*') but the confidence is
merely skin deep. There was a solidarity, a sense of belonging in the
youthful nihilism of *Rib of Earth,* now the adult world appears far
more treacherous.[55] The apparent calm of the volume, *Gods Can Die,*
dedicated to a wife of a good ten years or more, written by a father of
two, a poet who has a dream day-job at the university of his choice,
lasts only till the questions bubble to the surface. The simplicity of
the answer he had worked towards in *Rib of Earth* and found in *The
Cough of Albuquerque,* that his destiny lay in his nation, does not

---

53   Goh Poh Seng, *Bird with One Wing,* Lee Tzu Pheng, *New Country.*
54   *Interlogue,* Vol. 7, ed. Peter Nazareth (Singapore: Ethos Books, 2008), p. 200.
55   Ee Tiang Hong, *Responsibility & Commitment: The Poetry of Edwin Thumboo*
     (Singapore: SUP, 1997), p. 31: reference to his youthful nihilism.

appear so straightforward here. He struggles to find the same inner unity. As Virginia Woolf has suggested, like a good biographer he holds up mirrors at odd angles to view himself, to check his own response to different situations. Till at the end he arrives at a solution: yes, his future still lies with his nation but with a nation qualified by a certain set of personal ethics. It's the ethics that can give his public and personal selves a certain calming unity:

> But I am glad that others are powerful with compassion,
>   Who see before we do what troubles us
> And help in kindness, take ignorance in tow,
>   If not for such we lose our gods
>   Who lived but now are dying in our friends.

ET published *Gods Can Die* more than two decades after *Rib of Earth*. The volume is preceded by nearly seven years when he did not write any poems at all in the decade away from the university. When asked about this period of silence, he says he cannot pin down any reason.[56] But he speaks at length about what he did during those intervening years, when he civil serviced and the decade after when he joined the university where too, contrary to expectations, he was burdened by administrative work: 'Given the responsibilities I had, especially the administrative ones, my daily language was for explanation, problem-solving, in a mode that discouraged ambiguity . . . You might say the proportion between time spent on using language creatively and time spent on using language administratively rapidly grew in favour of the latter.'[57] Thus, for him, true to his poetic self, it was 'words' which he felt formed the first dividing wall, the line that delineated his personal from the public self. And maybe it is not surprising that *Words* form the first poem of the volume, words that can become 'part-anger, part-laughter, bruised', words that indicated the first

---

[56]   Interview 12 January 2018.
[57]   *Peninsular Muse*, p. 65.

split in his personality. It is significant that ET chose for the front cover of the volume a painting by Nanyang artist, Khoo Sui-Ho, a painting called *The Parade* which depicts a series of Picasso-style heads rendered in a surrealist style. He found it in the collection of Australian artist, John Watson, and perhaps chose it because it resonated well with the theme of his book—pure surreal automatism or the real functioning of the mind.

The volume includes the much anthologized twin poems on severing ties with Malaysia, a subject that has not been written about much in Singapore's aesthetic literature, *9th of August I & II*. What is surprising is that the second poem starts with a replica of the first stanza of the first poem and yet records a very different response. Instead of the resigned sense of pathos of the first, in the second he moves to a firmer need to vindicate the Singaporean cause:

> For us what then?
> Make strangers out of friends
> To face each other till the bitter end.

When asked about it, ET says he could not have settled for one response, for both to him were equally valid.[58] And this is the point where the inner dislocation happens, where he finds it difficult to arrive at a singular stance on a multi-headed situation created by many years of lived history and cultural complexities. It involves not only the controversy about whether for Singapore it was an eviction or voluntary exile, but also the loss of a crucial hinterland—a word that ET defines to be a 'portmanteau' term implying not only a geographical and political loss of a hinterland but also the loss of a common space where myths and legends have grown and where people have lived through a rich body of experiences.[59]

---

[58]   Peter Nazareth, *Interlogue*, p. 204.
[59]   Ibid, pp. 164–5.

Similarly is the bifurcation of the mind in *Walking My Baby Back Home*—the title is the opening line of a song by American jazz artist, Nat King Cole, and yet the poem is essentially an Asian love poem written in the imagist style of Ezra Pound and Arthur Waley. The simultaneous cultural existences that a Singaporean must live through is in the opening lines of *The Immigrant* as well:

> Days and Indian days stretch
> Beyond the grasping of his hands,

as is the tussle between the modern and the traditional in *Colour*,

> In the room they speak of social harm,
> Talk deep into the night,
> Beneath the surface of a modern calm,
> Prejudice sits tight.

The complexity of response that a particular situation can warrant is evident in poems like *Manikam*, a character sketch of a Jaffna Tamil who is brave enough to escape the confines of his small close-knit community to set sail on the high seas and yet returns to Singapore to claim his wedding dowry. The poet's voice is strong here, bristling with agitation at not only this circular exploitation of culture but also by the fact that his own young son, Julian finds him 'friendly', this in ignorance of Manikam's sexual dalliances while at sea, about which Julian's father can make a well-informed conjecture.

Yet interestingly, underneath this mind-splitting mélange of perspectives and cultures, the self-questioning has already started which will gradually move the volume towards the resolution it seeks in the ethical question. One of the first questions that ET finds himself come up against is the question of conformity in the poem of the same name. As he looks at Uncle Tan of the English-speaking Peranakan community which prides itself in conforming to British ways, sees through its ambitions, its calculating smiles and conniving quietness, he asks himself if he himself, as he progresses through life and achieves much of what he set out for, will soon be a part of the group of conformists. The days of the *Fajar* generation, of rebellion and grand nationalist ideals are long over, leaving in its wake some very mundane aspirations and family requirements. So does a quick fulfilment of needs mean joining the ranks of these traditional tea drinkers?

> Am I stolen,
> Indexed,
> Into this large conformity?[60]

This kind of a questioning occurs again and again. In *Commercial Politics* for example, where he equates the new-generation politician who kisses the 'electoral arse' to Judas of the Pharisaical mind who kissed to 'keep the status-quo.' Perhaps the catechism comes to a climax with *The Interview*, one of ET's strongest comments on contemporary Singapore—the trial of the radical Tan Jing Quee, the gradual wearing down of his resistance and final humiliating confession that was broadcast on national television.

But apparently the solution lies hidden in the climax. *The Interview* ends with thoughts on compassion,

> Let us see that kindness
> Has been tried and fell exhausted.
> Leaving such interviews as the only end.

And it is the same thought that is picked up by the titular piece, *Gods Can Die*, and effectively rounds off the volume. When asked about the last poem, ET speaks about fellow poet and novelist, Goh Poh Seng on whom it is loosely based.[61] It was the contact with Poh Seng

---

[60] ET, *Conformity*.
[61] Interview 12 January 2018.

that created the space for ET to start writing poetry again. After the
intense bonds of friendship from his university days had slackened,
his poetic consciousness had lain fallow for long years, missing the
presence of companions. Yet, soon ET noticed in his friend a change,
a change that was wrought by the proximity of power,

> The casual word, the easiness, the quick straight answer,
> The humane delay, the lack of cautiousness
> That gave ample laughter to our evenings
> Are too simple for these days of power

In response, ET found himself turning with renewed disappointment
towards those who seek power, but not a power qualified by
compassion. It is a certain ethicality that derives from spiritual
instruction so that it is more viable, with a capacity to expand and
renew rather than the rigidity of a strict moral code bereft of backup
religion.[62] So is the 'Gods' in the title a reference to his Christian
God of grace and mercy? The answer is a vehement no from ET.[63]
In 1977 when the collection was published, his full conversion to
Christianity was still twenty years away. As such 'Gods' is a reference
to the idea of goodness originating and renewing itself within man,
a seed of divinity in man that is urged by many religions. It is born
of his own eclectic exposure to religion, a syncretic amalgam of the
notion of godhead in Hinduism or the deistic belief of the Sufi
saints. Hence the use of plurality in the word. Yet, on the other
hand, he does not equate for a moment the death of gods to the
loss innocence. As he clarifies, in saying loss of innocence there is a
presumption that innocence is sacred, 'But I don't say that. I merely
say it is a part of growing up. Gods *CAN* die, and if they do, they do
so in us and because of us.'[64] Thus, it means the death of humanistic

---

[62]   Peter Nazareth, *Interlogue*, p. 219.
[63]   Interview 12 January 2018.
[64]   *Understanding African Poets: A Study of Ten Poets*, p. 43.

impulses, the goodness and divinity in man that can wither away under the pressures of a fast-changing, competitive world at the mercy of economic and political forces. But it can also be preserved if tempered by compassion.

As usual, in ET's world there is no turning away, no shutting off. Everything can be dealt with.

The Carver and His Nation

In one of ET's personal books on Christopher Okigbo there is a heavily underscored passage which obviously the poet had read with a great deal of attention.[65] It speaks of Okigbo's failure in managing to make the national and personal inferences cohere in the separate sequences of his masterpiece, *Labyrinths*. Apparently, Okigbo fails to resolve the problem of dealing both with the national and personal, the personal alone has the final vision. This issue is of the utmost importance to ET. Singapore never fails to be in his line of vision, even at the cost of tying him down to a narrow bandwidth of poetic expression. Seldom does he travel below to write 'me' poems, seldom does he move beyond to explore the metaphysical. And surprisingly enough, this is spontaneous, not born out of a compulsive need to be politically correct. As he explains, the nation and the self are always a part of the consciousness but the self is present as indirectly as possible, 'My ego is big, mind you. But I manage it well.' Or otherwise that, 'Quietly you are still looking for yourself but I try to be led by issues and formations rather than ego.'[66]

His African experience from this period is an important interlude when his consciousness of such issues was further heightened. As he repeatedly emphasizes, the poets that he encountered in Nigeria or Ghana gave him a 'tremendous' amount of confidence, though

---

[65]   Interview 12 January 2018.
[66]   Ibid.

none of them really influenced his style.[67] It was a time when large chunks of the African continent were caught in a similar moment of transition that Singapore too found itself in. Held in the incubator of change, the poets felt the urgent need for a personal quest and yet could not ignore the emotional call of the time to interpret the political meaning of their own country. As Day-Lewis aptly puts it,

> In me two worlds at war
> . . . heir and ancestor.

For ET one of the major take-away from his African experience was the compulsion to look at the past and to notice how the past makes space for itself in the present. In this context he speaks of Soyinka's poem *Abiku*, comparing it to Ben Jonson's *On My First Son*. Both are poems on the death of a child but, as ET points out, the grief in Ben Jonson is unbearable because it is so final.[68] While when Soyinka speaks of the child's spirit, the *abiku* returning to the world again and again, only to die and grieve his mother, it sort of 'takes away the sting'. This kind of an insight not only helped ET understand cultural differences better but also taught him that some awkward elements from the past remain, make space for themselves amidst all the modernity and continue to haunt the present. In his thesis ET points out how terrifying appears the *abiku* as Soyinka taunts the mother about the ineffectiveness of the ritual precautions: the placing of the bangles, the offering of goats and cowries, the deep burial of the body all prove futile.[69] Such reading of African literature would perhaps give ET's vision of his own country people's past an added empathy. It would compel him to take a closer look at characters like Manikam of the Jaffna-Tamil community or Uncle Tan of the

---

[67] Ibid.

[68] Interview 19 December 2017.

[69] *Understanding African Poets: A Study of Ten Poets*, p. 116; ET, *Personality, Intention and Idiom*, pp. 178–80.

Peranakan community who cannot escape the burden of community heritage—both positive and negative.

Africa would also beckon to ET with the possibility of creating a new psychic hinterland for Singapore, after the loss of Malaysia. He would find a great deal of commonality with Commonwealth cultures and later would take a closer look at the literatures of the Southeast Asian region as well as of Australia, India having been on his radar for many years anyway. Africa is a continent where he found languages spoken with a gay abandon—be it the colonial residue of French, English or Portuguese, or the national languages of the multi-national states—Wolof, Hausa, Yoruba, Ibo, Arabic and the many more, or the new African languages created by proximity to colonial masters—Krio in Sierra Leone or Pidgin in Nigeria and Swahili. It was not difficult to see language as a means of not only communicating but as a carrier of culture. Consequently, in the English department of NUS he started working towards an expansion of English studies beyond its canonical boundaries, involving a look at Asian Literatures in translation and Commonwealth Literature. Speaking of the time he says, 'After D.J. Enright left in the 1969–70 session, I was given charge of the department before Maurice Baker returned. Ban Kah Choon and I taught a Commonwealth Literature course with poetry and prose selected from Africa and Australia.'[70] The carefully selected course became a part of the syllabus in subsequent years but to his regret, after his retirement as Dean of the Faculty, the module on Commonwealth Literature was taken off the Arts and Social Sciences Syllabus from the 1992–93 session onward.

If there is an issue of tying himself down to the subject of Singapore, there is also a question of the degree of complexity ET allowed to percolate into his style, given that the English Literature of Singapore was then at a nascent stage. As his poetic idol Yeats has said, a country's literature normally grows through the stages of first, the narrative poetry, a period of epics and ballads when the nation and the

---

[70] *Peninsular Muse*, p. 58.

great national events form the subject matter; next comes the dramatic
period when characters and stereotypes who lived and wrought in the
times are written about and then comes the final, lyrical stage which
is the most complex with every kind of subtlety and obscurity of
mood and passion.[71] ET, when asked whether it was difficult to bend
his mind towards a certain simplicity demanded by his Singapore
audience, particularly keeping in mind the three stages and the huge
repertoire of literature he had personally thumbed through, denies it.
'I wrote the best poem I was capable of,' he says in a rather matter-of-
fact tone.[72] Though in an introduction to an edited volume of 1970
he does admit, 'We should restrain our sophistication . . . There is
need to demonstrate to the ordinary intelligence the relevance of what
is written.'[73] Perhaps in early years what was a conscious decision, later
became a matter of habit. Or perhaps it was a combination of both for
Gods Can Die does contain fairly simple poems like *9th of August*, as it
does a *Numinous* or a *Moses*.

Moses

Moses oh Moses
Smelt resurrection in the air.
Sinai had come alive—
Hot pursuit attending clash of arms,
Strong feelings in the fist of brothers
Frightened passaging of women,
Children of the tribes alarumed, misdirected
Here, there taken *en passant*
The burning bush.

---

71 *Uncollected Prose by W.B. Yeats: First Reviews and Articles*, Vol. 1, ed. John P.
Frayne (London: Macmillan, 1970), pp. 269–72.

72 Interview 12 January 2018.

73 Quoted in *Essays on Edwin Thumboo*, ed. Jonathan Webster (Singapore: Ethos
Books, 2009), p. 75. Originally from Introduction, *The Flowering Tree: Selected
Writings from Singapore/Malaysia*, ed. ET (Singapore: Educational Publications
Bureau, 1970).

Moses smiled; all seemed familiar.

Moses thought of the promised land,
Saw the Jordan and wept his thanks;
Touches her water, salty and dark.
Thus cleansed he sought his brethren.

On either bank they stood
Clad in green and sharpened steel;
Behind them, cunningly concealed
Their chariots growled, spewed destruction,
Fell upon each other, tore into the
Desert and the entrails of the hills.

Ram'ses and Joshua still alive?

Moses turned, sighed, fell
Into unquiet sleep.

He speaks in a similar vein of the censorship laws of Singapore, saying that he was not aware of for instance the particular Newspaper and Printing Presses Act of 1974 and if he did, he was also aware of the need of some control, some censorship particularly keeping in mind the racial riots of the past.[74] It was a society where racial nerves needed to be soothed or the incipient trade union movement needed to be controlled: '. . . a certain degree of self-censorship exists. Perhaps more than the kind of self-censorship which all individuals feel in all societies. In the case of Singapore, it may have to do with the fact that we are small, compact, well-organised, efficient, and therefore in some sense claustrophobic.'[75] For this reason perhaps he

---

[74] Interview 12 January 2018.
[75] *Peninsular Muse*, p. 62.

says he would not write a *Commercial Politics* now for its improper references to Christian symbols.[76]

Personally for ET, for all apparent purposes the 60s and 70s were a fulfilling period of his life—he married the woman he loved in 1964, by 1965 was the father of his first child, moved away from the civil service job he disliked, joined the university. His father continued to live in Singapore while he and his family moved first to Johor Bahru for his wife taught in Malaysia and then to various well-appointed university quarters. Yet, as the poems of *Gods Can Die* show, his mind never ceased to question. The easy unity of earlier poems eluded him, his mind splitting again and again on questions of ethics and change and perpetuation of the past. If in a poem like *The Way Ahead* he writes of the four perspectives of the Professor, much travelled and artistic, a Senior Civil Servant, who knew the way ahead, the Town Planner and I, the average man on the street, as they wrestle over the question of framing a City, it would have been possible that the four characters merely mouth opinions which are ET's own. Different perspectives which appear right to him at different times. But they were their views as expressed in the TV programme.

It is only in one poem in the collection that he stumbles on an unambiguous symbol of unity. In the poem *Renewal* as he gazes at a feminine form, for inexplicable reasons out of reach, the single rose, a soft anemone complete in her isolation,

> After such renewal
> I hesitate to enfold, to give
> What I receive;
> To touch, to reach
> This star, still not quite knowing,
> This sea's heart, soft anemone,
> Lovely even on her own.

---

[76] Interview 12 January 2018.

There are boundaries, subliminal ones—some drawn by the poet himself, some by his community, society, nation, religion— boundaries that he cannot escape.

IV

CITY ON THE MIND

Did the Seven Sages not lay its foundations? A square mile is
the city. A square mile date-grove . . . half a square mile the
temple of Ishtar . . . three square miles and a half is Uruk's
expanse.

—*The Epic of Gilgamesh*

Ask a question of any intersection and it will answer, not always
straightforwardly, allowing a quirk of the topography, the lie
of the land, a glimpse of a prospect to nudge you one way or
the other.

—Ivan Vladislavić, *Portrait with Keys*

Don't let appearances fool you. There is always one reality.

—Haruki Murakami, *iq84*

City Matrix

A city almost invariably has a certain multiplicity about it. And this is not entirely because of the Eliotesque image of a flowing crowd of dark bobbing heads that its mention evokes. It is in reality like the Mirrors Room in Salzburg where Mozart had performed for the Empress—with mirrors arranged to form corridors reflecting into infinity. A city's mirrors reflect and counter-reflect the same image till it recedes in the distant horizon, a tiny speck, almost invisible, yet not quiet.

The Way Ahead

We were to speak, to chat,
Involve our several minds on how
To frame a City.
We were asked, judiciously, to talk of beauty
In a town, how the town would change,
Turn supple, rugged, yet acceptable.

There were the four of us,
A Professor, much travelled and artistic,
A Senior Civil Servant who knew the way ahead,
The Town Planner and I; I?
The average man, the man-in-the-street,
Feeling nervous, struggling to free
Practicalities from dreams,
Leaving a small remainder hopefully sensible.

The Professor favoured China-town, not surprisingly.
His thinking was crowded, bred by city living.
The teeming interchange of word and gesture,
The odour of ordinary lives,
Intimacies overdone or underdone,

Privacy come to grief, private grief made public,
Were seen as energies of a proper order,
As breaking the loneliness of man.
It had the right perspective, he said,
In the middle of tourist China-town.
The flats were fine, but parcelled out too neatly.

The Town Planner took a different view.
Intricacies of change were based on principles;
A flat in the sun was to be had by everyone,
A spaciousness, part of the better deal,
Politics, economics, the re-deployment of custom,
Clan and tribe. Impulses of a national kind
Gave common rights. There has been talk of heritage.
There should be change, a reaching for the sky,
Brightening the City's eye, clearing the patches
From the shoulders of her hills,
For regiments of flats.

What could I say? Or think?

A city is the people's heart,
Beautiful, ugly, depending on the way it beats.
A City smiles the way its people smile.
When you spit, that is the city too.
A City is for people, for living,
For walking between shadows of tall buildings
That leave some room, for living.
And though we rush to work, appointments,
Too many other ends, there must be time to pause,
Loosen the grip of each working day,
To make amends, to hear the inner self
And keep our spirits solvent.
A City should be the reception we give ourselves,

What we prepare for our posterity.

The City is what we make it,
You and I. We are the City.
For better or for worse.

This possibility of infinitude is embedded in the very construct of
a city—the two intersecting streets which are laid out in the very
beginning. Not only from them sprout innumerable other cross-
streets, which in turn have cross-streets of their own, each successive
intersection represents a mélange of reality, experience, culture,
perceptions. For a city is not merely a physical space, but superimposed
on it is the complexity of human cognitive understanding and even
beyond human cognition there is something that is simultaneously
familiar and elusive—a kind of primeval force that defies mapping.
Thus there is Magdalena Tulli describing the city of Warsaw as the
growing of a tree, which even as it germinates, ripens and then rots,
holds within itself all possibilities at once, 'It is part and whole,
infinitude and a godforsaken backwater, a particle in the world and
at the same time an abyss into which the world vanishes—tiny as a
fly in the ointment.'[1]

For a city is marked by the imaginings of those who pass
through—the citizen, the town-planner, the urban, the well-
travelled, the scholar, the playful. Each interaction between
individual and space brings with it a dialogue between cultures, a
feverish translation between communities that throw up fragmentary
images of representative worlds, a moment of mutual illumination.
And when one brings into the matrix the possibilities of travel
and tourism, diasporas and labour migration, cinema and internet
cultures a single city is overlaid by many cities. The multiplicity of
the resulting texts staggers the mind.

---

[1]   Magdalena Tulli, *Dreams and Stones*, translated by Bill Johnston (UK: Penguin
       Random House, 2004), p. 8.

Yet, whether it is the Paris of Baudelaire or Kafka's Prague or the lost innocence of Dublin described by Joyce, many of these cities exist in the human mind, interpreted and reinterpreted, reflected and counter-reflected till the lived becomes the narrated and the narrated the lived. Thus when Italo Calvino has Marco Polo describe the cities of the world to the ageing Kublai Khan, the Emperor realizes the cities visited by the Venetian are always different from the ones he thinks of.[2] And when Khan finally asks Marco Polo to describe his hometown, a city he has never spoken of before, the latter replies, 'Every time I describe a city, I am saying something about Venice.' Thus, a city emerges shaped by the shifting pulse of individual experience, occupying a cognitive space between language and culture, between the visible and invisible. And just as it is marked by individual consciousness, the ideals the city embodies, the desires it excites in us tell us something about our own identity.[3] Thus, the city and the individual project their images, each on the other, and in so doing tie each other as binary shadows, a relationship as fundamental as of gnostic dualism.

Interestingly, ET's most well-known book of poems, *Ulysses by the Merlion*, published in 1979, has as its unifying theme the multiracial city of Singapore, a multiracialism where races had started speaking to each other only after independence through the English-educated. The volume rather intrepidly stakes its claim on a family tree that includes a Calvino, a Saramago or a Joyce. Indeed, it did result in upscaling both his professional and poetic careers—ET became the Dean of the Faculty of Arts and Sciences in 1980 and was awarded the Cultural Medallion of Singapore the same year. Perhaps this is what he means when he says, 'I wrote myself into the centre.'[4] When probed a little more about it, he speaks of always being a bit

---

[2]   Italo Calvino, *Invisible Cities*.

[3]   *The Cambridge Companion to the City in Literature*, ed. Kevin R. McNamara (NY: Cambridge, 2014), p. 4.

[4]   ET's confession in his first meeting, before the formal interview process started.

of an outsider, a half-caste, ragged in school and university as a *chap cheng*. He also speaks of the Chinese granduncle, later taken by the Kempeitai, who would call him a 'black devil' affectionately, 'There was so much of humour in what he said that I didn't realise the barb. It was only later that I started thinking.'[5] So when *Ulysses by the Merlion* finally happened, it was not only a personal foisting of himself into the centre but included in its broader sweep the multiracialism of Singapore. It was a journey of multiracialism into the centre of things, as a marker of identities, a multiracialism that ET held within himself. It was a journey shared by both the poet and his city.

The matrix as a structure is useful in understanding the poems of the volume. It can be interpreted at its most superficial level to represent two-dimensional array intersections. If in *The Cough of Albuquerque* he first spoke of binary arrangements that filled every moment of his life including those moments of loneliness when he was never really alone because of the images in his mind

Nor image, the strength of loneliness,
Cling together.

in *Ulysses by the Merlion* it is far more complex. Yet the complexity is neatly arranged in a matrix, without the mind-splitting conflict of *Gods Can Die*. If the naturalist, William Hornaday had compared Singapore to a large desk full of drawers and pigeon-holes where everything has its place, the poems of *Ulysses by the Merlion* are similar in finding a place for the multiplicity of Singapore. The poet finds himself at intersections he is familiar with—the rows and columns of language and culture, of passions and estrangements, of the real and the imagined that contribute to make the intersection a lived space. Friends appear frequently, in whom ET sees his own reflection. As he confided in an interview when asked about the theme of friendship, 'Yes, because, if not for friends, who are we? How do we extend

---

5   Interview 12 January 2018.

ourselves? Through our friends, and we extend them through us. Friendship is a sacred thing.'[6] Just as when he had travelled to Alexandria and in the hometown of Cavafy with its many cultures and a diasporic Jewish population found a reflection of Singapore, with friends he finds he shares the same experience. And as he does so, he finds his own identity and that of his city get more and more extended to encompass almost everything: 'It's like me starting off with a simple rope and then start weaving it and the pattern gets more and more complicated, bigger. One becomes others—I can't think of a better metaphor.'[7]

Beyond the intersections, Singapore is also the matrix or mould from which a relief surface is made, like an old-fashioned lead type or die used by a typesetter. So it casts into relief Singapore stereotypes like Mr Ang—married bachelor, gay, affable, who enjoys predictable welcomes because he tips generously.[8] And even beyond the interpretation of matrix as a mould lies the Latin root 'māter' or mother pointing to the meaning of 'womb' or a return to the origin. It is a single-point unity that ET finds amidst all the diversity and change of his city, an end to all the fragmentary images of successive perceptions, the shifting crowd of frenzied isolates. Tulli explains this kind of unity as,

There is hope . . . the uproar from which the ear loses all ability to distinguish sounds will be transformed into the mild silence of waking life, the same silence that endures inside stones. The crushing presence of thoughts that make the head throb with pain will in the end reveal a light, transparent void.[9]

---

[6] *Edwin Thumboo: Time Travelling, A Select Annotated Bibliography*, ed. Gwee Li Sui and Michelle Heng (Singapore: NLB, 2012), p. 77.

[7] Interview 12 January 2018.

[8] *How to Win Friends*.

[9] *Dreams and Stones*, p. 110.

Or in ET's words,
The City is what we make it,
You and I, We are the City.[10]

It is the discovery of an identity unified inextricably with his city, a
relationship as inevitable as that of gnostic dualism where there is no
'oneness' without the duality of the other.

Singapore on my Mind

There is a map inside ET's mind. In fact, not one but many maps—a
veritable cartographer's paradise. There are little pigeon-holes
with scrolls stowed away, catalogued as old and new, political and
topographical, cultural and religious. When he chooses, he picks out
one and though he continues to look at the person in front of him,
he unrolls the map in his head, follows with a fingertip the contour
lines, sharpens his vision of a tract with a cartographer's chisel, bends
over it in closer and closer scrutiny till it captivates him completely. It
is this that gives the spectator the sense of the 'other' when with ET.
The maps can be of many types. For instance, if he complements a
lady as 'elegant', his mind might move immediately to map elegance,
starting with the near-at-hand cheongsam and going up to Cleopatra's
headdress. Or if he dwells for a moment on a Chinese logograph,
his mind might map symbols of Freemasonry, the Jewish faith and
those which appear on the control panel of a cockpit. It is the old
childhood habit of noticing patterns—the series of hand movements
when his father would comb his hair or wash his hands, only made
infinitely more complex by his readings of history and literature and
mythology and anthropology and philosophy. A complexity that is
added to by the various personas that exist within him—the poet,
the scholar, the traveller, the citizen, the civil servant, the rebel, the
nationalist and perhaps even the observer of politics. To this if one

---

[10]   *The Way Ahead.*

adds his Chinese and Indian inheritance and family practices of old and mutated forms of Taoism, Hinduism and Christianity, the vision of a neatly catalogued and pigeonholed library appears too tame, perhaps even a flight of fancy. And all this even before one has taken into account the power of imagination!

Consequently, when ET speaks of Singapore the maps, more topological than topographical, that unfold are many, spread out with impatient rapidity.[11] There is of course the colonial map of the city—the cool colonnade of the Fullerton building, the carpark, the Singapore River with the departmental store Whiteaway Laidlaw for the 'memsahibs' and the Bank of China (the first Chinese bank to have a large building of its own) on its shores with OCBC (Oversea-Chinese Banking Corporation) down the road. Or the other square of civil service offices around the old Parliament in High Street with the PWD (Public Works Department) Headquarters to its right and a smaller building in its annexe which housed the treasury and was guarded by Gurkhas. Or 'old Coleman's house' in North Bridge Road, later torn down by the 'barbarians' and the luxurious spread of the Raffles Hotel. But there are also other kinds of maps that unfurl—the cultural map with white and brown-sahib culture in the Cricket Club, the Tamil/Indian culture of Serangoon Street with buffaloes and open fields where Tekka Market stands today, the Cantonese operas at the Nam Tin Hotel of Chinatown, or the Peranakan and Eurasians of Katong. There can as easily be a food map—the first Polar Café on High Street with its curry puffs ('no change there, can assure you'), the cakes at Adelphi in North Bridge Road, the *kway teow* at the Hock Lam Street food stalls or the shaved-ice stall in a hole opposite Aurora, the only Chinese Western-style departmental store of Singapore at that time. Equally possible is a map of the shops and small-time businesses that dotted the street sides—the Siong Lim saw mill near Syed Alwi Road where the old Victoria School used to be which would soak logs in the tidal

---

[11]   All details on Singapore in this section from interview 12 March 2018.

waves of the Rochor Canal, or B.P. de Silva of High Street which had beautiful Sri Lankan jewellery and Omega watches on display in its shop windows, or the reams of brocade and Chinese antique at Dragon House or the colours of Indian textile at Gian Singh's which was close to the Ensign Book Store.

The matrix that unfolds of the poet and his city is immense, the possibilities of combination infinite. For just as there can be spatial maps, there can also be maps of places traced over time. He speaks of the large tract of wooded country which stretched from Mandai over Yishun and Woodlands where tigers roamed in his grandfather's time, where ET found wild boars and squatters and later highways and skyscrapers as the city silhouette changed. There can also be maps which intersect culture with history—the Chinese schools where culture evolved with the political dynamics of China and the requirements of the diasporic community in Singapore, or the missionary culture that evolved under the highly organized network of Irish Catholic brothers and changed as colonialism came to an end and the schools fitted themselves around the more immediate trading culture of Singapore, though continuing to provide an education still cherished today. If the matrix is not complex enough, interweaving through its endless intersections is ET himself, evolving over time, embracing new interests, changing in perception. He remains as intensely present in front of the *rojak* pushcart selling cuttlefish and grilled Bombay duck by the canal at Balmoral Road with its carbide lamp and charcoal fire as the store windows of Oli Mohamed Jewellery in High Street, the appointed jewellers of the Sultanate. It is a city that has entered his bones—just as those shop windows are real, so is the reflection of himself in the plate glass—a young man with a bristling mind.

But what emerges as discussions on Singapore continue is how the city evolved, pulling out of the crawling multitudinousness and organizing itself into some semblance of order. He speaks of Singapore moving from a town to a city and finally a nation. According to him, though city status was conferred in 1951, the

British were merely being 'naughty' for Singapore remained a town—fragmented, modest in its aspirations, held together by nothing but its identity as an entrepôt. But then the first stirrings of nationalism were heard—with Separation in 1963, the sense of a nation was harnessed back to be restricted to the shores of Singapore. 'The shift to Singaporean nationalism from Malayan nationalism was almost instantaneous,' he says. Then with independence everything started changing, 'The PAP was always in charge' and with the Housing Development Board taking over control of public housing from 1967 onwards, the city skyline changed rapidly. While tracing this evolution, the first mention that ET makes is of the CBD or the Central Business District. According to him, a PAP innovation, the CBD became the heart of the city. What remains implied is that perhaps, more than the heart it was a declaration of serious intent to prosper. And more than a serious intent, perhaps the CBD became a unifying symbol—a cultural harbour where races took cover under words with a broad bandwidth—words like meritocracy, global investment and financial hub and nation building. The CBD was also a concept with a long shelf life, for using it as a scaffold Singapore would slide up on its economic graph, moving from trading towards higher-end financial services and wealth management. For Singapore citizens concepts like the CBD simplified some of the gridlines of the matrix, eased the weight of the many dividing lines. Or as ET puts it, 'Understanding made life endurable.'[12] Hence his emphasis on the verb 'must' in the lines,

Set all neatly down into Economy.
There is little choice—
We must make a people.'[13]

---

[12] *A Lighter Side of History: Writing Singapore—Themes & Perspectives*, talk by ET, 22 July 2017, National Museum, Singapore.

[13] *Catering for the People.*

Intersection I: Time and History

ET speaks of Eliot's *Four Quartets* in the context of time, a book he
read in school and had received as literature prize, long before he was
to read it as a part of his syllabus. This set of four poems, containing
some of Eliot's most overt comments on religion and drawn as much
from Orthodox Christianity as the Bhagavad Gita and Mahabharata,
forms the basis of ET's own formulation on time. Though he does
add as a note of caution that the realization about time was his own,
he merely uses Eliot's formulation because it is 'neat'.[14]

Burnt Norton, the first of the four Quartets, starts in a moment of
rare illumination, a moment in meditative practice when the garden
appears still, the sea is far away and the atmosphere of secretiveness
and enchantment is merely suggested rather than described. The trees
are full of children's excited laughter, containing their happiness. It
is a moment of clear light when memories appear full of promise,
possibilities that might have been,

> Footfalls echo in the memory
> Down the passage which we did not take
> Towards the door we never opened
> Into the rose-garden.

In the second Quartet, Eliot does indeed succumb to the lure of
memory, moving to *East Coker*, a village in Somerset from where his
ancestors had set out to explore the New World. *Dry Salvages*, the
third in the series, is a poem of adventure, describing the journey
that was embarked on, a journey that every man must undertake
amidst infinity and in search of awareness and rebirth. And with the
concluding, *Little Gidding,* there is a homecoming, a return back
to England. The poet visits the chapel in Little Gidding, it is dusk
with the voices of the children in the apple tree, it is a moment when

---

14   Interview 12 March 2018.

the fire and the rose appear to be one. The poet has moved from illumination to darkness, through blazing fire to translucence and a path has been found—a path that leads back to the beginning.

Four Quartets is all about finding echoes, poems in which ends constantly become beginnings and images endlessly repeat themselves in timeless circularity. It is essentially about the simultaneity of time, of the immanence of both the past and the future in the present,

> Time present and time past
> Are both perhaps present in time future,
> And time future contained in time past
> . . . What might have been and what has been
> Point to one end, which is always present.

Unlike the concept of time that ET had explored in his thesis on African literature, Eliot's concept of time is further extended with an extra dimension of divinity and pre-determined fate. Whereas what ET commented on in his thesis was how the past affected the present and the present found its way into the future, with Eliot it is how both the past and the future come together to unite in the present. It is a circular rather than a linear concept of time when the present moment remains fluid and ever-changing as it moves on the eternal cycle of time. The past never gives way to the present or the present to the future for each is present in each. As such the present is a moment in history that defies history itself because all of history lies in that moment. The present is also the moment that holds the key to all mysteries—it is the rose garden which is finally illuminated by the Pentecostal Fire in *Little Giddings*. And in holding both the past and the future within itself, the present is the signifier of the end of all duality—the stillness at the centre of a wheel that is born of the perfect balance between opposing forces.[15] It is the moment

---

[15]   Constance De Masirevich, *On the Four Quartets of T.S. Eliot* (NY: Vincent Stuart, 1965), p. 17.

when the contemplating mind becomes one with the object being contemplated upon, the 'oneness' of gnostic dualism,

> When the tongues of flame are in-folded
> Into the crowned knot of fire
> And the fire and the rose are one.

ET has spoken about the writer's sense of the past at many forums, one of his most recurrent themes. His emphasis becomes clearer when he compares the sense of history of Eliot with that of Yeats. He speaks of Eliot's poetry being touched by not only his American experience but much by the sophistication of European longing and that the lines that launch *Burnt Norton* carry a sense of 'history, of sequencing, of continuity.' He continues, 'His [Eliot's] sense of history is not the disturbed Irish history of Yeats but a synoptic one of European civilization . . . Eliot was more engaged with continuities, Yeats with revolutions.'[16] ET goes on to further clarify Yeats' stance on history—by the time he looked for his Anglo-Irish roots and tried to incorporate the realities of contemporary Irish nationalism into it, romantic Ireland was dead and gone. What replaced it was the energy and spirit manifest in Easter 1916 and incorporating this new present reality meant an internal realigning within Yeats, a shifting and assessment of historical forces. Consequently, according to ET, Yeats re-formed his sense of historical continuity, constructed it anew from indigenous, European and other sources but underpinned it with a 'potent grasp of the contemporary'. Thus, what ET speaks about is an interesting amalgam of Eliot and Yeats' ideas: a sense of history is important because of the continuity it provides, a certain homogeneity particularly in a multiracial society which involves inevitable shifts in sensibility from living in a culturally

---

[16] *The Writer's Sense of the Past: Essays on Southeast Asian and Australasian Literature*, ed. Kirpal Singh (Singapore: Singapore University Press, 1987), pp. 227–8.

binary world. But the past chosen for this purpose has to be underpinned by a keen understanding of the present. And this idea ET extends further in speaking of the author's role in representing history—as the past, present and future are but reflections of each other, the writer needs to consciously look for an extension of present symbols, images and metaphors in the past he chooses to incorporate in national literary discourse, 'For the construction was simultaneously a reaching out, an enlargement, an updating of the past into individual, intellectual, creative super structures.'[17]

ET's thoughts on the past and the simultaneity of time become clearer if one looks at three poems as part of a continuum—*A Boy Drowns* (*Gods Can Die*, 1977), *RELC* (Regional English Language Centre) (*Ulysses by the Merlion*, 1979) and *NTI* (*A Third Map*, 1993). All three are firmly rooted in Singapore history. The first has as its background the remnants of the Japanese Occupation, an eco-pool that is a part of what used to be the Raffles College and is the NUS campus and the Botanical Gardens now.[18] According to ET, during War the Japanese had their *butai* or armed forces headquarters there, 'The senior officers used to be there you know, and they had created a Japanese pool with koi and a little bridge— the whole lot. That strange combination of beauty and cruelty which is a part of Japanese culture.' ET had actually watched a body being fished out of the pool. By then Singapore was a modern metropolis, War was long forgotten and yet had the smell of gunpowder lingered in the air, a sense of brutality that had claimed yet another life? By the 1970s, the pressures of meritocracy was mounting on students, with the weaker ones pushed to the wall. The monolingual-bilingual streaming of the New Education System would be introduced in 1979, NUS would be formed the subsequent year. Yet, if there is a reference to the state's education policy in the poem, it remains unsaid, even on probing. What is

---

[17]   Ibid, p. 228.
[18]   Interview 12 January 2018.

expressed is the bald starkness of the death, as death always is - without reprieve,

> A boy drowns, in a campus pool,
> Not in flood-time, but quietly in cool waters
> While the afternoon sunned itself.

Death connects the young boy with the old men who stand around nodding, they know of *hara-kiri*, Japanese soldiers who had killed themselves in high honour. But then a young student carrying a sheaf of science notes comes and looks speculatively at the body, as though it were a scientific fact. And suddenly the tranquillity of the afternoon returns to hit the reader with renewed vigour—the quietness of latent violence which has lived on, which mars the beauty of the plate-glass face of the pool rippled by afternoon sunlight. Will the young science graduate be able to escape its force? Will Singapore actually be able to bury its war-dead?

The same theme of the present holding both the past and the future is in *RELC*, though with a clearer focus on historical continuity. It is dedicated to Tai Yu-Lin, the founding-director since 1967 of the Regional English Language Centre of Singapore. ET very consciously lays the poem at the doorway of history by speaking of Yu-Lin's father, Dr Wu Lien-Teh, the Malay-born Chinese doctor remembered for fighting the plague pandemic of China. He describes visiting Yu-Lin's home in Singapore, replete with her father's memorabilia, 'I would tell her, "Yu-Lin, it's impossible to walk in your house—everything I touch is 300 years old!"'[19] He also speaks of Dr Goh Keng Swee's tentative plans of closing down RELC in the mid-'70s when the institution was felt to have lost its relevance merely as a provider of English language training. But of course,

---

[19]   Interview 12 March 2018.

RELC would survive and reinvent itself as a centre for Southeast Asian languages.[20]

It is significant that the opening lines,

> Here our languages have a home
> Discover themselves, root and bole

are reminiscent of *Little Gidding*,

> . . . where every word is at home,
> Taking its place to support the others,
> The word neither diffident nor ostentatious,
> An easy commerce of the old and the new

For ET, RELC holds the potential unity of a Little Gidding, the place where fire and rose become one. It is at the Centre that the soft vocabulary is learnt which helps to enter cultures,

> Thus we enter the rhythms
> Of our many peoples, understand
> What colours move their laughter,
> The deep grammar of their hearts,
> As Thai, Bahasa, Filipino
> Mandarin and English meet.

He speaks of RELC's future role in the ASEAN (Association of Southeast Asian Nations), a region he increasingly perceived as Singapore's cultural hinterland. As such, RELC, like the stillness at the centre of the wheel, unifies binaries, eases out differences, helps create words for the past and the future. It is placed at an important intersection of the matrix where languages, cultures, geographies and histories come together, relatively free from fundamental upheavals.

---

[20]   The *Straits Times,* 31 January 1974, p. 5.

It is where 'we are our brother's keeper.' According to ET such icons, a particular locale, which touches all aspects of life and cumulatively defines major continuities are important as a particular image of history.[21] They need to be preserved.

The third poem, *NTI,* foregrounds the closure of the only Chinese post-secondary university of Singapore and its metamorphosis into the Nanyang Technological Institute. Founded in 1953 under the auspices of the Singapore Hokkien Association, it was merged with NUS in 1980 and turned into an engineering institute with a distinctly different ethos. Yet, surprisingly ET celebrates the transformation of this last bastion of culture, despite the historical past,

> A special place where history
> Turns and breathes in landscape.
> Among our memories, a stir of
> Earlier vision whose pulse transfixed

Why does ET accept the closure, notwithstanding the public outcry against it? This is where Yeats' thoughts on extending the present back into the past comes into play for finally the balance and the unity of the two are of paramount importance. Or as ET interprets it, the author needs to have a 'potent grasp' of the contemporary and armed with it he reaches for the right roots. Keeping modern Singapore in mind, technology is what can provide a neutral common ground, a site of engagement rather than rupture between overlapping generations, not a culture that has its roots in a different homeland. For ultimately it is the survival of the little island as a coherent entity that is vital,

> All feeding this mortal, invented island,
> Held above the foam, the world's fever.

---

[21]   The *Straits Times,* 31 January 1974, p. 5.

Among other Asian authors, ET is fond of K.S. Maniam, the Indian-Malaysian novelist and it is wise to cast a glance at what Maniam has to say about a writer's sense of the past. According to him, literature should harness all of human resources so that an individual (writer or reader) can move towards a 'completeness'.[22] For Maniam these include the cultural resources from the past which allow for a fuller human integration with Southeast Asian/Malaysian life. And for ET too, explorations of the past are undertaken in an attempt to make a spiritual contact with his land and he does so by reaching for enabling factors that facilitate transcendence over self-defeating social barriers. As he says in an entirely different context, 'One of the interesting things in Singapore is watching a commissioning ceremony for Colours for our young army. They are blessed by representatives from all the main religions in Singapore. You had that sense of the spiritual.'[23]

Intersection II: Culture and Mythology

ET is a great storyteller, able to weave a spell of mystery and magic even in a neon-lit Starbucks Café. He recounts an experience in Ireland, of sitting by a Celtic cross in Dublin.[24] He was at a point where three paths met, with his son, Julian, when the mists descended, 'You know the mists of Ireland, there are dark moments . . . yet something spiritual about them.' That day he had felt presences, presences which were not scary in the conventional sense but had overwhelmed him with the sense of something that was far stronger, sinewy than him. 'Demi-gods, part-god, part-human, part-animal . . . if I didn't know the myths, I wouldn't have felt it.' For ET that is the significance of myths—they open up possibilities of knowing, give lineage to instinct.

---

[22] Ibid, p. 218.
[23] *Interlogue*, Vol. 7, ed. Peter Nazareth (Singapore: Ethos Books, 2008), p. 218.
[24] Interview 06 June 2017.

Stories of the sea-serpent who encircled the island of humanity or of wolves who hunted the sun and the moon are important to ET for their colour and detail, but more so for the little grain of truth they hold. The great collection of Celtic, Nordic, Greek, Roman, Egyptian, Toltec, Mayan, Chinese or Indian myths that he holds in his mind give him a structure to understand a culture. They are an entry point. Or as ET puts it, 'They hold the fundamental values or "truths" of a society.'[25] And yet the relationship between myth and culture is not simple or single-dimensional, but infinitely recurrent. At the start of a human civilization normally comes a founding myth. Thus, the dual myths of the founding of Rome—one of the mother-wolf and the other of the Trojan-refugee Aeneas (though ET prefers the first because it is more organic to the land). And then as the civilization progresses, imparting to daily chores the sanctity of rituals, added to the repository are myths about agriculture, fertility or metallurgy—truths that are vital to the society at that moment in time. The truths remain as part of the social fabric and influence behaviour and from such behavioural norms and breaches come other myths, myths about gods, demi-gods and shadow-creatures. Thus, there is the pantheon of Egyptian gods which finds a place for not only the glorious Ra, the separator of light from darkness, but also Babi, the god of wild baboons who feeds on entrails, loves the wicked-dead of the Underworld. Each character personifies a human impulse and from them emerge the social 'types', right and wrong, paradigms and irregularities. They give structure to a society and yet as society evolves, breaks through the mould, myths are reinterpreted as well—the society taking from them what is relevant and contemporary. And so both myths and culture remain open-ended, tied to each other in infinite cycles of flux and reflux. Or as ET puts it, it is the continuity of cultures—for e.g., what many perceive as Greek culture today, has Egyptian origins.

---

[25]   Interview 22 March 2018.

In the context of myths, ET speaks of two things—Yeats and values.[26] Yeats because he reinvented himself from one hyphenated identity to another—from being an Anglo-Irish to being an Irish-Nationalist and in so doing reinvented Ireland's mythological past as well. And 'values' because for ET myths are important for they represent a continuity of values. In fact, he feels his poetry should be associated with religion rather than myths or at the minimum with myths that sit on the cusp of religious principles for all along he has looked at myths or folklores because they provide for a secular idiom for conveying new social concerns and fresh ideological options.

Yeats has remained one of the strongest influences on ET, stronger than Eliot or Shakespeare or even Ben Jonson because in him he saw his own closest extension. At the head of an essay on Yeats he quotes Kinsella,

'In Yeats's maturing poetry the tradition found a voice for significant events, and made its first move into modern poetry.'[27]

All three of ET's poetic missions are inhered here: the need to give voice to a tradition which is already part of a cultural fabric, to provide significant correlatives to an emerging culture in terms of 'events' or 'types' or 'places' and to be part of an evolving poetry which is born at the confluence of history, politics and value-systems. In Yeats he finds a psychic hinterland perhaps because of the Irish poet's inherent duality. To ET he remains an *Ariel* figure, one who, as his label of 'Anglo-Irish' indicates, partook of both the impulse to rule and to break free from that rule, one who belonged deeply to oppressor and oppressed.[28] Ireland was Britain's archetypal colonial testing ground, the original paradigm from which all other colonial paradigms were constructed. As such, Yeats knew well how intercultural dynamics worked based on proximity and contiguity,

---

[26]   Ibid.

[27]   *The New Oxford Book of Irish Verse*, ed. Thomas Kinsella (UK: OUP, 1986), p. xxvii.

[28]   *Conflicting Identities: Essays on Modern Irish Literature*, ed. Robbie B.H. Goh (Singapore: Unipress, 1997), p. 230.

the conduits between two well-established cultures and how contrasts muted, became familiar with sharing. Or as ET puts it, 'That sharing reduces the upper-case "Other" to a lower-case "other".' And in so doing it drew together the two halves of Yeats's own *Ariel* personality, the two halves that were rooted in two different worlds—the colonial and the indigenous which had started to confront each other with the forces of nationalism. The answer to this conflict was a need to change the overarching myth, a need to re-discover, re-negotiate, re-educate, re-work on the imagination of readers to create a new body of metaphors, a new paradigm and a new identity. As to Yeats, so to ET, the new myth would set the *Ariel* free.

Thus, ET speaks of Yeats's *A Vision*, a body of work he started while experimenting with automatic writing with his wife, where two characters of Yeats's imagination, Aherne and Robartes engage in a conversation. According to ET, *A Vision* contains the essence of Yeats's re-working, a distillation of mythology as he recasts the old Irish myth of lunar phases to describe the kinds of personalities found in each lunar incarnation. All except the 15th Phase or the full moon whose completeness of beauty comes from the agony of the many lifetimes lived in the Phases before, a painful approximation or an expanding calculus of the soul born of the past.[29] It is in *A Vision* that Yeats's thoughts on both myths and values come together, as does his conception that no human identity is complete without a multiplicity of individual elements.

So how does this Yeatsian vision of a new overarching myth which stands on an acceptable moral structure, accommodates and in turn influences and is influenced by a changing culture translated, when in Singapore? For ET it pans out in three different ways:

1. By creating vital correlatives with roots firmly entrenched in Singapore's multi-racial, post-colonial reality: the correlatives

---

[29]   Stuart Hirscheberg, 'Yeats's "The Phases of the Moon": Towards a Lunar Myth', *Notre Dame English Journal*, Vol. 9, No. 2 (Spring 1974), pp. 73–6.

can be in terms of places (ET's poems on the National Library or *RELC*), significant events (*9th of August* or *Vacating Bukit Timah Campus*) or Singapore 'types' as markers of the evolving society (*Ibrahim* or *How to Win Friends*).

2. By an unrelenting focus on the multiracial culture of Singapore, tracing it as it evolves and at the same time pointing towards the changing myth that supports it: if on his mind-map culture appears on the horizontal axis, then myth appears on the vertical and by shifting the myth to a fresh paradigm, he seeks to give the evolving culture of Singapore a better balance and scaffolding. Thus he speaks of the Chinese community as an example where poetry was born out of a sense of exile and the impact, especially among the young of the Communist victory over the Kuomintang.[30] Yet if the same themes or same set of values could be re-invented as a tradition of toil, a determination to surmount hardships, a powerful work ethic and this could be achieved along with a gradual admission of the local environment, a gradual localizing of roots, then it could gradually lead to a new identity—that of a Singaporean-Chinese. Moreover, the same myth as a determinant could draw under its sheltering wing the Indians, the majority of whom had come to Singapore to earn a living, to live frugally, remitting all they could to India and felt a sense of incompleteness within them as they lacked in high culture which strengthened their respect for education. As it could take under its wing the Malays who had the longest roots in the region. Yet with urbanization they had had to adapt themselves, break themselves away from a fuller Malay social structure extending from court to *kampong*, a feat that was particularly difficult since in Malaysia the Malay ethos flourished.

---

[30] *A Sense of Exile: Essays on the Literature of the Asia-Pacific Region*, ed. Bruce Bennett (Australia: Centre for Studies in Australian Literature, 1988), pp. 45–50.

3. By extending the determinant mythology to the psychological
    hinterland of Southeast Asia: he attempts to extend the notion of
    race and broaden sensibilities by pointing towards an aggregate
    of common inheritances. Thus, in poems like *Shiva* or *Krishna* or
    the more recent *Āyatana*, he draws a common rubric of religious
    beliefs and ideals that extend across the religions of the region.

A clearer insight into ET's paradigm of culture and mythology
emerges if one compares poems like *Ahmad* and *Ibrahim bin Ahmad*
which form a part of *Gods Can Die* with *John* from *Ulysses by the
Merlion*. According to ET, the first two are about a father and a
son, among the few poems written about 9th August 1963 when
Singapore separated from Malaysia. In the first he describes the
father and it is significant how cautious his words are as he speaks
of the commonly accepted stereotype of a Malay—his 'bronze
patience', the calm spirituality of fingers that turn the beads in
resigned submission and yet the anger that smoulders in his eyes, all
the more threatening because it remains unexpressed. The change
in ET's tone, the almost palpable relief is evident when he speaks
of the son, Ibrahim bin Ahmad. An entire generation has passed
since the separation and ET can sit now in 'quiet communion' with
Ahmad and yet can he really get beyond the curtain of communal
pride? Instead, they sit on either side speaking politely of Malay
heritage—the legendary Hang Jebat, the greatest *silat* exponent. A
conversation is now possible through the conduit of memories of
'uneasy times', of elders who 'stood for much' and yet the dagger
has merely been sheathed and the tense undertone remains with
talk returning to martial arts and a history of vengeful rebellion.
The crescent moon hanging low in the evening sky brings to mind
Islam, but also the Malay *kris*.

    In contrast is a poem like *John*, about a group of ET's personal
friends who share a common Christian name, John, and yet have
different surnames—Watson, Tan, Harniman, Raja, Cawelti,
Waiyaki, Sinclair, Richardson and Kasaipwalova—what ET calls, 'A

hell of a mixed gang!'[31] It a motley group consisting of Johns as varied in their vocation as John Watson, the editor of Heinemann who had published *Gods Can Die*, to John Kasaipwalova, a Trobriand Islander born during the Japanese Occupation, to John Tan, a teacher from Raffles Institution. Here one can see ET consciously making a move towards the *Ariel* or what he calls the 'hyphenated' identity of Singapore—the Singaporean-Malay, Chinese and Indian. The correlatives that he uses are specific to Singapore—the famous Emerald Room of Dublin Road where the proprietor Leong was a dear friend, the Malay fish-head curry eaten with Indian *chapatti* amidst a Chinese orchestra. Here in an environment bereft of any nervous edge, they tread freely on the holy ground of each other's cultures: 'Christ on the Mount of Olive', 'Arjuna's serene charioteer', 'Li Po lamenting absent friends'. And this crossing of boundaries having become possible, he decides to change the determining myth from memories of partition and communal violence to a common ground of collective admiration for Samia Gamal and Yeats, Shakespeare and Socrates. Here in the darkened interiors of a restaurant-pub amidst murmured conversation, even as they doodle on the tablecloth, they find comfort, the perfect balance between memories of inner inheritances and assimilation of outer cultures. In the humanistic centre of several spheres of existence the *Ariel* is set free,

> Turning all on soft conversation,
> Contemplating . . . man, proud man,
> Drest in a little brief authority . . .
> Among nine friends
> There is comfort.

Āyatana, a poem written in February 2018 to commemorate a re-installation by acclaimed Thai artist, Montien Boonma, placed at the National Art Gallery of Singapore, perhaps contains some of

---

[31]   Interview 26 February 2018.

ET's most matured and crystallized thoughts on the overarching myth. In the installation designed in concentric circles and titled, *The Pleasure of Being, Crying, Dying and Eating*, Boonma wishes to reflect on the cyclical and transient nature of human life. Surrounded by a ring of circular tables laid out for a meal, complete with smart red tablecloths, is an inner sanctum sanctorum, a circular column-like enclosure made of ceramic bowls. In fact such insertions appear repeatedly in Boonma's work to portray the sense of sacred enclosures from Buddhist texts which are cosmic centres of contemplation and concentration.[32] Through these structures of stillness with their sense of lightness and ascension, he wishes to walk into the space of soundless calm where the mind knows endless possibilities. As Boonma said of the Buddhist monk's alms bowl, 'Monks always hold the bowl . . . When I think about the space, I prefer to be inside this space which is separated from the outside world. I would like to place my mind inside the bowl.'[33] The fragility of the outer wall of these enclosures (for instance the ceramic bowls of the installation in Singapore) convey the insubstantiality of the human body—the physical outer layer that lies between the human soul and the outer world, a thin membrane that prevents the soul from unifying with the vastness of the cosmos. Once the wall is shattered, the soul is free to enter the eternal cycle of universal life.

ET names the poem *Āyatana*, to bring to focus the central thought of the installation—the sense-bases of the human body which connect the internal with the external, to highlight Boonma's thought that a meal, though a sensory act, can serve as a gateway to a deeper, more metaphysical experience. It is interesting how he connects Boonma's visual expression and interprets it in the Singapore context. Boonma, who had lost his wife to cancer and would die himself of the same affliction, had placed on the tables chopsticks which were 'bronzed finger bones', on the 'bowl-tower' a

---

[32] https://nga.gov.au/Boonma/edu.cfm; accessed on 05 April 2018.
[33] Ibid.

'yard of pink intestine' gleaming with mucous. These to ET become important correlatives to the essential uniformity of human form which hold together the multiracial framework of Singapore. Just as the bone and mucous are shocking in their nudity, so is ET's use of the most primitive of racial terms,

> We share bone, sinew and flesh, we SG Melayu,
> China, Kling, Serani. Demolish fish-head curry,
> take the Pledge, celebrate each other's Festivals.
> We keep ancestry, identity, major and minor feelings.

It is also significant that ET dedicates the poem to a couple, Leen and Mark, she Peranakan, for as he has always maintained, the English-speaking 'Babas' are one of the most remarkable races of the world who have moved into another language and yet have brought so much of their spirit and practice into that language.[34] It is the same thinking about crossing boundaries, arriving at the neutrality that lies at the centre of cultures or one of his original formulations of 'form and substance' that pervade the poem. Thus, the Buddhist alms bowls bring to his mind thoughts of Christian beatitudes, the Last Supper which lies at the foundation of his own faith, Boonma's blood-red napkins are reinvented as the Indonesian *sapu-tanga*. Grace and banyan, mantra and beatitude, bread and wine and the purity of a lotus mix and merge seamlessly till the whole of Southeast Asia becomes one throbbing, palpable quest for a more intelligible meaning to human life:

> Above all, live our Faith, Belief, *words of Divinity*.
> They infuse our senses, all six, to cope with the ebb
> and flow, mulling this swirling apology of a world.
> For me, the Beatitudes, and His gift of
> Bread and Wine at the Last Supper.

---

[34] *A Lighter Side of History*, 22 July 2017, National Museum, Singapore.

The overarching myth is of a moral coherence that holds together histories and geographies, races and religions. If in discovering this, ET's thoughts stop at the outer structures of religion, short of the spiritual experience that awaits him within the 'bowl-column', then it is a trajectory he will trace at a personal level.

Intersection III: Visible and Invisible

Edward Said quotes the French psychiatrist from Martinique, Frantz Fanon, while describing the effect of colonialism: it is comparable to a mother who keeps a child from knowing itself, protects it from its own ego, its own psychology and maybe even its own unhappiness which is its very essence.[35] In brief, colonialism is that malady that separates the individual from his instinctual life, breaks the generative lineaments of a nation's identity.

The notion of fractured identity emerges again and again as ET speaks about the Singapore where he was raised, an imperial metropolis which grew and changed with years of trade and migration. He knew well its geographical and topological spread, much as he knew its separating, psychological walls—its bifurcated spaces of culture and communal living which demanded distinctively different behaviour patterns of him. Thus, there was the colonial spread around the Singapore River—the mercantile banks, the fluted colonnades of the Fullerton or the out-of-reach windows of Whiteaway Laidlaw. They inspired awe, maybe even a sense of pride at the blinding elegance of his city. And then there was the *wayang* stage, his mother's favourite haunt, where he and his siblings would crowd into the back of a truck carrying stage props to get a better view. Or Mandai itself, where his father continued with his engineering hobbies, undeterred by mistakes. Mandai moved him with its vulnerability, a sense of protectiveness made all the more fierce because he knew it was a way of life not approved by white masters. It was a bifurcated world

---

[35] Edward Said, *Culture and Imperialism* (NY: Vintage Books, 1994), p. 287.

where he did not really belong to either of the two spaces—neither the first which disowned him, nor the second which he was taught to disown. Both brought a sense of inadequacy redeemed only by stirrings of nationalism.

The sense of the clandestine amidst the knotted, familial roots of Mandai is apparent in his very early poem, *Yesterday*:

> walk to the shadow of Mandai mountain
> I will show you a sleeping secret stream . . .

But all that changed with independence! He says with palpable relief washing his voice, 'By the time we became independent, we became one city, the invisible became visible. What was suppressed, fractured, marginalized—all came to the forefront, became unified, became SG.'[36] This sense of unity is evident in his poem, *National Library, 2007*. He sees reflected in the mirrored walls of the spanking new library his old friend, the stage actor, Seow Cheng Fong, reciting passages from Shakespeare's King Lear in earnest declamation. And suddenly the formal public structure becomes synonymous with long-forgotten evenings of Tiger Beer and oyster omelette in a Bugis Street still scarred by war. What is visible merges with what was subterranean—a roadside eatery which once was an alternative site of urban creativity. The Library is not only a triumphant testimony to lifelong learning, but a vindication of fate for the likes of Cheng Fong, bred on Shakespeare and yet denied the release of assaying a central role because of his skin colour.

In this context Yeats' attempt to retrieve subverted space given to colonialism remains relevant to ET. As ET says, 'I learnt to ask fundamental questions about change, permanence, identity and national identity. I learnt it all the more from him.'[37] Especially significant is the volume, *A Vision* in which the Irish poet explores

---

[36] Interview 22 March 2018.
[37] *Edwin Thumboo: Time Travelling*, p. 60.

the uncertain borderland between the separate parts of his own being, caught as he was in a hyphenated identity as an Anglo-Irish, and concludes that it all comes together in logical coherence and any part taken beyond a point makes a nonsense of the whole.[38] *A Vision* holds a complicated apparatus of Faculties and Principles and whirling gyres which arranges in intelligible order all of Yeats' knowledge and experience. And at the centre of every circle of his many-centred universe he finds 'One'—an awareness of a centrality against which he sinks back restfully in moments of exhaustion. *A Vision* is one man's defence against the chaos of the world, a welding together of scattered perceptions which brought with itself a discovery of the truth—for as Yeats said, without 'wholeness' there could not be any perception of truth.[39] It is a book that recognizes diversity, is full of combative energy and yet in essence remains the vision and salvation of one man alone. It holds Yeats' discovery that his conflicted, postcolonial soul needs to move through all the phases of the moon, walking alike through light and darkness to experience it all, for it is the wholeness of this experience that will bring him to the truth of 'One'—an emancipating unity born of the multiplicity.

So how does it work for ET? Did he find that post-independence the visible and the invisible parts of his identity imperceptibly and automatically coming together and that was the end of all conflict? But then what about the volume *Gods Can Die*, published long after 1965, where he finds his mind splintering endlessly over questions of morality and identity? What had changed between 1977 and 1979 when *Ulysses by the Merlion* was published? Perhaps what had changed was, ET now actively sought a unity of internal and external landscapes, deliberately finding in the external landscape extensions of his warring personality and attempting to repair the ruptured lines. As he says, 'We [the English-language poets] were actively looking for

---

[38] *Yeats: A Collection of Critical Essays*, ed. John Unterecker (NJ: Prentice Hall, 1963), p. 141.

[39] Ibid, p. 151.

unifying symbols then' and this unity he found in every aspect of his city.[40] He found it sometime in external symbols like the RELC or the National Library. Sometime in the coming together of romantic nostalgia over a lost past and the explosion of development that Singapore had seen in recent years—an inner instinct and an outer perception welded together under a rush of stars by a mechanic's torch to create permanent habitation:

> In time images of power,
> Our emergent selves,
> Will be familiar
> As, first the body learns
> This other song.[41]

As an extension of his thoughts on a binary unity appears the poem *Conversations with My Friend Kwang Min at Loong Kwang of Outram Park* where, while looking at Chinese artefacts in an antique shop, he finds scattered bits of his identity. It is probably ET's version of the Yeatsian wheel of incarnation for in the Chinese figurines he glimpses phases of the moon—faces of the human personality. Thus there is Kuan Yin on the lotus with her immense potency of limitless transcendence held in check under a feminine serenity, or Cheng Ho, the industrious admiral of the Ming Dynasty entrusted with imposing imperial control over the Indian Ocean trade, or Li of the Iron Staff who dispenses medicine to the poor from the gourd slung across his shoulder, or the great Hanuman, now Wukong the ravisher of the gardens of Heaven. Yet what is interesting is, under cover of their Chinese facades, every one of them represent unity, syncretic figures bringing together different cultures and different worlds: Kuan Yin who has as her predecessor Lakshmi the goddess of prosperity of Hinduism, Cheng Ho is the Yunan-born Muslim, the

---

[40] Interview 09 April 2018.
[41] *Island.*

castrated eunuch who transcends gender, Li of the Iron Staff is the
spirit that returns from visiting the immortals in Heaven and enters
the body of a beggar and so transcends the barriers of the living and
the dead, and of course the great Hanuman who rules alike Chinese
and Indian mythology.

But apparently ET does not stop here. For below the syncretism
are the singular universal values that each figure represents, which
coincidentally are the hallmarks of Singapore's national identity:
Lakshmi signifying the importance of economic activity, Cheng
Ho the spirit of industrious adventure, Li the empathy of a classless
society and Hanuman an adaptability to change. And even below
this is ET himself, who in these fragmented identities finds a gestalt
of himself—complete and yet restless to grow continuously, who
like Hanuman, must be 'absorbed' into this new milieu, 'given a
role'. In the 'contented' Singapore afternoon, the poet and his city
find each other in organic interplay, tied together in a relationship as
fundamental as of gnostic dualism.

The volume *Ulysses by the Merlion* ends with the poem *Shiva*—
one of the greatest syncretic figures bringing together both Aryan and
Dravidian traditions, in equal portions an ascetic and a householder,
a creator and a destroyer—benevolent and fearsome, equally active
in Shaivism and Shaktism—the two main streams of Hindu belief.
In front of this Hindu godhead ET places pomegranate seeds, a
Chinese symbol of cleansing, and lotus blooms which uniformly
portray purity across the religions of Southeast Asia. The short
piece, obviously another of ET's Sino-Indian poems with a haiku-
like simplicity in its pared-down imagery, is reminiscent of Arthur
Waley's Chinese poems. It ends with,

> I saw a pattern there,
> A rhythm in the evening sun;
> Your dancing feet will tear
> The fibres of the drum.

ET speaks about following the *kavadi-bearers* during the Thaipusam festival in Johor Bahru when he would watch the drummers dancing to the tune of their drums in frenzied ecstasy.[42] Yet at every juncture of the road, the rhythm of their dance would change and he would look at their dancing feet and wonder if the drumbeat had changed the dance or the dance had changed the drumbeat? Which came first, the internal or the external? Which changed first, the city or himself? Today, at a considerably advanced age, he no longer looks for an answer. He knows that the awareness that the self is placed at the confluence of the external and the internal, the visible and the invisible is enough. It is this self which is the 'One', a centrality born of its own multiplicity. He is the *Nataraja*, the cosmic dancer who stands circled by the all-consuming ring of fire, whose dance, the *tandava*, symbolizes cosmic cycles of creation and annihilation.

The answer lies in the question itself.

Ulysses by the Merlion

The poem, *Ulysses by the Merlion* represents a midpoint in ET's poetic career, the central, regenerative unifying vision. Before this he is on a quest for unity, after this it is a journey to find extensions to this central thought. It is the point where a river meets the expanse of the sea, dancing tributaries lose themselves in the ocean's solemn calm. The easier part of the journey is over, among frenzy and friends. The more difficult part remains with a solitary prow pointing to an ever-shifting horizon.

Ulysses by The Merlion
for Maurice Baker

I have sailed many waters,

---

42   Ibid. *Kavadi-bearers* carry pots of milk slung at either ends of a bamboo pole on their shoulder as a dedication to god.

Skirted islands of fire,
Contended with Circe
Who loved the squeal of pigs;
Passed Scylla and Charybdis
To seven years with Calypso,
Heaved in battle against the gods.
Beneath it all
I kept faith with Ithaca, travelled,
Travelled and travelled,
Suffering much, enjoying a little;
Met strange people singing
New myths; made myths myself.

But this lion of the sea
Salt-maned, scaly, wondrous of tail,
Touched with power, insistent
On this brief promontory . . .
Puzzles.

Nothing, nothing in my days
Foreshadowed this
Half-beast, half-fish,
This powerful creature of land and sea.

Peoples settled here,
Brought to this island
The bounty of these seas,
Built towers topless as Ilium's.

They make, they serve,
They buy, they sell.

Despite unequal ways,
Together they mutate,

Explore the edges of harmony,
Search for a centre;
Have changed their gods,
Kept some memory of their race
In prayer, laughter, the way
Their women dress and greet.
They hold the bright, the beautiful,
Good ancestral dreams
Within new visions,
So shining, urgent,
Full of what is now.

Perhaps having dealt in things,
Surfeited on them,
Their spirits yearn again for images,
Adding to the Dragon, Phoenix,
Garuda, Naga those Horses of the Sun,
This lion of the sea,
This image of themselves.

There is a mention of Ulysses in one of his earliest poems, *For Peter Wee*, in which he grieves for a friend, abruptly taken by accident, leaving nothing but a stray line of poetry on ET's mind.[43] Under cover of youthful nihilism at the loss of a friend, there is a rueful barb at the restlessness of his own mind: *The mind cannot quiver to a single purpose.* It is this journey from conflict to calm that the poet has traversed in the two decades or so since his university days. If in the ancient city of Byzantium Yeats had glimpsed a unity which had restored his poetic consciousness, the ever-itinerant Ulysses notices residing in the figure of the Merlion the same sense of calm stability,

---

[43]   Details in Chapter 3.

This lion of the sea,
This image of themselves.

The note of mature self-knowledge is palpable in the poet's voice. And perhaps because of this ET chooses the more seasoned Ulysses from Tennyson as the spokesperson for his poem rather than the Homeric Odysseus who still hankers for home and hearth. Here Ulysses is on the last voyage of his life, having assigned Ithaca to his son, Telemachus. He has seen it all and yet that niggling wanderlust remains when a journey is precious for itself and not for its final destination. When asked, ET says he chose Ulysses because he is the archetypal explorer, unaccepting of stasis, who chooses instead

to follow knowledge like a sinking star
Beyond the utmost bound of human thought.[44]

So, Ulysses arrives on the shores of Singapore and as the weathered traveller is able to transcend barriers and thrust into the inner life of the city. No nuance of sensation, tonalities of accent, emerging vitality of this new land escape him. And here he notices the Merlion,

salt-maned, scaly, wondrous of tail,

man-made and yet with an oneiric function. In this creature who so valiantly unites the land with the sea, he sees reflected the people, the variegated races of Singapore who

despite unequal ways, explore the edges of harmony.

It is interesting how *Ulysses by the Merlion* brings together ET's thoughts on time, mythology and that all-defining unity that is born at the intersect of the visible and the invisible. If in poems like

---

[44]　Interview 22 March 2018.

A Boy Drowns he had dwelled on the circularity of history when a present moment could never be free of the shadows of the past, in *UM* he notices much the same. Thus Ulysses sees the people of Singapore whose

> new visions, bright and beautiful, full of what is now

hold within them

> good ancestral dreams,

the aspirations with which their forefathers had set sail from India or China a long time ago. Similarly, in poems like *John* if he had indicated the need of redefining the determining myth of a community to bring the races of Singapore together, in *UM* too he mentions the people who

> have changed their gods.

They have done so not in bacchanalian neglect, intoxicated by the commercial culture but because they need to *mutate* in harmony, build a new identity. So

> they make, they serve, they buy, they sell,

making commerce their new determining myth.

Towering over the milling multitude, standing both as the perceiver and the perceived is the Merlion. In him coalesce the complex network of overlapping grids—the visible present prosperity and the invisible past when lions roared in the jungles and mermaids disappeared into the sea. He is as much the lion that once stood for British courage and pride as the lions on the pillar of Ashoka, the peace-loving king of India. He is the myth and the modern, the orient and the occident, the colonial and the postcolonial. He is a spatial expression of all that is temporal. As Barthes had written of the Eiffel Tower, he is an empty symbol that can signify everything.[45]

At a personal level, the poem brought with it an unwavering construct of identity, an identity that was born of overlapping grids of different realities. It also brought an inner connection with the figure of Ulysses, the eternal traveller who at the twilight hour sets sail into the unknown distance. ET speaks of the old man who rowed into the sunset towards the southern islands of Singapore. When the end comes, ET says, he would want it to be like that, while he is on a rocking boat, still travelling.[46]

Island of Fire

The Merlion poem brought ET fame, as it triggered criticism. It was sometime after the publication of the volume *Ulysses by the Merlion* that diplomat and Singapore's former representative to the United Nations, Tommy Koh, used the title of a poet laureate in ET's context and the moniker stuck, though never formally recognized by the state.[47] It is a label that ET 'enjoyed' for a while, but says it does not mean too much to him now. The poem also inspired a spate of other Merlion poems from acclaimed poets like Lee Tzu Pheng, Isa Kamari and Gwee Li Sui, so much so that it is believed writing a Merlion poem is a bit of a compulsion for Singapore poets.[48]

But criticism too has remained harsh, one of the strongest voices being of fellow poet, Lee Tzu Pheng, who wrote, 'To be quite frank, I got quiet irritated with Edwin's poem. I just felt it was false in some ways . . . I felt some of the things Ulysses was saying in that

---

[45]   Roland Barthes, *The Eiffel Tower & Other Mythologies* (US: University of California Press, 1997), p. 4.

[46]   Interview 26 February 2018.

[47]   Ibid.

[48]   *Reflecting on the Merlion: An Anthology of Poems*, ed. ET and Yeow Kai Chai (SG: NAC, 2009).

poem just comes (*sic*) too pat and too easy.'[49] Like many others in Singapore, her objection was towards the Merlion, a quaint man-made symbol designed by Fraser-Brunner for the Singapore Tourism Board in 1964, being chosen as a national icon rather than one that had naturally evolved from the culture of the country. It appeared to be a desperate attempt to 'manufacture' culture and ET in writing the poem was perceived as pro-establishment.

It is true. There is something distinctly plastic about the Merlion, its neatly serried plaster-of-paris scales, the chalk-blind eyes. But what is potentially more ominous is, as Tzu Pheng points out elsewhere, the Merlion represents how patriarchal laws work on a multiracial society—they push and pressurize and urge conformity.[50] For when ET's Ulysses sees the men who buy and sell or the bright and beautiful women who dress and greet, he sees a picture gift-wrapped by the state. It is a culture that encourages external compliance and maybe therefore an internal turning-away or at least definitely draws a demarcating line between public and private lives. And it is also true that the intersects ET crosses to arrive at the river bank where the Merlion stands, spewing out water, are rather carefully self-constructed. There is something factitious in the way, at every given junction, whether it is of history or of a culture-defining mythology, he chooses a path that leads back to this moment in time—the moment when the Merlion stands spinning urgent, luminous dreams.

The reason perhaps is twofold. Firstly, it is that all-determining factor—time. As he says, 'We are creatures of our time, we can't go beyond the premises that created us. Maybe we need younger people who will go for the real energies.'[51] For him that single rifle an

---

[49] 'Award-winning Poet puts herself between the Lines', The *Straits Times*, Singapore, 06 September 1997, p. 21.

[50] *ACLALS Bulletin*, 7th series, no. 2, Commonwealth Poetry, eds. Lee Tzu Pheng and Leong Liew Geok (Singapore: The Association for Commonwealth Literature and Language Studies, 1985), p. iv.

[51] Interview 09 April 2018.

Australian soldier had left, leaning against a coconut tree in Mandai is real—it had spelt war, the end of a happy, carefree childhood. For him is also true the racial riots he had witnessed, holed up behind the drawn shutters of his uncle's dispensary in Arab Street. Independence when it finally came and PAP took charge with its objective of building a socialist, multiracial Singapore brought with itself genuine relief.

The second reason perhaps is the question of a defining identity. As the child of Chinese-Indian parents, he had always felt the barb of an inner divide. For instance, he speaks of the Indo-Chinese border wars of 1962 when he did not know which side to support.[52] It is in the multicultural neutrality of Singapore that he found a definitive identity, a sense of pride and an end to inner fragmentation. He sees and appreciates the same unity-in-multiplicity in the merging colours of a piece of lapis lazuli or in the androgynous godhead of Shiva that he had seen in the Elephanta Caves of Mumbai. They give him goose-bumps, set his pulse racing. But it is Singapore that remains the touchstone of his personal identity.

His ties with his city become evident in different ways. Thus, we have him, as part of the *Committee on Street Names* formed in 1968, supporting to retain old street names: he insists Bukit Panjang should never be renamed because of the Malay resonance of the name with its meaning of a long hill.[53] 'It was probably called Bukit Panjang even before Raffles came,' he says and speaks about the way he went out of his way to convince S. Dhanabalan, the then Minister MND (Ministry for National Development), to prevent the name change. During the course of this conversation with the oral history department of the National Archives of Singapore, ET speaks repeatedly about respecting history and retaining names,

---

[52] Interview 09 October 2017.
[53] NAS interview transcript, 31 March 2005, reel 19.14, though finally not submitted.

'Names which you take and everything comes back.' This rushing back of memories is obviously important to him.

Similarly, when asked in this context how he manages to reconcile himself to the rapidly changing skyline of Singapore, his single-word reply is, 'Nostalgia!'[54] He speaks of travelling to Goa with its traces of old Portuguese culture or to Kyoto where the marqueed food stalls in the Nishiki Market remind him of old Singapore.

It is Singapore that gives him cohesion, holds him together and it is not surprising that the thought of losing his city spells to him the end of his poetic creativity,

> Deprived of you, history and sense
> Turn quicksilver. In my grieving side
> Grammars of living break their tense,
> Diminish tact, impatience, pride . . .[55]

It is a city where every slant of the light, every quirk of the topology is familiar to him, where he might look up to see eyes that pass him on the road and realize with a jolt that they are but extensions of his own.[56] Yet, even as the familiar merges with the familiar, as one street corner becomes another or a lace curtain blends into one from a different time, there is a sense of the same transparent void permeating everything. The void swallows details, returns an all-pervasive light. Every glance brings with it a sense of loss, a loss of separatedness.

---

[54] Interview 12 March 2018.
[55] *Temasek* from *A Third Map.*
[56] *For Peter Wee.*

V

STILL TRAVELLING

You get too much at last of everything: of sunsets, of cabbages, of love.

> —Aristophanes, *The Knights*

Now while the great thoughts of space and eternity fill me I will measure myself by them . . .

> —Walt Whitman, *Night on the Prairies*

I have a sin of fear, that when I have spun
My last thread, I shall perish on the shore;
But swear by thy self, that at my death thy son
Shall shine as he shines now, and heretofore;
And, having done that, thou hast done,
I fear no more.

> —John Donne, *A Hymn to God the Father*

Till the End of My Song

Different poets have been known to react differently to old age. Philip Larkin, the famous librarian-poet of England, had all but fulfilled his literary potential by fifty and was burnt out. In a few years he would fall into silence, remarking with weary sentimentality, 'What an absurd, empty life! And the grave yawns.'[57] An even younger Sylvia Plath for the last years of her life lived out her own pre-determined, self-destructive myth. Wordsworth and Auden fell into empty prolixity, others knew fears of poetic extinction even more crippling than the fear of death itself. It was a fear of 'inexistence', of the loss of senses and sensitivity, a tensed search for the revival of a once brilliant mind, now gone shallow, lacking in stirring obscurities.

Today Once More

Years ago, where that old Bedok road suddenly
Swung inland, I felt you breathe. Benedicting
Sunlight by the pillbox lit a curve in which I heard
My heart's first cry. It grew into a circling eagle,
Whose thermal eye kept clean our dome of blue.
Far below the tide rippled, turned and gripped,
Removing sand from under my feet. You held me
Citizen as I grew, from that wondering in awe
What made darkness come at noon, or why sea-salt
Bitterness, and the wind's lamentations, can cleanse.

Two points in time:
From there a tale of colony, war and occupation;
From here a past we made from careful politics
For better history, and bright embraceable evenings.

Hunting for a future leaves memories and images
Of crucial moments: gritty challenges which, for some,
Are high despair and doubt; a time to think of leaving,
Or stay and be damm'd, or prosper in our fashion.

---

[57]   James Booth, *Philip Larkin: Life, Art & Love* (NY: Bloomsbury Press, 2014), p. 398.

We re-arranged ourselves, besieged our hills, re-made
The contexts of our lives as we gardened city and island.
Now petal, shade, octaves in the night, and young faces,
Shift the mood and margins of our hopes, our seasons.
Side by side, old and young split Merlion thoughts, giving
Reasons, while savouring those two durians-on-the-bay.

Each generation has its songs and destinations that assert
A different destiny. Theirs more digital; keyboard-bound.
Mine mental abacus. No cables. Nothing battery powered
I learn, adapt; process words to stalk and refresh nostalgia.

Today, no smoke from burning half-dried wood to smudge
Our skyline's signature. Eyes tearful, not from fumes,
But the death of friends. Gopal and James now live in
That ever present past. So does Lim Boh Seng. I cross
The Padang as *banzais* echo again, rolling down city steps
As Coleman's demolished home haunts the new with gusto.
I taste the stalls in Hock Lam Street, feeling the chillies rise
As Ah Lau cuts his fruits. Foodcourts are far less friendly.
Regret? Yes and no. All is still here, as I pass the latest Bedok,
Knowing epiphany, tide, and crab are still a mile away,
Across our first reclamation, when land pushed back the sea.

It has been a long journey for ET since 1979 when *Ulysses by the Merlion* was published. Now in 2018 at the age of 85, he does not acknowledge the landmark year to have been a peak of his poetic career.[58] It merely coincided with a moment when for the first time he saw Singapore as a durable whole, an acquiescence that he found reflected within himself as well. Finally, the difference, the separation between his father's choice of the Malay *bangsawan* and his mother's choice of the Chinese Opera at the Happy World were reconciled. Unlike Caliban,

---

[58]   Interview 31 May 2018.

he found his release in his country's independence, contented to live within the two overlapping circles, linked by points of fusion. There was emerging unity. His release gave him confidence, he found hope in the 'hyphenated Singaporean', a new aspiration that the 'SG' part of the Singaporean's identity would gradually gain in importance and the country's ethnic inheritance would eventually be dissolved.

He had once been an admirer of Yeats' lyric enterprise. Like him, ET has continued to mingle a lifetime of service to the lyric Muse with vehement disclosures of his ongoing social attitudes. It is a persuasive vision which remains obdurately hitched to the fortune of his country. There have been criticisms, particularly hurtful when from those he considers intimate. He speaks of a 'frank conversation' with poet Lee Tzu Pheng, well known for her poems on Singapore.[59] She grumbled about him deserting midway his journey with the lyric Muse, of not walking down the proverbial poetic shoreline to struggle with his own daemons. His poetry has become too externalized, conscientious acts of will to feed his public purpose. Is he too much of a poet-laureate to be a poet at all?

In explanation, ET accedes to not having been able to evolve a style which is lyrical and yet public except rarely. At the same time, he also speaks of poetic responsibility. According to him, Singapore's government had worked out the economics of the country and yet there 'had to be those who would speak of the softer elements. The language, the poetry, the words. And I knew if I didn't write about it, no one else would to the same degree.' Hence came about his preoccupation with multiracialism, his discourse on language and indigenized English as a shared imaginative instrument. It gave him a rationale, a sense that in his public enterprise he rose above mere self-indulgence. To add legitimacy, he cautioned himself to base his poems on direct experiences, 'It was a lived experience for me. The poem *Little Boy Smoking* for instance, I actually saw it; it is a part of me. That's why these themes are very important to me.'

---

[59]   Ibid.

This also brings one to an aspect of ET which is most intriguing. Poets the world over have felt the gulf between the poet and the man. Larkin, for instance, at the height of fame, complained of 'making a good living but without a living at all.' The accumulation of wealth oppressed him, his public and professional commitments drove him into a private space that was claustrophobic in its insularity. ET too felt early the divide between his choice of private and public roles, the poems of *Gods Can Die* expressing some of his inner fragmentation. Yet in an interesting turn of thought, over the years he has allowed his public self to extend itself till it can accommodate his private self. Today he feels he is a composite whole with little inner conflict, 'Public is very private for me and at the same time very public.'[60] He might be playing different roles at different times—teacher, Dean, family man (an open-ended challenge for all men), friend (very important to me) and a Christian (work in progress)—but at every level according to him, he remains a poet, carrying the poet's language and sensitivity to every situation. At times he might be compelled to do a piece of work as a man that the poet in him does not enjoy. But that is where the division ends. Hence the strongly noticeable intertextuality between some of his prose and poetic pieces—they are inarguably distilled from the same imaginative energy. And hence also his sense of little conflict between religious and secular moral codes—he feels it is invariably the poetic code that wins![61]

Robert Pinsky in speaking of political poetry mentions the need a poet feels to respond to political change within his community.[62] It is this urgent need to answer that gives him a 'good sense' about his art. In this way the poet willingly ties himself down and yet reacts at the slightest inkling of social restraint. And if this sense of responsibility is not there, if his poetry is one of only protest

---

[60]   Ibid.

[61]   Discussed also in Ch. 1

[62]   *Politics and Poetic Value*, ed. Robert Von Hallberg (Chicago: University of Chicago Press, 1987), pp. 9–11.

and polemical didacticism then it subtly deadens his art. Thus, ET too remains tied to his community—he writes poetry which implicitly celebrates politically acceptable values and yet would balk at the idea of self-annihilating surrender, if there is ever an occasion. And so, post *Ulysses by the Merlion*, even while he allows his public self to engulf almost all of his private, the sense of tension remains. Surrender does not come easy and he seeks out different ways by which he can extend his sense of self. Hence his friends' poems, difficult imaginative metaphors of the self where he struggles to literalize his emotions. He speaks of his Buddhist friend, Boey Hock, who as a youngster unfailingly played the church organ every Sunday. Boey was the first of his friends to pass away. ET had watched him starving for oxygen in his bed, as he struggled with leukaemia. With his death a part of ET had also died. As he says, 'Friends are important because they act as feeders, they become extensions of yourself, a part of your perception.'[63]

On a similar vein he speaks of his travel poems, an easy way to venture out of the earlier provincialism of Singapore and seek out a universal cultural currency. He cites the example of an experience in Bagyo, Philippines, where he watched as American tourists threw coins at an old lady. As he saw her pick up the coins, her back bent with years of rice planting, he felt the old stirrings of anti-colonialism. ET could not stop himself from protesting and as he did so he sensed the crowd automatically dividing itself between Asians and non-Asians. Other Filipinos spoke up, came to stand behind him in natural solidarity. Such journeys are more mental than physical for him, they help him in relocating culture, extend sensibilities, enter other worlds. As he says, 'The individuals in any culture are good—they prefer to be good, not bad. And we have to establish these connections, bridges.'[64]

---

[63] Interview 31 May 2018.

[64] *Interlogue*, Vol. 7, ed. Peter Nazareth (Singapore: Ethos Books, 2008), p. 204.

His friends' poems as much as his travel poems are journeys that he makes to find himself, they are external symbols that anchor his inner self. Like a mountaineer's rope, they lead him to new destinations, discover inner obscurities.

Even as he has aged, this inner balance of private and public selves has become easier. What has not happened so easily, despite intense intellectual struggle, is teaching his unruly poetic mind to surrender. It is significant that he dedicated *A Third Map* (his fourth volume of poems, published after *Ulysses by the Merlion* in 1993) to his parents and wrote below their names, *Dono dedunt*—a Latin term with distinct religious connotations of surrender and devotion. The fact that there is conscious invocation of a mood of adoring piety in the context of his parents shows the intense need he felt at that time to succumb, to capitulate in all humility. He had been baptised in 1992, initiated into the idea of Christian faith and the complete surrender that it demands. Through his biblical poems he tries to enter into the spirit of Christianity like other religious poets and struggles to make space for invention in a devotional world where faith is fixed and delineated. For him every poem with a biblical theme is a personal journey, they teach him to rejoice in God's love, tell him how dangerous the human ego is. He says, 'The only question I still have is, why must all the apostles' words be treated as divine? I have difficulty in accepting this. As a poet I know what is inspired writing and what is not.'[65] But at the same time he also knows that any biblical poem he writes can never be the best for it is the prose of the Bible that he needs to contend with, the words of God himself.

Thus at eighty-five, his remains an active, vibrant, questioning mind. At times he does appear a touch pious, especially in the context of the younger generation. Sometimes his poems do take on a dated feel as he ruminates over the past a bit too much. At times one hears the struggle to assert an elevated poetic register against the drag of

---

[65]   Interview 31 May 2018.

despondent prose. Yet there is no weariness, no fake conclusions, maybe just some feeble lines. Most of all, he remains rooted in his own reality, never appears too effete to not be convincing. Thoughts of death come, but along with it comes a Lucretian belief that dying comes to all but 'death' to no one. The hunger for imaginative energy is still not over, there is no pathos in his last years. He still travels, looks forward with excitement to an imaginative conclusion to a poetic career, awaits a last flowering of his genius. The delightful literary critic of modern times, Harold Bloom, has said, 'Lastness is a part of knowing.'[66] ET, like at every stage of his life, still cannot wait to know.

Lyric Enterprise

As evening seals us,
This time with fervour,
It aches exceedingly.
. . . The road South deepens my
Yearning. The Beetle purrs
Uncharacteristically demur.
I pass Gunong Ledang there,
To the left. The night is black
But not dark. I still hold you.

Written in November 2015 for his wife, Swee Chin, the poem *Goodbye* was published in 2018. It forms a part of a series ET has taken to writing off and on when the mood suits him. Compressed, stylized, with emotions distilled to the richest purity, the short poems are dedicated to his wife. They go back to a time when he was courting her, a time of youth, of responding to life with sensibility rather than pragmatism, a time when life was bathed in

---

[66] *Till I End My Song: A Gathering of Last Poems*, ed. Harold Bloom (NY: Harper Collins, 2010), p. xvii.

limpid transparency and hope. Intensely personal, the poems are a part of his lyric enterprises, but more importantly they convey a unity of mood that ET at the time of the experience was perhaps not aware of.

Since the publication of *Ulysses by the Merlion*, ET has published four key volumes of poems: *A Third Map* (1993), *Friend* (2003), *Still Travelling* (2008) and *A Gathering of Themes* (2018). As the titles suggest, they are on different themes but what brings them together is the gestalt identity they hold forth. It was this identity that was his central discovery in *Ulysses by the Merlion*. In the Merlion he had seen expressed the multiracialism of Singapore and come to recognize the same in himself, manifest in growing ongoing processes from the early 1950s, expressed in the smallest aspects of life. For example, he knows, unlike his father's, his own cravings are distinctly multiracial—he looks for a proper *lontong* in a street-side stall and rarely for the plain-vanilla *thosai*. It is this third identity born of syncretic cultures that constitute the 'third map' of his existence. Thus, if *Ulysses by the Merlion* was his bildungsroman, then the later volumes are variations of the essential unity he had discovered within himself. And his lyric poems, though not too numerous, are the simplest, most crystalline expressions of this unity.

Long years back Cavafy had walked down the streets of Alexandria and looked outward as well as inward.[67] As he gazed, Alexandria had summoned up for him his youth and all of Greece of the recent past. When he gazed inward, he had found memories of the lost days in his heart and so his outer world and inner world had forged a partnership and lyric poetry was born which were true representations of his present-day reality. Similarly, as ET stares into the darkness of Gunong Ledang and up at the twinkling Mount Ophir, he experiences again the warm

---

[67]   W.R. Johnson *The Idea of Lyric: Lyric Modes in Ancient and Modern Poetry* (Berkeley: University of California Press, 1982), p. 11.

intimacy of holding Chin in his arms and it is the throbbing Beetle, uncharacteristically docile under his touch which becomes not only the metaphor for his ladylove but also the vehicle that takes him to her.

Lyric poetry that originated in Greek literature as poems to be sung to the lyre, popular in the island of Lesbos as intensely individual expressions, were later taken up by English poets.[68] In their poems all narrative or descriptive stories, all moralizing and analysis became secondary as communication of the emotional experience took centre stage. However, it was ET's favourite Yeats who actually reinvented the lyric poem. In his hands the landscape, the story, the poet and the audience are held together in unity as they go through the emotional experience that transmutes them to form a new whole.

Some of this lyric potential is evident in ET's early poems from *Rib of Earth*. Whereas there it is present more inchoately, in some of his later personal pieces of *Still Travelling* it is more of a consciously perfected art. Of course, in between there is a long hiatus. Tzu Pheng refers to this when she calls *Gods Can Die* 'extroverted poetry' with little self-searching.[69] In defence ET says, 'Lyric poem—that's where I started and that's the kind of poetry I like to write but I got sucked into writing about the nation, because I knew if I didn't, nobody else would.'[70]

Thus, in *Still Travelling* is the poem *Chin's Garden—I*, where in his wife's absence, as the substitute gardener ET tends her garden. He is the compliant subordinate, merely obeying her instructions,

> Water in the morning or when the sun is low,
> Just as evening begins releasing colours.

---

[68] *The Lyric Mood: An Anthology of Lyric Poetry*, Ed. R.K. Mottram (London: Oxford University Press, 1965), Introduction.

[69] Lee Tzu Pheng's Foreword to *Gods Can Die*, 1977.

[70] Interview 11 June 2018.

But as birds return to favourite trees and leaves which were yellow yesterday, curl brown, it does not take him long to enter their world. He feels with the extreme concentration of the moment, the mid-day heat that lingers between blades of grass, the flashing iridescence of honey birds, the moist molecules that rise into that tented air. He has always found it easy to cross boundaries and enter other worlds and here as he does so, in the chiku and custard apple, in the garlic creeper and allemandes, he finds the presence of his wife. The beauty of his surroundings, the silence, the fragrance—all suggest her. It is not only her physical presence, but the gradual unveiling of her soul. The garden suggests the careful meticulousness with which she tends her plants, her judicious vigilance in having them catch or miss the sun, the selfless love in her touch as she untwists branches that a careless wind has dishevelled. So, like children, the straining leaf, the petal, the tendril search his face for hers and in the fervent coming together of the last few lines, ET finds in Chin's garden the transcending unity of God's creation and man's love for it:

> You cool the breeze, hum songs adoring
> His walk in the Garden where all was one. Yours is.

Like the clear shaft of yellow light that brightens up many of William Turner's later canvasses, this is a transcending, enhancing unity that ties together the poet, the reader and the landscape in a sharply transmuting moment. And it is Chin's gentle humanity that is the correlative that takes us there.

Friend, bring out the sun

Friendship is one of the most important experiences for ET, so much so that he counts being a friend to be one of the most crucial roles he has undertaken during his lifetime, along with being a father or a husband. As he says of friends,

Before then we rely on him,
Each morning, to bring the sun.[71]

Consequently there is an entire anthology of friends' poems and yet what is intriguing is that some of the poems written to the closest friends remain an exploration of external experiences that they have shared, rather than a delving down deep into a more private space, casting aside the literary or intellectual clutter to look at the silent void that lies within. The rationale he provides is perhaps the unadorned truth, 'Some of the most important friends' poems will never be written because I don't have the vocabulary to externalize my feelings, certain subjects are so much a part of you—you just want to leave them there.'[72] So while the friends' poems are rhetorically confident exercises, written at a stage when he has perfected his craft and there is no falsity about them, born as they are of direct experiences, they lack in a certain plumbing of the depths of abstract existentialism. What the poems do achieve is they create a latticework of experiences around the poet and as ET traverses from one point to the next of the web, he extends himself to access a new idea of poetic inspiration, a further intensification of a personal relationship. Through this sharing his friends become important signifiers to the essential unity of life.

Fifteen Years After
for Shamus Frazer

That day when you left,
Taking for the safe keeping of us,
My figure from Bali,
Smooth, beckoning goddess
Urged to serenity by the lotus she stood on,
You too were poised in the brittle afternoon . . .

---

[71] *Friend*, from volume of same name.
[72] Interview 31 May 2018.

That day of incense I have kept to this.

You died recently. They say you died.

But no matter.
Image and breath persist,
Grow as I grow, would not suffer the mind's quip.
Your beard, dubious, smelling of cheese and beer,
Affectionate, still presides; your voice pursues,
Sweet or harsh, but ever itself.
Many sit in their rooms, remembering how
You took us through Christabel, Sohrab and Rustum,
Death's Jest-Book, The, Raven,
Brought new worlds to meet our own.
You lived—beautiful, precarious
Feeding us irrevocably on your self
While other gods shed their skin, withdrew,
Taking their notes with them.

But teacher and friend, white man,
What are they doing to you,
They, who come after?
Smaller, paler, full of themselves,
Suave, side burned, tousled? Setting up trade
In principles, freedoms, intellectual honesties?

They are eloquent,
These revivers of clichés, these late-comers,
Who strike a neat phrase, write letters to the press.

Old Shamus,
Your image and breath slip,
You are dying now,
When I need you most to live.

One of the most effective poems of the volume is *Fifteen Years After*, dedicated to his old English teacher at Victoria School, Shamus Frazer. Frazer was the Scotsman who was definitely the most important literary influence ET had, without whom he may not have gone into English at all, the good science student that he always was. It was in 1950 that he met Frazer, around the same time when he started dabbling in verse. Describing him ET says, Frazer had an excellent voice and would sometimes walk into the class reciting a poem, 'Poetry from the mouth of Frazer sounded beautiful, magical.'[73] He would rush through the set syllabus because many a lesson were spent discussing poems by Coleridge or Wordsworth—the *Lucy* poems or *Kubla Khan*—pieces which were not a part of the syllabus. The entire class was ill-prepared for the 'O' level exams, but he bred in them a permanent love for literature. His enthusiasm was infectious.

Fifteen Years After is a poem that moves from closure to closure. It starts with the day Frazer left Singapore, a day almost religious to ET, 'A day of incense I have kept to this.'[74] He had asked ET for his most precious piece of art and taken with him a statue from Bali, one of a goddess 'Urged to serenity by the lotus she stood on.' From here the poem moves to commemorate Frazer's death. But then disbelief at the news dawns on the poet and like the closures at the beginning, there is a corresponding movement in the second half of the poem as it moves from continuance to continuance. ET first moves to his youth when Frazer had 'Brought new worlds to meet our own', when almost like a parent he had allowed his students to feed 'irrevocably' on his self. The sadness at this thought triggers a peevish resentment, a comparison to other 'white' men who have come after Frazer, selfish men who feed on the milk and honey of the land and ET ends with a vow never to let go of the urgent need that he feels for his friend and mentor,

---

[73] *Peninsular Muse*, ed. Mohammad A. Quayum (Bern, Oxford: Peter Lang, 2007), p. 35.

[74] *Fifteen Years After* and *After the Leaving* from *Friend*.

You are dying now.
When I need you most to live.

It is ET's need that will continue to keep Frazer alive and it is the
same yearning need that holds this poem of contrasts together—the
closure and continuation, youth and maturity, Asian and European
worlds. The day Frazer left, ET had felt a poised rigidity in him as he
went statue in hand, holding memories of ET and Asia close to him.
At the end, ET retorts with the same taut tensity as he decides not to
let his friend sink to obscurity. He will continue to feed off the poet's
literary energies and the latticework will grow around them, perhaps
bringing them to a point of new discovery in the future.

After the Leaving...
for Ee Tiang Hong

There are two countries here:
One securely meets the eye;
The other binds your heart.

This is Perth, and yet Malacca.
Outside, suddenly spring arrives
In many wild, surprising flowers.
But no chempaka, no melor
Show that beauty of the heart.
You have lost more hair, though
Your spectacles perch as usual,
Looking quizzical, slightly anxious.

Beyond King's Park, the Swan
Whose neck nestles among vineyards,
Ministers to your dreaming home
To which I go again, in ceremony,

Remembering . . . your ukulele
Mastering the restless crabs,
Sunset upon the brow of Panteh 2;
Our shared tobacco; images of

Heroic days, court and kampong;
That great Tranquerah mosque,
St Paul's Hill, Sam Po's Well,
And other abodes of our gods.
But here the roads are happily
Waltzing with Matilda, leading
Through miles of bush to Laverton,
Abandoned mines, receding purple hills.

And as you hear the recurring
Soul of Voss adventuring Ayers Rock,
The Dream-time, purifying deserts,
Shore, sky and hinterland are yours.
But you return to Heeren Street,
Ancestral rooms, intricate histories,
Starting with a distant fracture
Of law, of order one quiet noon

Along uncoiling Amoy Streets,
Where the migrant, restless spirit
Took passion to an alien land.
You feel a deep possession.
Seven generations of the blood
Have stirred into the earth,
Gave sinew, fought fevers.
Held down swamps, added
Fertile patterns to the land,
Made the dragon speak
The brown language of the

Constant, Southern winds.

After the riots and the edicts,
You cried in the days of blight.
To leave again, after seven generations,
You must know so bitterly,
Is surely to return.

A similar poem of 'no closure' is *After the Leaving*, dedicated to Ee
Tiang Hong. Tiang Hong was a friend he met at the University,
with whom he discussed his poems the most, even more so than
Phui Nam or Tan Han Hoe.[75] He was one friend with whom never a
harsh word was exchanged, they had debates but not disagreements.
By the time ET caught up with Tiang Hong in University, the likes
of Goh Sin Tub, Beda Lim and Wang Gungwu had already moved
on to their chosen vocations, 'Fortunately, Tiang Hong was sitting
his Finals in English and History and was to stay for another two
years. We became firm friends . . .' They soon shared similar views
on the function of a Malayan literature in English and it was with
Tiang Hong that ET edited an issue of the *New Cauldron*, printed
two thousand copies, rented a car and sold it in schools, door-to-
door from Johor Bahru to Penang.

Tiang Hong was a Peranakan from Tranquerah, Malacca,
who would later feel compelled to leave Malaysia when Malay
rights became a bone of contention for non-Malays. As a seventh-
generation Chinese, he felt himself to be more of a son of the soil
than many Malays. Yet he would emigrate to Perth and consequently,
implications of identity and the conflict between home and exile
would provide the central themes for his poems.

After the Leaving opens at exactly this point with a mention of
the two worlds,

---

[75] *Peninsular Muse*, p. 57.

There are two countries here:
One securely meets the eye;
The other binds your heart.

A surprising spring has arrived outside Tiang Hong's dreaming home in Perth—the flowers are strange in their splendour while the chempaka and melor from his native land still nestle in his heart. ET returns to his friend's home 'in ceremony' as he used to visit his house in Tranquerah in Malacca, when Tiang Hong's mother would get medicinal herbs and make a nourishing soup for the two scraggy boys, both smokers.[76] A ukulele resting against the wall acts as the unifier of the past and the present—the times when the youngsters used to look out of the window to see the Methodist School girls walk past and Tiang Hong's mother would chide, 'Ayo, you boys!' and the present when the two elderly friends talk through the night and then breakfast on Australian bacon and marmalade. The double image of the neck of the Swan River, bringing to mind gliding twin birds on the edge of the water becomes a metaphor to their friendship.

But then suddenly do the waltzing blue waters of the Matilda Bay appear too tame, a bit too brazen in its gaiety? The heroic days of 'court and kampong' are long over when they felt with the keenness of youthful angst social and racial divides, when they conversed with their gods—the chaste ideals that gave them an uplifting righteousness and made life worth a fight? The placidity of a mellowed friendship is replaced by a searching restlessness in the second half as the poet returns to Heeren Street with an urgency, the tensed uncoiling of Amoy Street where seven generations have stirred their blood into the earth, in this homeland of swamps and fevers, of dragons and brown language and southern winds. The end is foreshadowed in the standing ukulele of the beginning—there is no escaping Malacca, they leave only to return,

---

[76] Interview 11 June 2018.

> You must know so bitterly, my friend,
> Is but surely to return.

The poem could have been written off as a poem of passing nostalgia, if it was not placed against an essay ET had written in 1968 for a Commonwealth Conference in Brisbane. Ironically, in the essay while comparing literary styles of two Malay poets, Tiang Hong and Mohammad Haji Salleh, he mentions that while for the former the past is important, his freedom and modernity are based on delivery from the past. And towards the end he goes on to vociferously argue that being tied to a community identity, severely restricts a poet,

> To take to it [community identity] would be to risk his personal identity, his own image of himself . . .
> And what profiteth a man if he gaineth National Identity, but loseth the power of his poetry?[77]

But as he discovers in *After the Leaving,* a poet draws his power from his community identity. Traditions might be diluted with time, fortified with syncretic understanding, but finally, there is no escaping it.

Edward Said in speaking of later works of a poet refers to a new spirit of reconciliation and serenity, a serenity that is born of not harmony and resolution but a certain sense of intransigence, difficulty and unresolved contradiction. Thus if *After the Leaving* ends in a moment of restless calm, an unwilling reconciliation after the mention of 'riots and edicts', then it is this sense of intransigence that ET reaches, walking down the latticework with his friend. And it is this intransigence that leaves the poem open-ended.

---

77   ET, 'Malayan Poetry: Two Examples of Sensibility and Style', *National Identity: Papers Delivered at the Commonwealth Literature Conference, University of Queensland, Brisbane, 9-15 August 1968* (London, Melbourne: Heinemann Educational, 1970), p. 187-96.

Visitor from Galilee

The very basis of Christianity if it was to be summed up in one sentence lies in the acceptance of divine sovereignty, the depth and scope of which is nowhere more evident than in the passion of Christ. It is the horrifying execution of one man that unleashed for the next three centuries in Rome a power to suffer and to love and to this day continues to shape the world. The single event takes us away from the cause to the purpose or meaning of the death. The apostle John referred to Jesus as 'the Word'—he was an embodiment of God's Word and in embracing the death God ordained, he embraced God himself. Christianity is all about this willing submission to a divine purpose and ET has spent a large part of his life trying to perfect obedience, a lesson that has not been learnt easily.

As he is fond of saying, ET was never an atheist.[78] He always knew and believed in a creator but with the panoply of religious influences in his family, it was more of an eclectic belief. It was with his conversations with his friend, fellow academic, linguist and lay minister, Jonathan Webster, that his faith took firmer roots.[79] They spent considerable time in each other's company during ET's stint in the City University of Hong Kong. Subsequently, on 22 August 1992, yet another friend had him baptised long after his wife and children had turned to serious Christian practice. It was S. Dhanabalan, former high-profile Singapore politician and Elder at the Bukit Panjang Gospel Chapel who ministered over the baptism, gifting him a copy of the King James' Bible with an inscription of the following words,

> Ye have not chosen me, but I have chosen you, and ordained you, that ye should go and bring forth fruit, and that your fruit

---

[78] Multiple interviews.
[79] Interview 11 June 2018; Lily Rose Tope, 'The Theory of Feeling: The Biblical Poems of Edwin Thumboo', *Essays on Edwin Thumboo*, ed. Jonathan J. Webster (Singapore: Ethos Books, 2012), p. 85.

should remain: that whatsoever ye shall ask of the Father in my
name, he may give it you. (John 15:16).[80]

That day strengthened a journey that has continued to the present.
The main struggle has been the quietening of the mind, acceptance
of a superior ordinance. He has come a long way from the distinctly
'cheeky' *Moses* or *Commercial Politics* of *Gods Can Die* when, self-
admittedly, he 'just knew the Bible, that's it,' when he would crack
jokes about Christianity, though never about God. It has caused him
considerable anguish to come not to the conclusion that there is a God,
but to realize and accept the thought that the God is Christian. The
belief has come gradually with a deeper reading of the scriptures and
the understanding that Jesus' life is actually a fulfilment of prophecies
of the Old Testament and that the prophecies were not interpolations
that can be discarded as mere inferences. In this, his study of Teutonic
scholarship of synoptic gospels as well as of English theologians like
B.H. Streeter or Charles Olmstead have been of assistance.

The result is a spate of biblical poems very different from his
earlier ones of *Gods Can Die*. Like his explorations of identity,
here too the poems are an attempt on his part to enter the world
of spirituality as much for personal reasons as for aesthetic ones. It
is interesting that a theme that surfaces recurrently is one of love,
that however great the sin, God's mercy is implied to be greater
and that love is the only path to reach Him. It is His infinite love
for man. It is also interesting to note the conflict between poet
and man. As a poet, in the tradition of Dr Johnson or Donne or
Blake, he is aware that he fights a losing battle, over the wit and
argument of his biblical poems hangs the knowledge of the futility
of his argument. Like Eliot had said that poetry of which the subject
matter is the doctrines of religion, can give only a 'limited kind

---

[80]   Email ET, 14 August 2018.

of pleasure'.[81] But on the other hand is the man who through his poetry fights his own religious battle and seeks an extension and fulfilment of himself. Thus, he tries to keep his literary impulse as strong as his religious impulse, exploring obscure corners, the complex interrelating of characters and historical patterns. Often, he goes beyond the famous laconic quality of biblical narratives to ponder over unexpressed psychological depths, indicating the divine election intervening in the accepted orders of society and nature. At all times he chooses moments of closeness to the divinity when in love and in grace God establishes his control over his people and leads them into reverential obedience.

By the Waters of Babylon
I
Behold, I have seen it, saith the Lord . . .
Cut off thine hair, O Jerusalem, and cast
It away, and take up a lamentation . . .
Your anger burns, O Lord; your wrath
Is crucible; save us, your people; break
Us in love, repair; we sinned exceedingly,
Whoring after strange gods; a rebellious
House, defiled, whose doors open wrong.
Yet, your words to Ezekiel who spoke.
Still your people; our feet seek Jerusalem.
Walls have fallen; jackals howl;
Scorpions scurry; vultures soar.

II
By the rivers of Babylon, there we sat down,
Yea, we wept, when we remembered Zion . . .
Our captors required of us songs . . .

---

81   *The Divine Poems of John Donne*, ed. Helen Gardner (Oxford: Clarendon Press, 1964), p. xv.

Among the willows, harps unstrung,
Silent, no rhythms rising; empty heaven.
Sad, strange waters lap bitter shores,
As they come, smiling into leprous days
Wanting music as we lament. Yet, squeeze
Our hearts, strengthen through sorrow,
O Lord. Great is thy faithfulness.
The Lord, ever my portion, knows my soul;
Therefore will I hope in him, even before fire.
Then will I cause you to dwell in this place,
In the land that I gave to your fathers,
For ever and ever. Your spirit lives in us,
Everlasting to everlasting.

ET uses lines from the Psalms (137:1) for his poem entitled, *By the Waters of Babylon*, a poem that describes the sadness of the Judean people exiled far from their homeland. Memories of the great ordeal of the Babylonian deportation, the crack of the whip, the rumble of wheels, the flash of swords are still fresh in the minds of the political and intellectual elite of Judah as they bemoan the downfall of Israel. The River Euphrates flows through the city while the opulent palace of Nebuchadnezzar on its banks becomes a symbol of decadence for the Jewish people as they live on in the hope that someday they will return to their beloved homeland.[82] As in the New Testament, in the poem too homeland and exile fit into the symbolical framework of heaven and earth as the lines resound with Jewish lament: 'Sad, strange waters lap bitter shores' and the 'leprous days' pass painfully. Yet the people of Jerusalem are strengthened by only one thing—their faith in their God's mercy. Hope, the true essence of spirituality, never ceases to rise in their hearts, perhaps a sign of God's blessing,

---

[82]   *Great Events of the Bible Times* (NY: Doubleday & Co. Inc., 1987), p. 108.

> The Lord, ever my portion, knows my soul;
> Therefore will I hope in him . . .
> Everlasting to everlasting.

Just as *By the Waters of Babylon* is ultimately a celebration of the bond of love that holds God and man together, where the only true exile is where one is debarred from the presence of God, *Jonathan before Gilboa* is a story of the selfless love that binds man and man, friend and friend, a bond that eventually leads one to God. Dedicated to the linguist Jonathan Webster, the poem foregrounds the friendship of Jonathan and David against the backdrop of an Israel divided by fratricidal skirmishes. It is the scene of Saul's last battle with the Philistines, when the mighty King's heart trembles violently as he climbs to the top of Mount Gilboa and looks in dismay at the expanse of the Philistine army.[83] He is a weakened king, who misses the advice of his old mentor, Samuel, is troubled by the prophecy of an occult practitioner.

In ET's poem, the scene shifts to Saul's son, Jonathan who knows with uncanny premonition that death awaits them. It is going to be the final encounter, an encounter made all the more deadly because his friend the almighty David, with his band of 600 followers, had joined the enemy as Philistine vassal. An empty hush dallies with awaiting death in a battle that will take the life of not only Jonathan himself and his father but also his brothers Abinadab and Malchishua. Saul, the founding King of Israel will be left virtually heirless and the house of Saul will be left at the mercy of David. And yet, even as images of death darken Jonathan's mind, he cannot find it in himself to berate his friend David, he knows in his heart that David, whose 'God-led heart slew Goliath', who in his innocence has countered the festering royal jealousy of King Saul, will remain superior. As ET says, 'Jonathan is very important for me. The greatest

---

[83] *The Great People of the Bible and How They Lived* (UK: *Reader's Digest*, 1966), p. 72.

thing in Jonathan is his love, he has qualities of a Christ in primitive form. His father is king, by rights he should be king too. But David takes the throne and yet Jonathan is not jealous. Instead he supports David, he is happy to walk behind.'[84]

> The poem ends in the tranquillity of Jonathan's acceptance, a calm
> that ET hopes to achieve,
> Night falls. I have no shadows left. Only that empty
> Hush dallying with death before battle. I yearn for still
> Waters and perfect Garden walk at Eventide. Selah.

It is not so much the fear of death but the preparation for death, both for poet and his protagonist and this starts with the calm of acceptance.

Revisiting

There is something liberating about later works. This is when the artist has a fuller understanding of his weltanschauung, knows well the expanse of both his outer and inner worlds of creative energy. He finds it easy to lift off from his moorings and make a transition from one world to the other. The outer world is beautiful in the density of its familiar details, but the inner world is even more radiant with the thoughts and memories and moods that they evoke. The details he dwells on but only for the short while it takes him to make the transition. And then it is like floating on a ray of light, a rippling blue expanse of translucent limitlessness where borders are but sleeping embankments which lead to other rivers, another stream of thought.

Later works is all about expressing this inner luminosity. This often takes the form of abstract expressions in visual artists. Thus, as a prime example of Turner's mature style are canvasses where the objects—be it the mast of a ship or a steam engine are barely

---

[84]   Interview 20 June 2018.

discernible. Instead he uses oils even more transparently to create the effect of pure light—the light shimmering on water, the radiance of skies and fires—the light which to Turner was the emanation of God's spirit. Similarly, in the artwork of the Singapore painter, Lim Tze Peng, as old age confined him to his studio and he shuffled through old memories in search of new inspiration, he found his paintings were a departure from his earlier practice, turning more and more towards abstract expressionism.

This is exactly the kind of escape into incandescence that ET speaks of in *Memories—II.* A stretching tranquillity on the brown banks of a stream in stillness brings to mind the rugged, comforting face of his grandfather. From here it is just a short flight of stairs through a couple of olfactory images—a slug of opium, a pot of fragrant tea and the poet surges into the unending,

> Above, two eagles ride thermals of your thoughts,
> Their widespread wings inscribing free-geometry.
> I rise into that unending, ripple blue, the sky's rush,
> The colour of your surge. I cling happily.

A similar poem of revisiting is the recent *Bukit Panjang: Hill, Village, Town.* He turns yet again to his old haunt, Singapore and searches for fresh inspiration. If in the Merlion he had sighted the racial and cultural harmony of Singapore, then the Bukit Panjang Hill becomes a site of geographical unity.[85] He speaks of the spine of the long hill which runs through a large section of the city, passing the University's Bukit Timah Campus and ending only downtown near Cathay Theatre. It has different roads with different names cutting across—at Jurong, the Ford Factory, Singapore Polytechnic or the 6th Avenue but the single spine, supine like a sleeping dragon remains a unifying symbol.

---

[85]   Ibid.

Part I of *Bukit Panjang: Hill, Village Town*

Long Hill . . . way up, semi-north:
Time-traveller; master of winds: you
Culled our seasons years before we
Glimpsed your contours. You
Rolled south to be the tip of Mother Asia,
Picking up names like Bukit Batok. You
Finally stopped for tectonic breath, at Mt
Sophia; your last spur is Fort Canning.
Still steady stately un-stressed, you
Our vigilant secret dragon saw further
Than Brit radars, tireless atop your peaks.
They genuflexed setting sun, rising moon,
Trying to spot Konfrontasi: a word, a fear,
A rant, an impunity that briefly sired a little
Neighbourly bloodiness. Pray wars have
Killed themselves, that skirmishes and riots
Miss our little red dot while we work to
Push coasts against the tide, flats higher,
Float IPOs, plant splendours-in-the-park,
Though we are yet to parcel out the sky.
Granite, soil, sub-soil; beds of moss: you
Flew our flag umpteen years; covenanted
Ten faiths and more, aligned and bonded
Immigrant syllables for our daily bread.
That we, too, did, as undergrads scouting
Wild mid-50 ridges, skirting colonial camps,
As butterflies rode winds, tilting to joust
Fragrant moments as swifts snatched morsels.
When we got merdeka and you, sub judice,
We tickled your knuckles and your toes;
Bit and dressed them; trimmed; dressaged;
Progressed; installed occasional oddities.

Those were . . . the days . . . my friend
Not the ones . . . with . . . deadly ends.

ET is not new to place poems. He has written extensively about
Singapore landmarks, the poems on the National Library for instance
where the library becomes a symbol of Singapore's knowledge
economy, a reason for its invincible growth. Here too he tries to
capture the spirit of the hill, portraying it both as a geological entity
as well as a symbol that holds together not only the urbane city built
on principles of order and regularity but also primeval, vegetative
processes of birth and decay, morning mists, long-rooted Jurassic loam
and threatening darkness. The visible setting becomes a complete
world, a cosmology of sentiments and consciousness shaped by the
location. For the Bukit Panjang Hill has been a part of Singapore
history, its resolute spine spearing together the times of the 'vigilant
secret dragon' as well as the times of the 'Brit radars', the Konfrontasi
to the modern times when development has wiped out the rich
variety of regional differences, replacing them with homogenized,
'efficient' settings—'regular brick blocks carefully aligned'. Like the
hill runs parallel to the city, so does ET's life-experience run parallel
to the country's history. It starts with when during war his father
worked for the MAS and ends at the doorstep of the Bukit Panjang
Gospel Chapel where he was baptised. In between it spurs during
his university days when with his friends he would trek the hill,
when rose-apples, rambutans and chikus juiced his shirt, when faces
'beamed innocence'.

However, it is neither the theme of unity nor the fact that the
poet's personal experiences run parallel with Singapore history that
make the poem remarkable. It is the fact that, despite it being another
of his 'place' poems, the setting of the poem does not enjoy the same
status as in his earlier poems. Setting is not overemphasized, it is
not a part of a declamation like in earlier pieces where he claimed
Singapore as a part of his national identity. He has decided to put
the minor irritant of colonialism aside. And so, setting is merely

a part of a shared, experienced milieu, a familiar and meaningful backdrop that is the cause of resonance. He is already reconciled to the wholeness of his identity, the concept of nationalism has finally been outlived.

It is also significant that he depicts the narrator as descending rather than climbing up the hillside. From the peak where the hill is 'Time-traveller', 'master of winds', from where can be viewed the contours of its slopes it is a long and meandering climb down in real terms and in terms of memory to where Singapore lies, complacent with success, spread out at the foot of the hill, smug with a self-congratulatory flatulence,

> Improvements? Perhaps. One thing's certain.
> You are getting plump with amenities.

There is a sense of calm, gentle rhythm, a languidness in the words which indicate a harmonious coexistence. There is little conflict between past, present and future, between primeval nature and the new chiselled skyline of the city. It is a new city with a new support system.

It is this new calm, an acceptance of change that makes it a poem of 'revisiting'. There is no sense of fragmentation or displacement in the debilitating effects of urbanization. Instead the recent developments are a part of a pattern of growth and evolution, another opportunity for creative hybridization. Just as the poet continues to travel by the MRT that criss-crosses through the city, the city too continues to grow and change,

> Soon the MRT arrives, me still travelling . . .
> Long Hill . . . way up, semi-north, time adventurer;
> Master of winds, culling our seasons, in all mood
> And weather, as we glimpse your changing contours.
> You will be here, expanding, when we
> Have gone.

For the poet there can be only death, no dying. The cycle of life will continue and by participating in the physicality of existence he hopes to transcend it.

Still Travelling

The traveller as a leitmotif has been a part of ET's literary vision right from the outset. This is because travelling holds an almost sacred place for him. It is *The Cough of Albuquerque*, one of his early poems that holds the key to this. Inspired by his 1954 trip with Professor Tregonning to Wat Arun on the banks of the Chao Praya River, he had written,

> Lord Buddha, shaman with the wheel
> Was in the loaves of Christ.

The temple of the Sun God had stirred something deep inside, he had seen the underlying aquifer of grace that waters every faith and arrived at one of his first formulations: the distinction between form and substance—that forms can differ, but substance cannot. The formulation had held true through his studies of not only religions, but cultures and histories and even human stereotypes and he had increasingly felt that it was the traveller who was best equipped to see these founding unities. This was because it was the traveller who crossed boundaries, entered other worlds, like St Thomas visited another country as an apostle and ended up understanding it as well as his own. This is why he speaks of Cavafy in Alexandria or Hanuman who transcends borders to enter China as Wu Kong. This is also why *A Passage to India* remains one of his favourite novels— the climactic scene in the Marabar Caves where words are reduced to incommunicable echoes, which possess nothing but a quintessential nothingness older than creation. It is in the caves that the characters stumble upon reality, the truth that lies within themselves far below the barriers erected in pursuit of imperialism or theological conformism.

In ET's words it becomes,

> We need to build these bridges because in every culture, I am convinced there is a centre, a humanistic centre. The humanistic centre sometimes is outward-looking, sometimes inward-looking. There is a chance for communication between these centres . . . there is this kind of penetration, not necessarily agreement, but understanding.[86]

It is perhaps an understanding of this basic universal unity that makes it easier for ET to reconcile his own inner differences, why he says, 'When you are half this and half that, you don't become a split personality as a result—you are a functional whole.'[87] It is this essential unity that Magdalena Tulli refers to when describing the city of Warsaw as a cosmology of humanity—as one street corner becomes another or a lace curtain blends into one from a different time, there is a sense of the same transparent void permeating everything. The void swallows details, returns an all-pervasive light—the same golden sun that engulfs Turner's later paintings.

Thus, ET straddles two continents in his poem, *Take a Plane*, in his journey to understand two conflicting cultures. On facing pages appear two parts of the poem—one in the Suvarnabhumi International Airport of Thailand and the other in New York. In the first we hear the righteous ring in his poetic voice as young American undergraduates berate a group of Afghans—softly elegant in their flowing white jellabiyas. 'I wonder where these goats are from?' they laugh complacent in their foreign cynicism even as the quiet group of bearded men hug and part, sharing a little secret. But on the facing page the site shifts to NYC, the

---

[86]   *Interlogue*, Vol. 7, ed. Peter Nazareth, p. 166.
[87]   Interview 2 January 2018.

Twin Towers and the thought of 'all that instant dying' where 'tragic loss lay flat in images'. The white of the jellabiyas is reflected in the crested waves of the harbour waters, the group of American youth from Thailand—he sees them strewn all around, this is their homeland and despite the sunny winds, he sees the descending darkness,

> Pain still circulates; finds its own moments, words,
> Perhaps when we line along to a homeward plane.'

Yet another travel poem is *Little India*. Though set within Singapore, it gives the feeling of a little detour just as the real Little India does. It is also a poem that dwells on the theme of form and substance as ET sets out to discover the centrality of a culture, on the way deftly capturing the essential duality of Little India—its outer veneer of busy commerce as a community pursues its destiny and the inner quietness that can be sensed only by residents. The 'circuits of electronic deals' which find their counterpart in temple bells and 'self-renewing' hearts raised in prayer. The physical duality leads to a deeper reflection on the duality that is inherent to every culture—where outer forms vary with time and place, but the bedrock of essential truths remain unchanged. Thus with the tidal waves of passion of every age the way Indian culture manifests itself has changed—there have been the times of the great battles of Kurukshetra, the colonial cultures of Kambuja or Champa, the expanding kingdoms of the Chola dynasty or the touristy souvenirs which are sold in kiosks now. But all through, the central giving heart of India has remained the same, rooted in religion, in gracefully memorialized metaphysics and freely shared divinity. It is significant that ET dedicates the poem to his friend Dhanabalan and his wife of Teochew ancestry, Christine. They beautifully portray the duality of the poem, the humanistic centres of two cultures held together by a bond of love.

Beyond

river mouth, jade-green valley door,
bird on the wing, crinkles in our lives,
is a some-how room. Without walls,
cracks, keyboard, compromise, report.
There, behind shutters, ego-id-super ego
argue to unlock, control, deploy, relay
revelations. Free of echoes and semantic
by-ways, they get re-born. Revise their Tao.
Ours too. Harmonious once more, my heart
and inner self scale down. My shirt is simple.
My pen, soft-tipped black. My poems less
Knotty, shorter. My mind balanced in deep
glow where clear waters up-lift rainbows.
Closed by fresh imagining, my eyes see
clean. Starlight is brief. Days are fervour.
New towns bloom lilac and jacaranda. Little
India is Divali. Orchard Road Chrismassy.
The news is economy, share indexes, fusion,
upgrades, the Next Fifty. We project, scenario
plan. Shave margins of error.
I will not be here.
Except for words, leave nothing. Shift for clues
to that room. You need it. It is you . . . and us . . .
Que Sara Sara

Another poem of an internal journey is *Beyond*. After a long hiatus
of some of his poems from *Rib of Earth*, he is again alone, looking
inward. There he had stared into the waters of Ayer Biru, a picnic
spot desolate of campsters and mused,

Blue waters, I mutter,
Blue waters.

It was a time when he sought a purpose in his life and found it in nationalism. Now he looks at 'beyond' life, but the tone of earnest solemnity remains the same, it is an equally interesting moment in life. And maybe the poet recognizes the similarity of mood for the opening line contains a reference to one of his friends from the time, Goh Poh Seng, and his sequence of poems, *Bird with One Wing*. His thoughts are erratic, like the one-winged bird as he consciously withdraws from life, retires into the 'some-how' room, a room with no walls, no keyboard, no report, as ancient and primeval as the Marabar Caves of Forster.[88] It is a room of no compromise where he cannot look away from himself and is confronted by the self in all its ugliness and glory. 'Finally it's only you,' he says 'I think the real interpretation of the Marabar Caves was missed. It is a mirror, it reflects what you bring in with yourself. You see all the ugliness within yourself, there's no escape. That's why it is a renunciation perhaps even beyond what Buddha did.'

Beyond is a poem about renunciation as he wrestles with the Buddhist-Christian-Tao concepts of ego and superego and seeks a renewal of the self. It is a personal resurrection as he finds himself denuded, stripped down and at peace,

> . . . Harmonious once more, my heart
> and inner self scale down. My shirt is simple.
> My pen soft-tipped, black. My poems less
> knotty, shorter.

He speaks of the Hindu philosophy of the four stages of man's life. This is *sannyasa*, the final stage when one withdraws, the struggles with vices and virtues are over. It is just an essential void of perfect balance, like the clear waters that 'uplift rainbows'. As he says, 'Like the Vikings I want to go to death with joy.'

---

[88] Interview 31 May 2018.

A Poet Reading

It is rather surprising that among the numerous books and articles of literary criticism on ET, there is a strange absence of any that can be called definitive. A possible reason could be that like Yeats, ET for a large part of his career did not wish for singularity but a new and modern species of essentially Singaporean or Southeast Asian poetry. As was his expressed purpose, he wished to chronicle Singapore's social history, all that had happened beyond the stupendous economic development the country has known. Like Yeats, he wanted to familiarize readers with the imaginative periods of Singapore history so that they responded to it intuitively even if they did not know it with a scholar's accuracy. But a keen sense of nationalism and a desire to construct historical continuity did mean a wilful veiling of his persona. Quite clearly for the early part of his career he was not looking for individual distinctiveness or a portrayal of the inner-scape. In addition, was the exaggerated belief of the difficulty of his verse and this meant his poetic persona remained even more heavily cloaked to the public eye in supposedly arcane allusions.

The publication in 1979 of *Ulysses by the Merlion* was a turning point. After this, the strands of self and country become more clearly discernible in his poetry, with his poems on friends or travel or otherwise lyrical themes. Perhaps it was a conscious decision in the face of criticism as reproach became louder that behind his exuberant intelligence and delight in the surface pleasures of language, he sought to support the edicts of the government or more particularly the PAP. Perhaps it was an inherent obduracy (of which he is well aware) which makes complete surrender of individual will impossible. Whatever the cause, the fact remains that in later volumes the carefully considered system of ideas behind the eventual outburst of seemingly spontaneous poetry becomes clearer as the poet wills a disclosure of himself.

Despite this gradual change of poetic stance, if a definitive volume of study is yet to appear it is perhaps because of the continued training of arc lights on the public purpose of his poems rather than his private quest. It is often overlooked that the two are mostly inseparable, tightly interlocked like the pendentive of a dome, the structural columns of his personal consciousness allowing the piers of his poetry to receive the weight of his ideas. As he said in one of his last interviews, 'My poems are closely linked to my personal life, one reflects the other. A poet's life and his other occupations cannot be separated from his poetry.' This is a dead giveaway, as crucial a clue as a kingpin of a drug cartel or a hypothesis to an argument—if taken away the whole structure of understanding crumbles, dissolves.

But the statement is also a bit of a double-edged sword. It is true that his personal life—the ravages of war, the push-backs he encountered for being of mixed race, help to explain his search for some unifying principle in his poems. It is also his past that explains some of his need for a certain collective security—the reason why his poems are so warmly and endearingly populated by friends and family, why the cartography of his country and maybe even his continent and region are writ so large in his imagination. He noisily argues against street names being changed, seeks unity in the slogan campaigns of Singapore—they keep the population together, give them a sense of past history as well as future purpose. He dislikes change unless change brings with itself a sense of national solidarity, appreciates social order for like Caliban he wishes to 'belong' to the island and unlike the unfortunate Caliban, finds eventual release in the independence of his country.

But in reverse logic, his poems too throw backlight on him. Like luminescence that makes the dark waves of the sea more visible, sometimes a closer mapping of the man and the poet hints at a certain dichotomy, this despite his claim that rarely has he felt a gulf between the two. To illustrate, one could look at *A Poet Reading*, a piece that is top-of-the-pile when ET speaks of important poems. A long poem in four parts, it has each part separately looking at the intricacies of the poetic process—from conception, release, crafting to articulation.[89] Yet what is interesting is the way it speaks of universal unifying principles at various levels. Firstly, it is a poem that breaks the fourth wall, drawing the reader deep into the poetic process and thereon the reader and the poet journey together, the reader privy to a process that the poet as the central protagonist might not be. It is also a poem that begins and ends its lengthy discourse in the same moment as the poet sits, reading her poem in a sunlit garden, laced with flowers. The garden and the completion of a circle act as strong correlatives in evoking an image of the basic unity of life, of moving from dust to dust, from nothingness to nothingness. And then there is the central protagonist of the poet, a figure self-confessedly inspired by ET's wife. She is at once a wife, a mother who nurtures as the light of the sun, a poet and a Muse who inspires. With the clear intent of conveying unity, ET chooses her to be a woman,

> Enshrined within a tactile moment,
> With no beginning, with no end,
> Her brow, gently by rising lotuses,
> Receives the sky's deep reverence
> As her eyes watch seven golden koi
> Swim serenely into provinces of silence.

This concept of continuity in a moment, with no beginning and no end is repeated in different ways and at different levels through the poem. The first section ends as the Muse becomes the sunlight once again, waiting to be yet another poem and in the coda too, as she reads in the glass hall,

---

[89] Also mentioned in introduction of *The Best of Edwin Thumboo*, ed. Lily Rose Tope (Singapore: Epigram Books), 2012.

She quivers, stakes her space in several memories,
Is transmuted into many distances.

Creation is not only a never-ending, continuous process, it is also akin to its Sanskrit counterpart, *Shristi*, which implies a certain projection, rather than a new beginning. It lies quiescent in every moment, it was there when the universe was in a primal state, as it is now in the age of modern sciences. It is an infinite force that rises and falls in cycles, moving from finer to gross and from gross to fine again. It is only the energy or vibrations that lead to its springing forth at certain moments as *Shristi*—in this case it takes the form of a poem. It is only the external senses that make it apparent, it is a part of the internal for infinitude.

ET has obviously traversed a long distance from when he saw Singapore's multiracial unity projected in the Merlion or even the cultural unity he glimpsed in Multatuli or *Harp of Burma*. Today it is a unity that is more cosmological, making all barriers not only flimsy but also meaningless. It is the unity that Mrs Moore catches a glimpse of in the Marabar Caves when she suffers from a collapse of will as she drowns in the nothingness and realizes good and evil are but one. But the question remains, that once this kind of unity becomes apparent, and particularly after leading a large part of his life believing in syncretic religions, how is it possible to turn to Christianity now? On what basis does he separate his own faith from others and feel he must submit to its rigid discipline? How does he bridge the gap between art and morality? After a lifetime given to dualism and plurality, contrast and antithesis—modes of comparison which allow things to reveal their particular differences and yet point to their fundamental relationships—how does he settle for the linearity of ethics? As Hopkins concluded about this irreconcilable relationship,

> There is an important difference to be noted here. In art we strive to realise not only unity, permanence of law, likeness, but also, with it, difference, variety, contrast: it is rhyme we like,

not echo, and not unison, but harmony. But in morality the
highest consistency is the highest excellence.[90]

One wonders if the answer to this lies in his family of devoutly
practising Christians or is it his own social need of acceptance into
a community? For as he vehemently says more than once during the
year's conversations, it was never difficult for him to believe in God,
but a very difficult decision to believe in the God of Moses, the God
of his family. In a life where his senses have always been tipped by
intellect, where he has come to assimilate even sensate experiences
through an intellectual rationalizing, such unquestioning submission
has not come easily. Through his biblical poems he has tried hard to
expand his poetic consciousness to include religion. Rather than the
immediacy of an epiphany, it has been a slow meditative process and
perhaps he has submitted to its rigour only because he seeks a final
unity, a unity that will leave him completely fulfilled.

This is the final leg of the journey, this search for ultimate
perfection, a plenary, thirst-quenching completion. It will set him free
of all the struggles he has known as a poet—the compulsions of being
both ordinary and informed, the dilemma between spontaneity and
artifice as he strove to externalize the most internal of experiences, of
knowing himself as both holy and profane, of making poetic capital
out of love and self-abrading thoughts on drawing inspiration from
artistic wantonness. But it is a journey that he will have to undertake
alone. His life marked by symbols of friendship, by poets and painters
and books of fiction that have shaped his identity, sprawls around
him. Books have been given away to libraries, his eyes well up in
memory of friends who departed a bit too early. It is a moment when
he realizes the mountaineer's rope was nothing but an apparition.
And yet he will have to continue the climb. He speaks of retreating
into himself, of learning to live in the pure bliss of God.

It will be a wrench very hard to bear.

---

[90] R.K.R. Thornton, *Gerard Manley Hopkins: The Poems* (London: Edward Arnold,
    1973), p. 22.

APPENDIX I
JANUARY TO SEPTEMBER 1953

If we look at the key periods in our personal growth, there are very, very few utterly crucial ones. We realize that there are two, three or four which were deep, broad and central periods of extreme development, of opening up great areas of interest that remain a core of our enlarging mind, behind fructifying and managing ourselves. What makes us what we are, as individuals. The me, the I. Looking back, I believe the most vital one was when we were entering the beginnings of manhood.

These all too rare junctures are induced, initiated, created by a host of different causes. They range from the death of one's father to doing well in a major examination. There is pain of preparation and the joy of getting over them. It is often both, as when a prince or princess becomes king or queen. What were Elizabeth II's thoughts when she was crowned? She had lost her father, married a Greek prince with strong German family ties. That she soon toured West Samoa, Australia and South Africa to strengthen the link between royalty and the Empire turning into Commonwealth was obvious.

In January 1953, I was between school and university. I had taken the School Certificate in November 1951. The University of Malaya Entrance Examination was in mid-March 1953. We expected to go up in September of that year. We were the first to undergo nearly two years of Post-School Certificate before university. We were being prepared for the University's Entrance Examination. The Advance Level school certificate was available but not formally required for admission to the university here. I had entered for the A-level but did not take the examination.

As there was shortage of graduate teachers, Post-school Certificate classes were only available at Raffles Institution, Victoria School, Anglo-Chinese School, St Joseph's Institution and St Andrews. The last three were founded by Methodist, Catholic and Anglican missionaries in the nineteenth century respectively. And we should remember that the Peoples' Action Party has governed Singapore ever since it took power in 1964. Remarkably, it moved us from Third to First World in about thirty years. But the nine months of 1953 I am looking at were not remarkable in any way. On the contrary, it was still a period when the United Kingdom was still recovering from WWII. The USA had rendered material help to her before she joined the war and she had to be re-paid. We traded in rubber and tin which was sold to the USA. But the American dollars earned was not for us but for Britain, the Colonial power. In 1955, I taught at the YSC Institute of Commerce in Carpenter Street during the university's long vacation. I met Sathasivam—my brother-in-law as we married two sisters—who needed US$60/- per month to supplement his scholarship at Sacramento University, California. He failed to get any American dollars from the Colonial Government in Malaya. Britain needed all the American dollars she could get.

I only had the March 1953 Entrance Examination, nothing else. The last two years of School had been active: the Literary and Debating Society, the Civics Club, first eleven hockey and cricket, the cadet corps, the Schools' magazines and editing *YOUTH*, the combined secondary schools, magazine. Each week was full of school. And the group of close friends who kept in touch as they, too, were facing similar problems. And favourite teachers: Shamus Frazer, Kenneth Owen, Vera Curran, Chan Chew Kiat, Roy Jansen,

Andrew Yeo and Major Fam Fong Hee. And Ahmad our office boy who lived by the school's main gate. The closest contact was with Frazer and Owen. I was composing poems, spending much time with Frazer, listening to his comments and learning, Owen was a Welsh nationalist. When he felt he could trust me, he started talking of Welsh nationalism, making it clear that the Welsh were marginalized into a compart zone by the Oxbridge establishment that ruled the UK. I heard Welsh nationalist songs in his beautiful voice. He spoke of Llewellyn, Owen Glendower and other nationalists who resisted the English. He described the racism in the UK; how the English dominated the Welsh, Scots, Irish and Cornish. I had suffered because of my Tamil-Teochew.

I started to see Singapore's racial inheritance. All our groups—Malay, Chinese, Indians and Eurasians—had sub-groups. The Malaya had Bugis, Bataks, Achenese, Javanese and others. The Chinese had Hokkiens, Teochews, Cantonese, Hainanese and so on. The Indians were far more complicated. We should remember that India as a single nation is a Colonial invention. 6,000 British administrators ruling the dominion. We have Tamils, Malayalees, Bengalis, Gujaratis, Kashmiris, Sindhis, and so on. Each from a full society, distinctive and separate, yet sharing much of their religion and caste system. Our fourth group, the Eurasians, have links to the UK and Ireland, and on a far smaller scale, central and southern Europe.

I saw that Singapore was likely to be multi-racial. There was much each group could contribute. But we had to get our attitudes and perceptions right, or fail badly. As a Tamil-Teochew, I had suffered from those who believed in 'racial purity'. My last experience in November 1953 during ragging in Dunearn Road Hostel was a release, turning pain and embarrassment into relief. I was called a half-caste. Beda Lim, who became the Librarian at the University of Malaya in Kuala Lumpur, said I was among the first Malaysians. Victor Gopal was mixed like me; we started calling each other 'Countryman'.

Nationalism was gathering further strength. We wanted independence. While I was somewhat aware of likely developments, my main thoughts were about my own change as I moved to a more significant stretch of life in an increasingly adult world. At the university I would be meeting Malayans for the first time in quantity. They outnumbered us by three to one at the university. But what engaged me more was the kind of place Singapore was to become; what I hoped it would be, in reality. The Malays would control Malaya. Their interests would prevail. In Singapore the Chinese formed the largest majority, at about seventy-eight per cent. Any links with Malaya had to be on special terms. We were not a Malaya state, like Negri Simbilan or Pahang. Yet to be a Chinese enclave would be odd for internal and external reasons. Historically, this far south in Southeast Asia was Malay before colonialism. It stretched from Ache, southern Thailand Malaya, Sumatra, Java, Celebes, Borneo, Brunei, the southern Philippines to Timor. A Chinese pimple in an extensive Malay Muslim belt. For this and other cogent reasons we needed to be multi-racial. Especially for me and my family who would be less open to abuse. Fortunately, being racially mixed—and English educated—I was far more open to the issues involved, able to see where the problems were, and how they were to be tackled. That was and is at the centre of my search for attachment, relevance and meaning which leads to the sense of reality.

And when you look at RACE closely, especially the dismantling of its barriers, you find a host of other issues: language, various customs, taste, nuances of family structures, management of colour and shape, literature, music, dance, painting, sculpture, religion, and their histories and traditions especially. A Singaporean Identity would emerge. It would combine what we grew up with, in early life before school, and what we acquire in school and at play and the computer, and beyond them. It is there in my poems. It is one of the themes Nilanjana treats.

Edwin Thumboo
June 2020
Phoenix Heights
Bukit Panjang

APPENDIX II
OFFICIAL TIMELINE OF THE 'UNOFFICIAL' POET-LAUREATE

Name: Edwin Nadason Thumboo

Title: Emeritus Professor

Present Appointment: Professorial Fellow, Department of English Language and Literature,

National University of Singapore (01/10/2005–)

Date & Place of Birth: 22/11/1933; Singapore

Citizenship: Singaporean

Marital Status: Married (with a son and a daughter)

Qualifications: BA (Hons.) Singapore, 1957

PhD Singapore, 1970

Website: http://go.to/thumboo

Appointments: Assessment Officer, Income Tax Dept (Nov. 1957–May 1961)

Admin. Officer, Central Provident Fund (June 1961–Sept. 1965)

Asst. Secretary, Singapore Telephone Board (Oct. 1965–June 1966)

University of Singapore/National University of Singapore

Asst. Lecturer (June 1966–June 1969)

Lecturer (July 1969–June 1971)

Senior Lecturer (July 1971–June 1974)

Associate Professor (July 1974–Dec. 1978)

Professor of English (January 1979–Nov. 1995)

Director, NUS Centre for the Arts, National University of Singapore (01/03/1993– 31/09/2005)

Professorial Fellow (Dec. 1995–present)

Emeritus Professor (Sept. 1997–present)

University Positions Held

Vice-Dean, Fac. of Arts & Social Sciences (June 1974–June 1977)

Acting Dean (June 1976–April 1977)

Head, Dept. of English Lang. & Lit. (June 1977–Nov. 1993)

Council Member, i) University of Singapore (January 1977–December 1979); ii) National University of Singapore (January 1980–December 1982)

Dean, Fac. of Arts & Social Sciences, (July 1980–June 1991)

Visiting Appointments:

Fulbright-Hayes Visiting Professor, Pennsylvania State University, USA (1979–1980)

Writer-in-Residence, Institute of Culture and Communication, Hawaii (July–August 1985)

Ida Beam Professor, University of Iowa, Iowa City (September–December 1986)

Honorary Research Fellow, University College, University of London (March–September 1987)

Senior Fellow, Dept of English, Australian Defence Force Academy, University of New South Wales, Canberra, ACT, Australia (March–April 1994)

George A. Miller Visiting Professor, Centre for Advanced Study, University of Illinois, Urbana-Champaign, USA (October–November 1998)

Visiting Professor, University of Innsbruck (2002)

Visiting Professor, City University of Hong Kong (March–April 2007, January–May 2008, Jan–April/Sept–Oct 2009)

Distinguished Visiting Professor, International Islamic University Malaysia (July–August 2008)

Started/Founded/Co-founded/

Initiated:

Centre for Advanced Studies, Faculty of Arts, NUS

Centre for the Arts, NUS

Singa: Literature & the Arts (Founded in 1980 with the support of Masuri S.N., V.T. Arasu and Wong Yoon Wah. Ceased publication in 2000)

Singapore Writers Week 1986 (renamed *Singapore Writers Festival* in 1991)

An Annual 5-day Residential Creative Arts Programme, jointly organized with the Ministry of Education for 150 secondary school students (1990–present)

Chief Editor, *The Arts* (April 1995–May 2004; thirteen issues in all)

Pan Shou and Singapore Culture (1998 Symposium)

Symposium in honour of Braj Kachru (1999). Paper published as *Three Circles of English*

Symposium in honour of Frankie Sionil Jose, National Artist, Philippines, December 2005.

PoetryWalls Singapore (2015)

Singapore National Poetry Festival 2015

Editorial Affiliations:

Consulting Editor, *World Englishes* (Oxford, UK and Cambridge, MA, USA: Blackwell Publishers)

Editorial Consultant, *Westerly* (published by the University of Western Australia)

Founding General Editor of *Writing Asia: The Literatures in English* (Series that will look at all aspects of the literatures in Asian Englishes, 2007–)

Groups and Programmes	NUS Dance Synergy
Founded/Initiated/Supported	NUS Jazz Band
as Founding Director,	NUS Dance Blast
NUS Centre for the Arts:	NUS Lion Dance

NUS Chinese Drama

nu (STUDIOS) Film Productions

NUS Singa Nglaras Gamelan Ensemble

Kent Ridge Ensemble

Chinese Instrument Courses and Examinations

NUS Arts Festival (2006–present)

Conferences / Seminars

Started English Language Proficiency Unit, Faculty of Arts and **Organized** Social Sciences, University of Singapore in 1970 and ran it till 1977.

First Seminar for Pre-University students with the Ministry of Education (1970)

Solidarity Conference of Asian Writers, with Francisco Sionil Jose and the participation of Moktar Lubis, Sulak Sivaraksa (1976–1986)

Biennial Symposium on the Literatures and Cultures of the Asia Pacific Region (with Bruce Bennett with the University of Western Australia), (1982–present)

The Writer as Historical Witness (The 1986 Conference of the Association of Commonwealth Language and Literary Studies)

English in South East Asia: Malaysian Writing; The Writer Speaks (1994). Symposium and book exhibition.

First World Chinese Mini Short Story Conference; organized with the Singapore Association of Writers (1994)

Annual Creative Arts Programme with the Ministry of Education (1990–present)

Wu Teh Yao Memorial Lectures (1995–2001)

Seminar on Malaysian Chinese Literature (1995)

East West Studies: Traditions, Innovations and Transformations. Conference in Honour of Professor Chiu Ling Yong, held at the Centre for the Arts, NUS and jointly organized with the Departments of Chinese Studies of NUS and Hong Kong Chinese University (1998)

International Conference—Man & Nature: Literature on the Environment (1999)

Reading-cum-Signing Session by Francisco Sionil Jose of the Philippines (2000)

An Afternoon with Vuyelwa Nana Mthimkhulu from South Africa (2001)

Biennial International Conference on Tamil in the International Arena (2002 & 2004)

Contemporary Literature and Human Ecology: International Conference on Chinese Literature in Southeast Asia, organized with Singapore with the Singapore Writers Association (2003)

Symposium on Literatures of the Asia Pacific, NUS Centre for the Arts (2005)

Honours & Awards:

National Book Development Council of Singapore 1978 Book Award for Poetry in English published between 1975–77

Southeast Asia Write Award 1979

National Book Development Council of Singapore 1980 Book Award for Poetry in English published between 1978-79

The Cultural Medallion Award, March 1980

Public Service Star (BBM), August 1981

ASEAN Cultural and Communication Award (Literature), August 1987

Public Service Star (Bar), August 1991

National Book Development Council of Singapore 1994 Book Award for Poetry

Raja Rao Award for contributions to the literature of the Indian Diaspora, University of Illinois, Urbana-Champaign, October 2002

The Meritorious Service Medal, 2006

Distinguished Service Award 2008 presented by The International Association for World Englishes for his exceptional scholarly contribution and insightful leadership to all of us involved in the study of world Englishes.

APPENDIX III

TEN MOST IMPORTANT POEMS: ET'S CHOICE

1. A Poet Reading
2. Conversation with my Friend Kwang Min at Loong Kwang of Outram Park
3. Island
4. Jonathan before Gilboa
5. Mandai
6. May 1954
7. Path of our Spirits
8. The Way Ahead
9. Ulysses by the Merlion
10. Uncle Never Knew

BIBLIOGRAPHY

Ahrens, Rudiger, ed. *Anglophone Cultures in Southeast Asia.* Heidelberg: Universitatsverlag, 2003.

Barthes, Roland. *The Eiffel Tower & Other Mythologies.* US: University of California Press, 1997.

Bedient, C. *Architects of the Self.* Berkeley: University of California Press, 1972.

Beier, Ulli, ed. *Introduction to African Literature: An Anthology of Critical Writing from 'Black Orpheus'.* London: Longman, 1967.

Bennett, Bruce, ed. *A Sense of Exile: Essays on the Literature of the Asia-Pacific Region.* Australia: Centre for Studies in Australian Literature, 1988.

Bloom, Harold, ed. *Till I End My Song: A Gathering of Last Poems.* NY: Harper Collins, 2010.

Booth, James. *Philip Larkin: Life, Art & Love.* NY: Bloomsbury Press, 2014.

Chatterjee, Partha. *The Nation and its Fragments.* NJ: Princeton University Press, 1993.

Davis, A.R., ed. *Search for Identity: Modern Literature and the Creative Arts in Asia.* Sydney: Angus & Robertson, 1974.

Fieldhouse, D.K. *The West and the Third World.* UK: Blackwell Pub, 1999.

Fox, Robin. *The Tribal Imagination*. UK, USA: Harvard University Press, 2011.

Fraser, Robert. *West African Poetry: A Critical History*. Cambridge: CUP, 1986.

Frayne, P. John, ed. *Uncollected Prose by W.B. Yeats: First Reviews and Articles*, Vol. 1, London: Macmillan, 1970.

Furbank, P.N. and Lago, Mary. *Selected Letters of E.M. Forster*. London: Collins, 1983.

Gardner, Helen, ed. *The Divine Poems of John Donne*. Oxford: Clarendon Press, 1964.

Gibb, James, ed. *Critical Perspectives on Wole Soyinka*. Washington DC: Three Continents Press, 1980.

Goh, Robbie B.H., ed. *Conflicting Identities: Essays on Modern Irish Literature*. Singapore: Unipress, 1997.

Goodwin, L.K. *Understanding African Poets: A Study of Ten Poets*. USA: Heinemann, 1982.

Gungwu, Wang. *The Revival of Chinese Nationalism*. Leiden: IIAS, 1996.

Hallberg, Robert Von, ed. *Politics and Poetic Value*. Chicago: University of Chicago Press, 1987.

Hong, Ee Tiang. *Responsibility & Commitment: The Poetry of Edwin Thumboo*. Singapore: SUP, 1997.

Hughes, Ted. *Poetry in the Making*. UK: Faber & Faber, 2008.

Johnson, R.W. *The Idea of Lyric: Lyric Modes in Ancient and Modern Poetry*. Berkeley: University of California Press, 1982.

Kai, Poh Soo, Quee, Tan Jing and Yew, Koh Kay, eds. *The Fajar Generation: The University Socialist Club & the Politics of Postwar Malaya & Singapore*. Petaling Jaya: SIRD, 2010.

Kinsella, Thomas, ed. *The New Oxford Book of Irish Verse*. UK: OUP, 1986.

Klein, Ronald D., ed. *Interlogue*, Vol. 4. Singapore: Ethos Books, 2005.

de Masirevich, Constance. *On the Four Quartets of T S Eliot*. NY: Vincent Stuart, 1965.

McNamara, Kevin R., ed. *The Cambridge Companion to the City in Literature.* NY: Cambridge, 2014.

Men in White: The Untold Story of Singapore's Ruling Political Party. Singapore: SPH, 2009.

Moores, Gerald, *Modern African Writers: Wole Soyinka.* UK: Holmes & Meier, 1971.

Mottram, K.R., ed. *The Lyric Mood: An Anthology of Lyric Poetry.* London: Oxford University Press, 1965.

Multatuli. *Max Havelaar or the Coffee Auctions of the Dutch Trading Company.* London: Heinemann, 1967.

Nazareth, Peter, ed. *Interlogue*, Vol. 7. Singapore: Ethos Books, 2008.

Ngara, Emmanuel. *Ideology and Form in African Poetry: Implications for Poetry.* Nairobi: Heinemann Kenya, 1990.

Nielsen, Niels C., ed. *Religions of the World,* ed. NY: St Martin's Press, 1988.

Nkosi, Lewis. *Tasks & Masks: Themes and Styles of African Literature.* Harlow, Essex: Longman, 1982.

Okara, Gabriel. *The Fisherman's Invocation.* London: Heinemann, 1978.

Patke, Rajeev S. and Holden, Philip. *The Routledge Concise History of Southeast Asian Writing in English.* Oxon: Routledge, 2010.

Quayum, Mohammad A., ed. *Peninsular Muse.* Oxford: Peter Lang, 2007.

Quayum, Mohammad A. and Wong, Phui Nam, eds. *Sharing Borders: Studies in Contemporary Singaporean-Malaysian Literature.* Singapore: National Library Board, 2009.

Rajan, B. *W.B. Yeats: A Critical Introduction.* London: Hutchinson University Library, 1965.

Said, Edward. *Culture & Imperialism.* NY: Knopf, 1993.

Said, Edward. *Culture and Imperialism.* NY: Vintage Books, 1994.

Singh, Kirpal, ed. *The Writer's Sense of the Past: Essays on Southeast Asian and Australasian Literature.* Singapore: Singapore University Press, 1987.

Sui, Gwee Li and Heng, Michelle. *Edwin Thumboo: Time Travelling, A Select Annotated Bibliography*. Singapore: NLB, 2012.

Sui, Gwee Li, ed. *Written Country: The History of Singapore through Literature*. Singapore: Landmark Books, 2016.

Suryadinata, Leo. *Chinese Adaptation and Diversity: Essays on Society and Literature in Indonesia, Malaysia & Singapore*. Singapore: Singapore University Press, 1993.

Tagore, Rabindranath. *My Life in My Words*. India: Penguin Books, 2006.

Tagore, Rabindranath. *Nationalism*. ND: Fingerprint Classics, 2016.

Takeyama, Michio. *Harp of Burma*. Tokyo: Charles E. Tuttle Co. Inc., 1966.

Tay, Eddie. *Colony, Nation & Globalisation: Not at Home in Singaporean and Malaysian Literature*. Singapore: NUS Press, 2011.

Thornton, R.K.R. *Gerard Manley Hopkins: The Poems*. London: Edward Arnold, 1973.

Thumboo, Edwin and Kandiah, Thiru, eds. *Perceiving Other Worlds*. Singapore: Marshall Cavendish, 2005.

Thumboo, Edwin and Chai, Yeow Kai, eds. *Reflecting on the Merlion: An Anthology of Poems*. SG: NAC, 2009.

Thumboo, Edwin. *Literature and Liberation*. Philippines: Solidaridad Pub. House, 1988.

Thumboo, Edwin. 'Conversion of the Tribes: Societal Antecedents & the Growth of Singapore Poetry'. *World Englishes*, 9(2), 1990.

Thumboo, Edwin, ed. *The Flowering Tree: Selected Writings from Singapore/Malaysia*. Singapore: Educational Publications Bureau, 1970.

Thumboo, Edwin. *Personality, Intention and Idiom: A Framework*.

Tope, Lily Rose, ed. *The Best of Edwin Thumboo*. Singapore: Epigram Books, 2012.

Tulli, Magdalena. *Dreams and Stones*. UK: Penguin Random House, 2004.

Unterecker, John. *W.B. Yeats: A Poem by Poem Analysis.* NJ: Prentice Hall, 1963.

Unterecker, John, ed. *Yeats: A Collection of Critical Essays.* NJ: Prentice Hall, 1963.

Waley, Arthur. *A Hundred and Seventy Chinese Poems.* London: Constable & Co., 1918.

Wayang: A History of Chinese Opera in Singapore. Singapore: The National Archives, Singapore, 1988.

Webster, Jonathan. *Return to Origins: The Poet & the Tao.* Singapore: Ethos Books, 2009.

Webster, Jonathan, ed. *Essays on Edwin Thumboo.* Singapore: Ethos Books, 2009.